Critical Acclaim for Chantal M. Roberts, CPCU, AIC, RPA

"You are such a wealth of knowledge!"
— *Leana Massey, CPCU*

"To date, the best explanation in detail
(of a reservation of rights letter) I have seen or read."
— *Alex Shaw, AFIS*

"Chantal is one of those women to watch in this decade and the next."
— *Nancy Germond, MA, SPHR, SHRM-SCP, ARM, AIC, ITP*

"Chantal Roberts is a passionate observer and commentator in the landscape of insurance claim handling. A seasoned practitioner who blends practical know-how with insights understandable to those within and outside the insurance claim industry, she has the rare ability to translate insurance concepts and terms and make them intelligible."
— *Kevin M. Quinley, CPCU, ARM, AIC, ARe, AIM, RPA*

THE *Art* OF
ADJUSTING

Writing Down the
Unwritten Rules
of Claims Adjusting

CHANTAL M. ROBERTS
CPCU, AIC, RPA

Tilting at
Windmills
Press

ISBN: 978-1-7374268-0-6 (paperback)
      978-1-7374268-1-3 (ebook)

---

1 But it has to be a good book review. If it's a bad book review, I'll have to call your mother because you didn't listen to her when she taught you, "If you have nothing good to say, don't say anything at all."

Disclaimer

I am not an attorney. The information in this book does not convey any legal or professional advice of any kind. Each insurer handles their claims differently, and readers should keep in mind this book is intended for informational purposes only.

The opinions expressed in this book are those of the author.

Nothing in this book is intended to recommend a specific course of action. If specific information is needed, please consult with an attorney or me. My opinions may change based on the specific circumstances of your situation. The coverage discussions are based on the standardized ISO policy forms.

Indemnity

You agree to defend, indemnify, and hold harmless the author and the copyright holder(s) from and against all the liabilities, claims, damages, and expenses (including reasonable attorney's fees and costs) arising out of your use of this material; your breach or alleged breach of this agreement; or your breach or alleged breach of the copyright, trademark, proprietary or other rights of the author or copyright holder(s).

For information, please contact:

Chantal M. Roberts, CPCU, AIC, RPA
P.O. Box 4676
Olathe, KS 66063
TheArtOfAdjusting.com

Book cover design by Chantal M. Roberts
Interior design by Laura Orsini, Panoply Publishing LLC

Dedication

To all the claims I've loved before...

Contents

Author Notes

I began to write this version of this book after my expert witness business, CMR Consulting, came to a complete halt due to the COVID-19 pandemic. Because of the pandemic, trials were delayed and there was no need for expert witnesses.

Wondering what to do with my time, and not wanting to learn how to bake bread badly enough to actually do it (although I would someday like to acquire that skill), I began to explore other experts in my field, many of whom have written books about our chosen specialty of adjusting claims. I have written articles and I started a vlog as a soft marketing campaign, so I felt it was time, again, to try to write a book.

Except that I didn't want to.

I say again, as this is not the first time I have tried to write book about insurance adjusting. Fortunately, before I got too far on my first endeavor, I received a big assignment and gladly pushed the book to the back burner. Somehow, although I do love talking about it, I did not enjoy writing about insurance claims adjusting.

It occurred to me that the reason I didn't enjoy writing a book about adjusting claims, but do not mind writing articles, might be because articles are short.

I have a formal writing style for which I blame the Registered Sisters of Mercy and Ms. Riley, my 9th grade teacher. Whilst endeavoring in a scholastic writing, one should be formal in one's language. You should not jolt the audience by changing subject usage and thrusting them into the reading. Passive voice is frowned upon. And one should not start a sentence with a conjunction. One should not use a preposition to end a sentence with. Bad incomplete sentences.

Then there was the whole misconception of what a book was and the kind of book I wanted to write. And the new usage of "they" as a singular pronoun, instead of "he or she." Which, by the way, I have addressed with the editorial decision to make the claims adjuster feminine and the insured (and other players) masculine throughout my book.

I wanted to write a book because it bugs me that the only aspects of insurance taught in universities' risk management degree programs are sell-ing insurance and underwriting. In the unlikely event you can find a class about claims, it is one semester – more often, just one chapter in a larger book. Claims is usually an afterthought. Therefore, my original goal was to pen an academic, how-to tome to be carried by universities with Finance & Risk Management majors. I thought, nefariously, if I could worm my way into universities, I would have a steady, passive income stream since students would be forced to buy my book (insert maniacal laughter here).

So, I started to write my claims book, complete with exercises, examples, and glossaries. And it was hard and boring and I hated it. Not to mention the fact that books like this already existed—most notably from The Institute. I didn't know how (and still don't know how) to write a book that imparts my knowledge to someone else. I especially hated the part where I had to justify my knowledge with citations. A college professor I know is writing an article for publication in a scholarly magazine. She complains that you have to have 137 sources for one sentence, which of course has to be reworded so you are not accused of plagiarism. The reason for so many sources is that you have to cite the source where you found the material, then cite the source for that, then cite the source for the source for the source, all the way back to the guy who first made up this bit of information and had a good enough poker face to make us all believe him.

I really can't be bothered to do all that work. Besides, I'm pretty sure some Insurance Rules are just not written down because we all "know what the rules are." That is, however, one of the reasons I began writing the book. I wanted to put some of those unwritten rules into writing. Maybe they are already written, and I'm just really bad at Googling. Regardless, if that's what interests you, skip to Chapters 10 and 11. I will warn you, though, some of the unwritten rules come in the guise of helpful hints, which are peppered throughout the book, like how to write good claim notes (Chapter 9). And yes, I put all the good stuff in the back of the book so you have to read the whole thing for it to make sense.

I also couldn't figure out how to organize an introductory claims handling book, because when it comes to claims, everything touches something else. It's like a gear tooth in a cog: everything fits together. If I describe a homeowners policy and talk about endorsements (*See Chapter 2*) but haven't explained what endorsements are, how can I use that example? But if I talk about all the bits and bobs first, without any examples, then it's just another textbook about insurance, dry as burnt toast.

Or it's like a knitted sweater: pull the thread and the whole thing unravels. So, where does one start?

This consideration led me to a new possibility: I would write the book in a conversational tone, using everyday examples as a way to teach how to handle and adjust claims. I would also assume the reader had some prior insurance/adjusting knowledge. In essence, this is an *intermediate* claims adjusting book. I am assuming (and you know what that means) the reader of this book has a few years of adjusting claims under his/her belt and wants to gain a bit more knowledge.

I also want to tell you about a small, little quirk that drives my editor nuts.[2] The caption *Insurance in Action* uses real claims I've either handled or overseen[3], but (*allegedly*) I will randomly indent a few paragraphs which discuss a claim for illustrative purposes. I will not put these examples under the caption *Insurance in Action*. It's just that I want to make sure you understand one specific point of the main issue and I'm afraid if I break off into another caption, there will be no direct way back to the main idea. So, pay attention. I'm not done talking.

Yeah, threads in a sweater...

I believe you can't build a house that will last on a weak foundation, so the first few chapters are things an adjuster learns, ideally, in the first year of her career. This is a property and casualty insurance claims book. I do not discuss other lines of business.

Or, maybe this is Claims 201, and I did turn it into university coursework.

---

2 There really are a lot of my quirks that drive her nuts, but, well, I do have a method to my madness. Kinda.

3 Names have been changed to protect the guilty.

Insurance Concepts

I'm a firm believer of starting with a good foundation before launching into intermediate courses. So although this book is designed for advanced claims adjusters in the 5th to 10th year or so of their careers, in the first few chapters, I'm going to cover the definitions, rules, steps, and methods adjusters should already know. Besides, it never hurts to have a refresher.

Insurance is a practice in which one party (the insured) transfers the risk of a loss (pays a premium) to another party (the insurer).

Insurers have accountants who review prior losses to determine the likelihood of the same event occurring in the same place. This is part of how premiums are set. This is also why the owner of a home located on a flood plain cannot obtain insurance from a standard carrier and would have to buy flood coverage from the National Flood Insurance Program. A property insurer would find the risk of a flood unacceptable since the possibility of the home flooding (due to being on a flood plain) is high. Alternatively, if an insured had a house on the top of a mountain, a standard property insurer would likely offer flood coverage, although it would probably be a waste of money from the standpoint of the insured, as chances of flooding would be low.

Insurance books of business, or classes, are underwritten first as a group, and then individually. For example, auto insurance underwriters/accountants review types of accidents, locations of these accidents, the people involved in said accidents, and the varying amount of damage incurred to arrive at a base premium. Then they review the specifics of individual seeking the policy. If the prospective insured is a better than average driver, his premium might be lower than his neighbor; if he is a worse driver, his premium would likely be higher.

The Affordable Care Act, the national healthcare coverage passed under President Obama's tenure, generated considerable discussion, both pro and con. The Act penalizes people who failed to obtain healthcare insurance. Many laypeople and members of Congress believed the Act would mean paying for others' insurance, expressing that they did not believe this was the purpose of insurance.

This, literally, is how insurance works. You not only pay for your risk, but you also pay for your neighbor's possibility of loss as well. Likewise, you effectively transfer the possibility of your risk to someone else.

Because liability insurance on automobiles is mandatory for everyone, the premium for the transfer of risk is (usually) affordable. If you drive in a rural area, where there are fewer cars, your premium will likely be lower. If you drive in an urban area where there are many opportunities for an accident, your premium will tend to be higher.

Most insureds would be unable to afford to self-insure against the possibility of their own car accidents. The amount of money the insured would need to hold aside for payment/liquidity would be based on the frequency of the type of claim and the maximum value of a claim. Most auto claims are small property damage and bodily injury claims; however, if there were serious injuries to the other party in the auto accident, such as permanent paralysis, or even death, payment of this kind of claim would likely be more than one individual could sustain. This is why everyone's premiums are pooled together, enabling the insured to "pay" for the loss—even though the insurance carrier is really the one writing the check.

What it comes down to is you are using both yours and your neighbor's premiums to pay for your car accident. And when the neighbor has an accident, he is doing the same, because both your premiums and his premiums go into a "pot" that is reserved to pay such claims.

Insurers can get into trouble if they underwrite too heavily in a single area. For example, say the mythical carrier Gulf Coast of America insures only residential homes located within five miles of the Gulf Coast. Now a hurricane comes along, creating damage along the Louisiana coast. All premiums pitch in so that all insureds are covered. Then, two months later, Houston is hit by an even more severe hurricane. More premiums pitch in. By the time a hurricane hits Florida, on the far side of Gulf Coast of America's 400-mile coverage area, all the premiums would already have been paid out, and the insurer would go bankrupt. In real life, Montana pays for damage due to Houston hurricanes, while Arkansas helps cover California wildfires, and Illinois pitches in for Oklahoma's tornadoes.

There are ways for both the carriers and the insureds to avoid biting off more than they can chew.

Risk Management

Both insureds and insurers alike can simply avoid a risk or loss exposure: insureds do so by choosing not own the item (or live in the place) which causes the risk; an insurer can do so by issuing an exclusion for the risk or refusing to underwrite the risk.

The insurer can lower its risk of large payments for accidents by offering larger deductibles or large retention agreements with the insured. A retention agreement is when the insured agrees to retain a specific amount of the loss. This is commonly called "self-insurance" or "self-insured retention."

Often the insured will enter into agreements with others who will agree to pay for and to protect the insured from a loss. These are called noninsurance transfers or indemnity agreements. As a side note, the person or organization who is paying or protecting the insured from a loss will usually its own insurance policy and it will be that carrier who handles the claim. So, although this is called a "noninsurance transfer," a is carrier involved and insurance is available.

What Insurance Covers

An insurance policy is a contract between the insured and insurer. The specifics of what is and is not covered will be discussed in later chapters. The contract must contain an insurable interest for the policy to be applicable for a loss.

Insurable interest is any legal or monetary relationship one person has with the property that is insured. The insured will have an insurable interest in her home; the mortgage holder or lienholder will also have an insurable interest since it lent the insured money to buy the residence and wants to be sure said residence is protected.

Insurance policies cover risks. Risks, also known as hazards or perils, are conditions that increase the possibility a loss will occur. There are three types of risks:

- *Physical hazard* is a feature of an item which will cause or increase the opportunity for a loss. An example of a physical hazard would be locating a log cabin in the Western United States, because such a cabin would be kindling for the wildfires that tend to burn often throughout these states.

- *Moral hazard* is the risk that a loss will increase in frequency or severity of damages based on the actions of the insured. An example of a moral hazard would be when the insured places dried brush close to the log cabin and neglects to remove dead trees from the property which could increase the frequency or severity of a fire.

- *Morale hazard* is the risk that a loss will increase in frequency or severity of damages based on the attitude of the insured. A morale hazard is very similar to the moral hazard, but in this instance, the insured knows there is an increased possibility of fire, but he does nothing to decrease the risk because he "has insurance" which will pay for any damages.

Insurance Regulation

Insurance is regulated at the state level through the McCarran-Ferguson Act of 1945, which declared that states should regulate the business of insurance and confirmed that the continued regulation of insurers by the states was in the public's best interest.

The Financial Modernization Act of 1999, also called Gramm-Leach-Bliley, established a broad network to allow relationships among banks, securities firms, and insurers. It also affirmed that states should control the business of insurance. The main reason for insurer regulation is to protect laypeople (insureds and claimants). State regulation is geared toward several key functions, including insurer licensing, agent licensing, adjuster licensing, policy review and approval, market conduct, financial regulation, and complaint reviews.

An insurer's failure in regulatory compliance may cause suspension or revocation of its license in that particular state. The states also have the ability to assess fines for these violations.

This book specifically focuses on claims; therefore, it will not discuss regulation relating to other aspects of the insurance marketplace. However, most states require insurance adjusters to pass a test to receive a license to practice the adjustment of claims. This information can be found on each state's department of insurance website.

The National Association of Insurance Commissioners (NAIC) published model unfair claims practice acts which most states have adopted. Every adjuster must be aware of his state's Unfair Claims Practices Act and what constitutes unfair acts while adjusting claims in order to avoid bad faith. The NAIC also serves as an advisory board and a place for all the states to discuss issues in order to present a (somewhat) uniformed supervision of insurers.

Insurance Contracts

As mentioned previously, the insurance policy is a contract. The first party of the contract is the insured; the second party is the carrier. Although the claimant is not an actual party to the contract between the insured and the insurer, the claimant is referred to as a "third party" since they are tangentially related to the contract.

There are four parts of a legal contract:

- Agreement
- Consideration
- Competent Person
- Legal Purpose

Agreement: The people who enter into a contract must agree on the specifics of what the contract will contain. When it comes to insurance policies, there is usually little negotiation between the insured and the insurer, since the average insured cannot amend the policy. However, by signing on the dotted line and paying the premium, the insured indicates his agreement with the carrier about the policy.

Consideration: Not only does the insured "agree" with the insurer about the policy when paying the premium, but consideration has just occurred. Consideration is defined as something of value (premium) being given by one person (insured) to someone else (insurer) for something (policy of coverage). This is listed in the insurance policy as the "Insuring Agreement."

Competent Parties: Both people must enter into the contract understanding the duties and obligations of the contract. A corporation is a legal "person." So, in the case of an insurer, which is a corporation, the insurer (or its representative, who is a live human) is a competent party.

Incompetent people include minors, intoxicated people, anyone who wants to adjust claims for a living, and mentally incapacitated persons (who may also be adjusters), to name just a few examples.

Legal Purpose: The contract must be about something that is legal. The example often used when discussing whether a contract is legal is a contract with a hitman.

> John hires Bill to kill Darren. (Competent Person/Contract)
>
> John and Bill are in agreement about murdering murder Darren. (Agreement)
>
> John makes a down payment to Bill for the murder-for-hire. (Consideration)
>
> We have three out of the four things necessary for a contract. Where things fall apart is that it is against the law for Bill to murder Darren, and it is against the law for John to hire Bill for murder. Therefore, there is no Legal Purpose, so the contract is not legally binding.

A murkier example is insurance policies for marijuana-related businesses.

> Though marijuana is federally illegal, many states have legalized its use, and states control the regulation of insurance. (Contract)
>
> Insurers offer policies for marijuana businesses. (Competent Person/Contract)
>
> However, if insurers accept money from dispensaries, are they laundering drug money, which would be illegal? (Consideration?)

Is there a Legal Purpose? And who would make the legal determination about this? Federal courts would say the contract was illegal and non-binding; state courts might rule differently.

Insurance contracts also have some distinct characteristics which affect how courts interpret them.

Contract of Adhesion

An insurance policy is, for the most part, a contract of adhesion. This means the insured does not have the power to change the contract wording. While endorsements are a way for the insured to change policy language, the endorsement is still written by the insurer.

Since the insurer writes the policy and the insured has no say in how it is worded, in the event there is confusion or ambiguity over a word, courts tend to rule against the insurer. If the word in question is not defined in the policy, courts will use the "everyday meaning" of the word. The everyday meaning of a word is usually one found in a dictionary. The logic is that the insurer had the opportunity to word the policy in the manner it chose; so if the carrier were unclear in its language, that is the fault of the carrier. Coverage would likely be awarded to the insured.

This concept is important for adjusters to understand because it comes up often while handling claims. Let's explore the following example.

> The insured is a landlord who has a base form of CP 00 10 10/12 and a Special Cause of Loss form, CP 10 30 10/12. The building is split into separate offices and rented to separate tenants. Tenants are responsible for paying the electricity, including heat and air, for their spaces, while the landlord is responsible for the heat and air in common areas, such as the lobby and hallways.

> A tenant moved out without telling the landlord, and turned off utilities. Over the weekend, a pipe in the now-vacant office froze, creating water damage. The CP 10 30 10/30 states the insured (landlord) must maintain heat in the building for there to be coverage.

CAUSES OF LOSS – SPECIAL FORM

Words and phrases that appear in quotation marks have special meaning. Refer to Section G. Definitions.

...

B. *Exclusions*

...

2. *We will not pay for loss or damage caused by or resulting from any of the following:*

...

g. *Water, other liquids, powder or molten material that leaks or flows from plumbing, heating, air conditioning or other equipment (except fire protective systems) caused by or resulting from freezing, unless:*

(1) *You do your best to maintain heat in the building or structure; or*

(2) *You drain the equipment and shut off the supply if the heat is not maintained.*

The carrier denies the claim, stating the landlord did not maintain heat in the "building," but building is not defined in the contract. The landlord argues only a portion of the building did not have heat maintained. In this case, the adjuster should review the policy and review the common, everyday definition of the word "building" before arriving at a coverage decision.

Unilateral Contract

Most insurance policies are unilateral contracts—meaning one party makes a binding promise. The promise in this case is that the carrier will pay for covered losses. While it's true the insured has conditions upon which the promise of coverage/payment is based, the insured does not have any promises to the insurance company *per se*.

Conditional Contract

Insurance policies are also conditional contracts because the insured must do certain things for the contract to be valid. There are conditions within the contract which must be met before the contract can begin, and there are conditions which must take place after a loss occurs for coverage to be granted.

The conditions which must be satisfied before the policy/coverage can begin are called "condition precedent." For example:

- The insured must pay the premiums.
- The insured must promptly notify the insurer of a loss.

"Conditions subsequent" are the conditions the insured must carry out after the loss occurred. For example:

- The insured must cooperate with the carrier's investigation.
- The insured must file a police report in the event of a theft claim.

Aleatory Contract

An insurance policy is also an aleatory contract, meaning an agreement wherein the involved parties have to perform no particular action(s) until a specific triggering event occurs. The insurance policy is contingent on the occurrence of a loss which may never happen. An insured can pay premiums for years and never suffer an accident, thus he does not "need" his policy; likewise, an insured can obtain a policy and suffer a large loss within months of the policy effective date.

Contract of Good Faith

Both the insurer and the insured must be transparent with one another when entering into the insurance contract. The insurer relies on the honesty of the insured when it assesses the insured during the underwriting phase. The insured's statements on the application are called "representations" and are used to determine whether the policyholder is insurable and how much premium should be charged. Misrepresentations are false statements of a material fact on which the insurer relies to write the policy; however, as will be discussed later, it is possible for the adjuster to misrepresent coverage, which can lead to waiver and estoppel issues.

An insurance contract is voidable if any representation is:

- Material
- Relied upon by the insurer
- Known to be false by the policyholder

"Material facts" are facts which, if they'd been known to the carrier, the insurer would either not have underwritten the risk or written the policy with higher premiums or a higher deductible. Misrepresentations are also indicative of fraud, which will cause the insurer to rescind, or void, the policy.

Rescinding the policy means the policy is assumed to have never been in existence from the beginning (*ab initio*). In such an instance, the insured is refunded the premium.

As mentioned previously, the carrier must also act in good faith and pay the claim when a covered cause of loss occurs. Failure to do so leads to violations of Unfair Claims Handling regulations and allegations of bad faith claim handling.

People Involved in Insurance

Adjusters

An adjuster is a person who works for an insurer to discover and determine the amount of any loss or damage payable under a property, casualty, or workers' compensation insurance policy. The adjuster then handles the case in order to settle the claim, loss, or damage.

As of the writing of this book, these 15 states and the District of Columbia do not require an adjuster to have a license to handle claims:

- Colorado
- District of Columbia
- Illinois
- Iowa
- Kansas
- Maryland
- Missouri
- Nebraska
- New Jersey
- North Dakota
- Ohio
- Pennsylvania
- South Dakota
- Tennessee
- Virginia
- Wisconsin

If an adjuster lives in a non-licensing state, she will need to apply for a Designated Home State (DHS) in order to have reciprocity with other states that do require licenses. For example, if the adjuster lives in Kanas, which does not require an adjuster license, she can ask for another state to become her Designated Home State. Adjusters usually choose Texas as their DHS, since the Texas adjuster license is reciprocal with almost all other states.

In order to obtain a license in a home state, the adjuster must pass that state's test. The state's department of insurance will have study guides and testing locations.

There are three types of adjusters:

- *Staff Adjusters* are adjusters who work for insurance companies. Staff Adjusters can also consist of Field Adjusters who examine property damage or photograph locations where accidents occurred to determine how much an insurance company should compensate the insured or claimant. The property can be anything from a house to a business or vehicle. They might look at police reports, talk to witnesses, do research, or consult with experts like architects, construction workers, or doctors to create a better understanding of the claim.

- *Independent Adjusters* are adjusters who work for companies other than the insurance company. The insurer will hire these adjusters to perform all or part of an investigation for them. Independent Adjusters are usually hired when no staff or field adjuster is close or available. Independent Adjusters can do almost all of the jobs of the staff adjuster; however, since the independent adjuster is not an employee of the insurer, the independent adjuster usually cannot accept or deny coverage or liability.

- *Public Adjusters* are adjusters hired by the insured to help with the adjustment of his claim. Not all states allow public adjusters.

Adjusters look at all the information from photos, video, and audio evidence, interviews and on-site evidence to determine if coverage and/or liability is available.

As a side note, I will refer to desk adjusters as *adjusters* and those insurance professionals who go into the field and investigate losses as *appraisers*. I find that using the terms "desk adjuster" and "field adjuster" is not enough of a distinction for lay people. However, it should be noted that given the correct training, a desk adjuster can "appraise" the damage of an item; therefore, she also can be an "appraiser."

Agents

Insurance agents and brokers, also known as producers or retail agents, must be licensed to sell insurance and must comply with state laws and regulations governing their activities. State departments of insurance regulate agents' activities in order to protect laypeople's interests while buying insurance.

Like adjusters, agents must have continuing education to ensure that they meet high professional standards.

Underwriters

Underwriters are the people who are responsible for determining whether a risk is acceptable and, therefore, whether a policy should be offered. The underwriter prices the premium of the risk and tries to balance the price to be competitive with other insurers and also profitable for the carrier.

Insured

Insureds will be discussed in more detail in Chapter 2, but an insured is the person who has obtained the insurance policy.

Claimant

The claimant is the person who is making a claim on the policy. This is an important distinction, as many adjusters do not consider insureds to be claimants, but in first-party claims, a policyholder is a claimant to his own policy of insurance.

Wrap Up

When it comes to insurance underwriting, there are simply too many concepts for any single book to capture. I'm not even going to try. For this reason, I assume an adjuster reading this already has a few years under her belt, and can use this book as a springboard into more complex ideas. I have attempted to place the concepts in sequential chapters which make the most sense.

2

Insurance Policy

The first thing an adjuster should do upon receiving a new claim is to review the loss notice and the policy together. The adjuster is looking for coverage. She is looking to make sure the details of the loss fit within the four corners of the policy.

Types of Policies

There are many types of policies to cover all types of losses. They usually fall into one of two categories: (1) property and (2) liability.

A property policy will cover events when the insured experiences a loss as the result of damage, destruction, or loss of use of property. Examples of a property peril include fire, water, wind, and vandalism.

In a liability loss, a third party, called a claimant, will file a claim against the insured's policy as a result of something the insured did or did not do. An example is a slip and fall or trip and fall in a grocery store which results in bodily injury to the claimant. Auto accidents are another liability example most laypeople are familiar with – but they can fall into both the property and liability categories. The claimant's car, while property, would be filed on the insured's liability policy if the insured were at fault. The insured, on the other hand, would file a claim on his auto property policy because he would have a property claim for his own car.

Other types of policies, such as cargo, while encompassing damage to inanimate objects or cattle, is actually a type of liability policy because damage to the item being hauled might be the result of something the insured did or did not do.

Essentially, if the damage to the insured's item was not self-caused, the claim would fall on the property policy; if the insured caused damage to another's property, the claim would show up on the liability policy.

Parts of the Policy

Policies have 5 parts, and an easy way to remember this is the mnemonic "DICE."

(1) Declarations
(2) Insuring Agreement
(3) Conditions
(4) Exclusions & (5) Endorsements

The Declarations Page will detail the perils, or risks, or a list of what is covered in the policy. Policies cover many different kinds of loss, but all policies have the sections listed above. I use a commercial property policy Declarations Sheet as an example. Though this example is for commercial coverage, the same principles would apply to a homeowners policy.

1. DECLARATIONS

The Declarations Page is the who, what, where, when, and how much of the policy. It is a summary of the coverages offered to the insured.

COMMERCIAL PROPERTY
CP DS 00 10 00

COMMERCIAL PROPERTY COVERAGE PART
DECLARATIONS PAGE

POLICY NO. SP000024892   **EFFECTIVE DATE** <u>02</u> / <u>21</u> / <u>2020</u>   ☐ "X" If Supplemental
                                                          Declarations Is Attached

NAMED INSURED

Insured Works, Inc.

DESCRIPTION OF PREMISES

Prem. No.	Bldg. No.	Location, Construction And Occupancy
01	01	123 Main St., Little Rock, AR 72211, joint masonry. warehouse
02	01	17264 Priest Dr., Little Rock, AR 72211, joint masonry, tenant

COVERAGES PROVIDED — Insurance At The Described Premises Applies Only For Coverages For Which A Limit Of Insurance Is Shown

Prem. No.	Bldg. No.	Coverage	Limit Of Insurance	Covered Causes Of Loss	Coinsurance*	Rates
01	01	Bldg.	$200,000	Special	80%	See sched.
01	01	Contents	$150,000	Broad	80%	See sched.
02	01	Bldg.	$ 75,000	Special	80%	See sched.
02	01	Contents	$150,000	Broad	80%	See sched.

*If Extra Expense Coverage, Limits On Loss Payment

OPTIONAL COVERAGES — Applicable Only When Entries Are Made In The Schedule Below

Prem. No.	Bldg. No.	Agreed Value			Replacement Cost (X)		
		Expiration Date	Cov.	Amount	Building	Pers. Prop.	Including "Stock"
					01	X	

Prem. No.	Bldg. No.	Inflation Guard (%)		*Monthly Limit Of Indemnity (Fraction)	Maximum Period Of Indemnity (X)	*Extended Period Of Indemnity (Days)
		Bldg.	Pers. Prop.			
02	01			1/3	12 months	

*Applies to Business Income Only

MORTGAGEHOLDERS

Prem. No.	Bldg. No.	Mortgageholder Name And Mailing Address
01	01	City Bank & Loan
02	01	City Bank & Loan

DEDUCTIBLE

$2,500 Exceptions: Wind/hail Deductible: 5%

FORMS APPLICABLE

To All Coverages: CP0010, CP1030, CP0030, CP DS00, IL0017, CP0321

To Specific Premises/Coverages:

Prem. No.	Bldg. No.	Coverages	Form Number

CP DS 00 10 00   Copyright, Insurance Services Office, Inc., 1999   Page 1 of 1   ☐

Who

**COMMERCIAL PROPERTY COVERAGE PART
DECLARATIONS**

Policy No. SP00024892   Effective Date: 02/21/2020
Insured: Insured Works, Inc.   12:01 A.M. Standard Time
                                   ☐ Supplemental Declarations is Attached

The "Who" of the Declarations Page is the *First Named Insured*, the person or entity who is insured on the policy. In the example above it is shown as "Insured Works, Inc." The First Named Insured has some rights and obligations granted by the policy which other insureds do not. The First Named Insured is responsible for payment of the premiums. He also has the right to cancel coverage.

Other people or entities can be insureds.

- *Named Insureds* aka *Additional Named Insureds*: These insureds also are listed on the Declarations Page. There are no Additional Named Insureds in the sample Declarations Page above. The Additional Named Insured is usually found in a liability policy. She does not have the same rights and obligations as the Named Insured, although, unlike the Additional Insured, the policy will cover all of the same actions she takes as the insured.

- *Additional Insured*: This person has been added to the insurance policy, usually a liability policy, via endorsement because he has a contract or indemnity agreement with the Named Insured that requires it. The agreement states the First Named Insured must accept the transfer of risk for the Additional Insured. However, unlike the Additional Named Insured, the policy will only cover the Additional Insured for his acts performed by or on behalf of the First Named Insured.

- *Defined Insured*: This is the person who may not be named on the Declarations or Endorsement but may become an insured based on the definition in the policy.

  For example, Peter Smith is married to Mary Smith for 14 years. Their homeowners policy, HO 03 05/11, lists Peter Smith as the only Named Insured on the Declarations Page. The policy would list Mary as a defined insured, based on the following:

DEFINITIONS

...

B.   *In addition, certain words and phrases are defined as follows:*

...

5.   *"Insured" means:*

   a.   *You and residents of your household who are:*

   (1)   *Your relatives; or*

   (2)   *Other persons under the age of 21 and in your care or the care of a resident of your household who is your relative...*

This also means Peter and Mary's 14-year-old niece, Samantha, who is spending the summer with them, is also a defined insured because she is under the age of 21, staying at Peter and Mary's house, and in their care.

Peter and Mary have a 19-year-old son, Bill, who rented an apartment with his boyfriend, Barry, while attending an out-of-state university. Both men qualify as "full-time students" by the definition of their school. Bill would be a defined insured, but Barry would not, based on the following policy language:

DEFINITIONS

...

B.   *In addition, certain words and phrases are defined as follows:*

...

5.   *"Insured" means:*

   ...

   b.   *A student enrolled in school full-time, as defined by the school, who was a resident of your household before moving out to attend school, provided the student is under the age of:*

   (1)   *24 and your relative; or*

   (2)   *21 and in your care or the care of a resident of your household who is your relative;*

It is very important for adjusters to know who the insured is at all times, since notifying the insured of coverage issues/questions will often involve notifying all the insureds.

An Additional Named Insured is entitled to 100 percent of the benefits and coverage provided by the policy. An Additional Insured is not. Therefore, the insurer may have obligations to the Additional Named Insured that it does not have to the Additional Insured.

What

Prem. No.	Bldg. No.	Coverage	Limit Of Insurance	Covered Causes Of Loss	Coinsurance*	Rates
COVERAGES PROVIDED		Insurance At The Described Premises Applies Only For Coverages For Which A Limit Of Insurance Is Shown				
01	01	Bldg.	$200,000	Special	80%	See sched.
01	01	Contents	$150,000	Broad	80%	See sched.
02	01	Bldg.	$ 75,000	Special	80%	See sched.
02	01	Contents	$150,000	Broad	80%	See sched.

*If Extra Expense Coverage, Limits On Loss Payment

Prem. No.	Bldg. No.	Agreed Value			Replacement Cost (X)		
OPTIONAL COVERAGES		Applicable Only When Entries Are Made In The Schedule Below					
		Expiration Date	Cov.	Amount	Building	Pers. Prop.	Including "Stock"
					01	X	

	Inflation Guard (%)		*Monthly Limit Of Indemnity (Fraction)	Maximum Period Of Indemnity (X)	*Extended Period Of Indemnity (Days)
	Bldg.	Pers. Prop.			
02	01		1/3	12 months	

*Applies to Business Income Only

The "What" is indicated on the sample policy by listing what the policy insures. In this example, a building, its contents, property of others, and business income and extra expenses are covered. Business income, also called business interruption, is listed under "Optional Coverages." Insured Works, Inc. paid an additional premium for this coverage.

Where

DESCRIPTION OF PREMISES

Prem. No.	Bldg. No.	Location, Construction And Occupancy
01	01	123 Main St., Little Rock, AR 72211, joint masonry, warehouse
02	01	17264 Priest Dr., Little Rock, AR 72211, joint masonry, tenant

Above is the Description of Premises, which is the "Where" of the Declarations Page and provides the address for the "What" that is insured. It is commonly referred to as the coverage territory.

When

COMMERCIAL PROPERTY COVERAGE PART
DECLARATIONS PAGE

POLICY NO. SP000024892   EFFECTIVE DATE 02 / 21 / 2020   ☐ "X" If Supplemental

The coverage dates are the "When" of the policy, usually called the "policy period." This policy doesn't give an end date—it simply shows the beginning or effective date. Almost all policies are for one year. If they are not, there will be an endorsement stating how long the policy is.

Coverages

The coverages are in two locations. The first states "Covered Causes of Loss." This Declaration Sheet is for a commercial policy in which there is not a package policy, but several policies which must come together in what I call a "cafeteria plan" to fully cover the insured.[4]

COVERAGES PROVIDED   Insurance At The Described Premises Applies Only For Coverages For Which A Limit Of Insurance Is Shown

Prem. No.	Bldg. No.	Coverage	Limit Of Insurance	Covered Causes Of Loss	Coinsurance*	Rates
01	01	Bldg.	$200,000	Special	80%	See sched.
01	01	Contents	$150,000	Broad	80%	See sched.
02	01	Bldg.	$ 75,000	Special	80%	See sched.
02	01	Contents	$150,000	Broad	80%	See sched.

*If Extra Expense Coverage, Limits On Loss Payment

OPTIONAL COVERAGES   Applicable Only When Entries Are Made In The Schedule Below

Prem. No.	Bldg. No.	Agreed Value			Replacement Cost (X)		
		Expiration Date	Cov.	Amount	Building	Pers. Prop.	Including "Stock"
					01	X	

Inflation Guard (%) Bldg. Pers. Prop.		*Monthly Limit Of Indemnity (Fraction)	Maximum Period Of Indemnity (X)	*Extended Period Of Indemnity (Days)
02	01	1/3	12 months	

*Applies to Business Income Only

---

4 As a quick reference, a package policy is one that, well, is packaged together, meaning property and casualty risks are together in one coverage form. Homeowners, Personal Auto Policies, and Businessowners Policies are examples of this. Cafeteria plans – and I have no idea if that's the Official Insurance Term for a non-packaged policy – are those in which the insured, agent, and insurer cobble together a unified set of policies which, hopefully, doesn't leave the insured with a large uncovered loss. Commercial policies frequently use this process. For example, an insured business needs a property policy, a liability policy, a cyber policy, an equipment policy, and possibly an additional theft policy since employee theft is not covered in the property policy. Since no package policy will cover all of those elements, the parties involved come up with what I refer to as a "cafeteria plan" for complete coverage.

In this section, the Declarations Sheet is telling the adjuster, insured, agent, and anyone else reading it, which types of risks are covered (Special and Broad in this example).

The second, noted as "Forms Applicable," informs the reader which policy forms the insurer is using for this insured. This allows the adjuster to know, specifically, which forms to use.

FORMS APPLICABLE

To All Coverages: CP 00 10, CP 00 30, CP 00 90, CP 10 30

Unfortunately, this Declarations Page is incomplete.

The Insurance Services Office (ISO) writes standardized policy forms many insurers use. Some insurers will use the wording as it is, and others will change a few parts of the coverages to adapt it to their specific risk tolerances. Regardless, every ISO policy has a 10-digit alphanumeric code.

The first two slots are letters, indicating the type of policy being used. This is a "CP" policy, telling the adjuster it is a "commercial property" policy. An "HO" policy would be a "homeowners" policy, while a "BP" policy would be a "businessowners" policy. (There is a difference between Businessowners and Commercial Property policies, but we won't discuss that here.)

The next two slots are for the "level" of the policy. An introductory or "base form" policy is usually denoted as 00.

The following is the type of policy. In our Insured Works, Inc. example, CP 00 10 means the "property" or building and contents policy. The CP 00 30 is the business income policy.

All of the above are represented in the "Forms Applicable" section of the Declarations Page. What is missing are the last four slots which will instruct those reading the policy about the exact language they need to review. The last four numbers stand for the month and year ISO published the policy form.

All policies will be updated at some point. Some updates are minor and hardly noticeable. However, this Declarations Page does not tell the adjuster whether she should be reviewing and using the 10/12 edition or the 06/07 edition. Therefore, the adjuster does not have the entire policy, and cannot determine if there is coverage until she knows the date of the edition the underwriters intended to use.

There is a further problem in this Declarations Page. Comparing the

Covered Causes of Loss with the Forms Applicable, the adjuster notes the "Broad" form Cause of Loss is to be used for Insured Works, Inc.'s contents and the contents belonging to others which Insured Works, Inc. has in its possession. But this form is not listed in the applicable coverage forms.

The Special Form Cause of Loss (for the building and business income) is CP 10 30 (no edition date), but there is no listing for the Broad form, which is CP 10 20 (MM/YY).

FORMS APPLICABLE

To All Coverages: CP 00 10, CP 00 30, CP 00 90, CP 10 30

Again, the adjuster cannot adjust this loss until she reviews all coverages. The missing form number may simply be a "Scrivener's error," which is the legal term for a typo. If that is the case, there should be an endorsement noting the edition dates of all the Forms Applicable and the inclusion of the Broad form.

If it is not a Scrivener's error, then there should be an endorsement stating the policy should read that the only cause of loss form is the Special Cause of Loss form, CP 10 30 (MM/YY).

Either way, when reviewing policies, the adjuster must make sure she has all the correct forms before coverage can be determined. This shows how coverage can hinge on the meaning of one word or four numbers.

Co-Insurance

COVERAGES PROVIDED			Insurance At The... A Limit Of Insurance Is Shown			Coverages For Which
Prem. No.	Bldg. No.	Coverage	Limit Of Insurance	Covered Causes Of Loss	Coinsurance*	Rates
01	01	Bldg.	$200,000	Special	80%	See sched
01	01	Contents	$150,000	Broad	80%	See sched
02	01	Bldg.	$ 75,000	Special	80%	See sched
02	01	Contents	$150,000	Broad	80%	See sched

*If Extra Expense Coverage, Limits On Loss Payment

OPTIONAL COVERAGES		Applicable Only When Entries Are Made In The Schedule Below					
Prem. No.	Bldg. No.	Agreed Value			Replacement Cost (X)		
		Expiration Date	Cov.	Amount	Building	Pers. Prop.	Including "Stock"
					01	X	

		Inflation Guard (%)		*Monthly Limit Of	Maximum Period	*Extended Period
		Bldg.	Pers. Prop.	Indemnity (Fraction)	Of Indemnity (X)	Of Indemnity (Days)
02	01			1/3	12 months	

*Applies to Business Income Only

The Limit of Insurance and Coinsurance are located on the same line and show that these two items are linked. An insured is required to have his building insured up to 80 percent of its *insurance* value (not retail value). Failure to do so makes the insured a co-insurer (or another insurance carrier) of its loss. In other words, if Insured Works, Inc. doesn't have enough insurance, it must pay the portion of the claim that is not covered because it does not have enough insurance.

Adjusters are taught the following formula to calculate the amount owed when a coinsurance adjustment is required:

$$\left(\frac{Did}{Should} \times Loss \right) - Deductible$$

If you'd like to skip ahead to Chapter 10, I discuss another method which is more beneficial to the insured:

$$\left(\frac{Did}{Should} - Deductible \right) \times Loss$$

Coinsurance Adjustments

Since we're on the topic of coinsurance, almost every adjuster I know (including myself) calls the coinsurance adjustment the "coinsurance penalty."

Don't do this!

The policy doesn't mention penalties. People get their hackles up when you penalize them.

Do not write the word "penalty." Do not say the word "penalty." Do not think about the word "penalty." Do not pass go; do not collect $200.

Deductible

DEDUCTIBLE
All perils: $2,500; wind/hail deductible: 5%

This is the amount the insured owes before the insurer will pay. It is different from co-insurance. For Insurance Works, Inc.'s policy, there are two types of deductibles: (1) an "all peril" deductible of $2,500 and (2) a wind/

hail deductible of 5%. Usually that is a percentage of the total insured value (TIV).

There are two ways to interpret the reading of ambiguous instructions regarding application of the deductible, and I've seen it done both ways. The more conservative method, and thus the better method for the insured, is to apply the deductible to the total insured value of the line of coverage. For example, if there had been a hail loss to building 1, the deductible would be $200,000 x 5%= $10,000.00. However, an alternate school of thought says the total insured value would be the policy's total insurance limit. In this case, totaling all the limits would amount to $1,050,000. If the 5 percent deductible were applied, the deductible would be $52,5000.00. This is not at all advantageous to the insured.

The adjuster should review the policy to see how it is worded to apply the deductible, and lacking that, discuss it with her supervisor.

Mortgage Holder

If the insured does not own the item being insured (a building, car, etc.), then there may be a lienholder or a mortgage holder. If a payment is being issued to the insured, the lienholder or mortgage holder has an interest in the settlement and should be listed as a second payee on the settlement check to the insured.

MORTGAGEHOLDERS

Prem. No.	Bldg. No.	Mortgageholder Name And Mailing Address
01	01	City Bank & Loan
02	01	City Bank & Loan

2. INSURING AGREEMENT

The insuring agreement is the promise the insurer makes to the insured. This statement tells the insured what the carrier will do in the event of a loss.

The Dwelling Property Special Cause of Loss form (DP 00 03 12/02) insuring agreement is:

> *SECTION I*
>
> *DWELLING PROPERTY 3 – SPECIAL FORM*
>
> *AGREEMENT*
>
> *We will provide the insurance described in this policy in return for the premium and compliance with all applicable provisions of this policy.*

It really is that simple.

The insurer ("we") states it will provide coverage for the insured's property in exchange for money ("premium") and the insured's cooperation ("compliance") with policy provisions (conditions of the policy).

Since the arrival of COVID-19, many attorneys believe this statement covers everything, because it doesn't specifically state what the policy doesn't cover. In everyday speech, the policy attached to this Special Cause of Loss form is called an "all-risk" policy, a term I very much dislike. There is no such thing as an "all-risk" policy. There is an "everything-is-covered-except-what's-excluded" policy, which is more cumbersome and not nearly as sexy as saying "all-risk" policy. This inaccuracy tends to create a great brouhaha in the legal sphere, which is why adjusters should stick to calling the Special Cause of Loss form a "Special Cause of Loss" form. Do not call it an "all-risk" policy; and when explaining coverages to the insured, take great pains to educate the insured that, despite what he might have been told by the agent or the internet or his neighbor's cousin's brother-in-law's friend who is an attorney, there is no such thing as an "all-risk policy."

3. CONDITIONS

This part of the policy states the requirements of the insured and insurer and describes how certain situations will be resolved. For example, the policy will describe how the claim will be paid in the Conditions section, the duties of the insured, subrogation and appraisal rights, and how notice of a claim should be provided to the insurer.

Policies may have Additional Conditions, which discuss co-insurance and payments to mortgage holders.

Some policies will have the ISO Interline form, IL 00 17 11/98, which refers to "Common Policy Conditions" and includes cancellation, changes, the insurer's right to inspections, premium, and the transferring of rights and duties. Because the Common Policy Conditions is a separate form, it is an endorsement, adding additional conditions which must be met in order for there to be coverage in the policy.

4. EXCLUSIONS

Exclusions are the part of the policy lay people may have heard the most about when it comes to insurance claims. This is, after all, why their claim is not being paid. Insureds may believe their policy is nothing but exclusions; however, this may boil down to having bought the wrong policy or misunderstanding the role and purpose of insurance.

Insurance is not a warranty policy. If the roof simply wears out, the insured cannot make a claim and expect to be paid for it. There must be a covered cause of loss. Likewise, if the insured does not provide for continued maintenance on his building, the insurer will not replace the roof unless the insured opted for replacement cost coverage (RCV). Even then, the insurer is not obligated to replace the entire roof if replacing part of it will suffice and there is no local ordinance stating otherwise.

In reality, exclusions are the parts of the risk the carrier does not want to insure. Either it is:

(a) too expensive to do so (for example, Buckingham Palace does not have insurance)

(b) too rare or too specialized a risk (although it is true some specialized risks can be covered – I knew an agent who obtained insurance for dinosaur bones while they were being transferred from the archeological dig site to a museum to be studied)

(c) the carrier simply has no appetite for the type of risk (for example, many insurers do not underwrite homes on the Gulf Coast, due to the numerous hurricane/windstorm risks)

There are some "smaller" exclusions, which do not entirely delete coverage from the policy. These would not properly be called "exclusions" as much as "limits of liability."

This is a carving out of coverage—somewhat like an exclusion, but not really, because the loss is still covered. It may not be covered to the total amount of the loss. For example, in the HO 00 03 05/11 coverage of contents, there are some instances when the carrier wants to limit the amount of money it would pay for a particular kind of loss.

C. Coverage C – Personal Property

...

3. *Special Limits of Liability*

The special limit for each category shown below is the total limit for each loss for all property in that category. These special limits do not increase the Coverage C limit of liability.

a. *$200 on money, bank notes, bullion, gold other than goldware, silver other than silverware, platinum other than platinumware (sic), coins, medals, scrip, stored value cards and smart cards.*

b. *$1,500 on securities, accounts, deeds, evidences of debt, letters of credit, notes other than bank notes, manuscripts, personal records, passports, tickets and stamps.*

...

c. *$1,500 on watercraft of all types, including their trailers, furnishings, equipment and outboard engines or motors.*

d. *$1,500 on trailers or semitrailers not used with watercraft of all types.*

e. *$1,500 for loss by theft of jewelry, watches, furs, precious and semiprecious stones.*

f. *$2,500 for loss by theft of firearms and related equipment.*

There are more limits on the amount which would be paid, but this provides an example of how coverage can be carved out in a policy, but not necessarily completely excluded.

5. ENDORSEMENT:

I explain coverages as thus: There is the policy. It states what is covered (Declarations Sheet). Then the Underwriters taketh away (exclusions), and then the Underwriters giveth back (endorsements).

As mentioned previously, there is usually some insurer somewhere who will write coverage for something that is excluded. Endorsements are additions to the policy in which a risk is added back to the policy for coverage. Endorsements are often found "outside" the base form of the policy—meaning they are on different sheets of paper with different form numbers. Exclusions can either be in the base form, or they can be separated from the base policy.

Like the exclusion, an endorsement does not necessarily mean the entire risk is added back. Depending on the carrier's appetite for the type of risk or the amount of premium, the risk may be partially added to the policy.

Covered Causes of Loss

The causes of loss are the occurrences which could cause the policy to respond, but not all causes of loss are covered, which creates some confusion for lay people who believe because they've suffered a loss, they have coverage.

A direct loss is a claim sustained due to uninterrupted physical damage to property. This means there is no intervening incident between the cause of loss and the property damage. These are usually the named perils listed in the Cause of Loss forms.

A second type of loss is an indirect or consequential loss. This claim or damage would be as a consequence of the direct loss. For example, if the insured suffered a fire loss, its business would be closed while it rebuilt/repaired the structure. We will assume the insured has a Business Income policy which would pay for the loss of customers while the insured rebuilds/repairs. This policy and payment are as a consequence of the fire.

On Insured Works, Inc.'s Declarations Page, there were two Causes of Loss listed for coverage: Special and Broad. These were briefly discussed above. The types of risks covered vary according to the insurer. The vast majority of adjusters and laypeople are familiar with three types of covered causes of loss:

- Basic Cause of Loss
- Broad Cause of Loss
- Special Cause of Loss

Often these will be numbered as 10, 20, 30 in commercial policies and 01, 02, 03 in homeowner or dwelling policies. The HO 00 03 (MM/YY) is the Special Cause of Loss form for homeowners; for a dwelling policy, the cause of loss is written DP 00 03 (MM/YY); in commercial insurance, it would be written as CP 00 10 30 (MM/YY).

Basic Cause of Loss forms are the narrowest of the named peril policies. "Named Peril" policy simply means there is only coverage for the perils (causes of loss) named. It is opposite of an "Open Peril" policy where "everything-is-covered-except-what's-excluded" (aka Special Cause of Loss form as previously discussed).

The named perils of the Basic Cause of Loss form are:

- Fire
- Smoke
- Riot
- Vehicles,
- Sinkhole Collapse

- Lighting
- Windstorm
- Civil commotion
- Vandalism
- Volcanic Action

- Explosion
- Hail
- Aircraft
- Sprinkler leakage

The Broad Cause of Loss form are the above-named perils, plus:

- Falling objects
- Collapse from specified causes
- Weight of snow, ice, or sleet
- Water damage (from appliances that leak)

The Special Cause of Loss form is the most inclusive of perils; it is an open peril policy. When adjusting a policy with a Special Cause of Loss form, adjusters need to pay special attention to the exclusions section of the policy to ensure they are not inadvertently paying for something that is not covered.

A little-mentioned maxim of cause of loss forms is how they are applied when working with the insured. The insured must prove his loss if there is a Named Peril policy. This means the insured must show the insurer that a Named Peril caused the damage. Alternatively, the insurer has the burden of proof to show that an exclusion is applicable and, therefore, there is no coverage when the insured has an Open Peril Policy.

Insurance in Action

Insured Works, Inc. suffered roof and interior water damage due to a tropical storm. It has a Special Cause of Loss for the building, and the adjuster is checking with the underwriting department concerning the cause of loss form for contents.

Tropical storms are a wind event; therefore, the damage to the roof caused by the wind is a covered cause of loss because there are no exclusions which prohibit coverage. Once the adjuster receives the estimate for the roof damage, she should issue a Proof of Loss (if required by the carrier) and pay the claim.

Insured Works, Inc. also suffered interior water damage due to localized flooding which damaged its structure and contents. Water is not excluded in the Open Perils policy, but flooding is not a covered occurrence; therefore, it is up to the adjuster to prove the interior water damage to Insured Works, Inc.'s structure is due to flooding and not the damage to the roof, which may have created an opening for water to enter, and thereby damaging the interior of the building.

To prove the cause of the interior water damage, the adjuster would review the photographs of the Insured Works, Inc. roof, review the local news or check with neighboring businesses for flood information, and perhaps even review some flood maps. If Insured Works, Inc. is located in a flood zone and its neighbors also experienced flood damage, that is a good indication Insured Works, Inc. also had flood damage. However, this evidence does not allow the adjuster to deny coverage for the interior water damage yet.

In reviewing the roof photographs, the adjuster sees damage to the roofing materials, but there are not any obvious openings created by a covered peril. Likewise, the appraiser/field adjuster did not note any water damage near the ceiling of the building. Now it seems likely the interior water damage is completely related to flood.

The adjuster's next step would be to discuss coverages (or lack thereof) with the insured and send a Reservation of Rights letter, followed by a Letter of Declination if the final investigation showed there was no coverage for the interior.

However, imagining the adjuster did see damage to Insured Works, Inc.'s roof which encompassed an opening in which rainwater could enter, there is a co-mingling of flood water and wind-driven rain. This means there are two causes of the interior's damage. Wind-driven rain is a covered cause of loss because it is not excluded; flood is still an excluded occurrence. What does the adjuster do in this instance?

The adjuster must determine how much damage is as a result of the water coming from the opening in the roof and how much damage is as a result of the flood. Of course, this is a nearly impossible task.

See our example photograph above.

Logic must be applied in not only this circumstance, but in every claim adjusted. After Hurricane Katrina, Louisiana stated property adjusters were not able to simply use the "flood line" in this image (red straight line) and determine that everything beneath this line was "flood" and, therefore, everything above it was a result of the windstorm (blue arrows).

There are some tell-tell signs, however, demonstrating the damages. Generally, damage on a ceiling will be from the roof opening. Even if there is a floor above—the rainwater could enter the structure and then seep into the floor, gradually making it to the first-floor ceiling per the law of gravity. In such a case, photographs will show water stains on the ceiling. For our example, this is the blue line on the house.

Wind broke the window on the first and second floors (blue arrows); rain came into the house through the first and second now-opened windows damaging the interior of the home. The first-floor ceiling will have damage from the second story window as mentioned above.

Mud and debris on the first floor will be left behind by receding flood waters (red arrow). And, flood waters will leave a line (red straight line).

In the above example, along the left wall, there is obvious structural damage (white arrow). However, an adjuster would not be able to tell whether the damage was a result of the wind/hurricane or the levy breaking and flood damage. How would the adjuster determine what is covered (and therefore pay the claim) and what is not covered (and send a Declination of Coverage Letter) for this damage?

The property adjuster is not handling Insured Works, Inc.'s flood damage because it's not a covered peril. Hopefully Insured Works, Inc. has a flood policy. For the sake of our example, they do. The flood adjuster would not handle the roof damage, as that is excluded in his policy.

The property adjuster should coordinate her appraisal with the flood adjuster, and the totals of their two damage estimates (property and flood) should match closely enough that they do not leave Insured Works, Inc. with a large uncovered loss.

I want to stress a common-sense approach to handling a claim such as this—cooperation between insurers. Unfortunately, this is, in my opinion, an uncommon occurrence. My experience is that all too often insurers are so steeped in their rules and guidelines that they forget their purpose is to indemnify the insured, which means the adjuster must adjust (or move) the settlement figures sometimes.

I'm going to take a step even further back, since it occurs to me that I am assuming everyone knows this basic step of cooperation. I apologize for the rudimentary lesson, seeing as this is an intermediate adjusting book, but I figure it's best not to assume this is known and to make sure it is part of the foundational information about handling claims.

When there is a covered and uncovered loss, the respective adjusters should ask the insured for the contact information of the other insurer/ adjuster. It should not be the insured's task to coordinate his insurers and ensure he is fully indemnified for his loss which is covered between two insurance carriers.

In this example, Gail Force, our windstorm adjuster (*Get it? Wind? And the adjuster is named Gail Force?*), knows there is flood damage to the property. She contacts the insured, who informs her that Lotta Wadda is the flood adjuster (*if you're not ROTFLOL right now, I just give up on you*). Gail and Lotta contact one another to coordinate inspections.

Even though there are computer programs which help write the estimates, the appraisal process is not science. By coordinating inspections—or even using the same appraiser to write the estimate—the two insurers can ensure their mutual insured is not, as mentioned earlier, left with a large gap or uncovered claim.

For example, the two adjusters may decide to split the damage in this manner:

Damage	Flood Policy	Property Policy
First floor ceiling	0% of damages	100% of damages
Second floor interior	0% of damages	100% of damages
Left wall	100% of damages	0% of damages
Front (outside) wall	75% of damages	25% of damages
First Floor	85% of damages	15% of damages

It is not the goal of insurance to pay as little as possible. The policy's goal is to put the insured back to where he was prior to the loss (some of this is explained further in Chapters 5 and 10). There is, literally, no way to tell what damage is caused by which peril. Therefore, Gail and Lotta are going to adjust their estimates to match the damages and fully indemnify the insured.

In our make-believe example, we only have one exterior photo, and we can't see the interior of the house. In reality, we'd have several photographs of the damage, including a photo showing the first-floor ceiling which collapsed because of water coming in from the top floor window (blue arrow). Assuming that's the case, then rainwater would have fallen into the interior of the structure to the first-floor ceiling (blue line), so the property insurer would owe a portion of the first-floor damage—although not all of it, because the majority of damage is from flooding.

It could confuse some that the property adjuster is paying 25% of the damages for the front (outside) wall and 15% of the damages for the first floor. As mentioned previously, we cannot know whether the damage to the left wall is structural damage resulting from the flood, or if the damage is due to wind. Therefore, giving the insured every benefit of the doubt, the property insurer should pay for a portion of the damage, and the flood policy should pay the other portion in order to avoid a gap in coverage.

Still confused as to why Gail would pay for alleged uncovered damages? And why Lotta might pay for damages her flood policy doesn't cover? Let's get into some (slightly) more advanced adjusting concepts.

Imagine the flood claim had never existed. Let's say, for the sake of argument, a tornado came through, picked up the house and slammed it back down. This is what caused the broken windows and structural damages. What would the property carrier pay? It would have to cover 100% of all damages, even the first-floor interior water damage, because all of the damage was caused by wind.

There's no question here. This is pretty straight forward.

Now let's add the flood back into the claim, with a tornado thrown in just for fun.

Scenario A

The levee breaks and flood waters slam into the insured's house, knocking it off its foundation and causing structural damage, and as the flood waters recede, a tornado comes along, picks up the house, and slams it back down breaking the windows.

One could argue that Gail doesn't owe any of the first-floor damage (except maybe the first-floor window) because the flood waters created the first-floor damages to begin with. All Gail would owe is the second-floor damages and interior water damage around the broken second-floor window.

Scenario B

A tornado comes through, picks up the house and slams it back down, creating structural damage. Then the levee breaks and floods the first floor. How much does Lotta pay? She could argue "nothing," because the house was already damaged and the peril she covers (flood) didn't damage the insured any further than what he was already damaged. In other words, you can't break something that's already broken.

Reality

In reality, there is literally no way to tell which came first—the flood or the tornado, even if these perils are separated by days, unless there are time-stamped photographs showing one type of damage before the other.

When I handled Hurricane Katrina claims, the hurricane left and the levees didn't break right away, but because of the widespread damage, the government did not allow appraisers into the neighborhoods while they secured the areas and looked for survivors. *Then* the levees broke. I had no way of knowing if the damage was from the hurricane or the flood. I contacted the flood adjuster and we split the house (if it was located in the Nineth Ward) right down the middle.

Sound farfetched? What made it even worse was Hurricane Rita, which followed Katrina a month later. There was so much destruction from Katrina, the appraisers in New Orleans hadn't even been able to inspect all of its damages before Rita hit. Now adjusters had to split one house between two hurricanes and two floods. How do you do that?

As a final note on this damage, I made up the example of the split percentages between the two carriers. In reality, the two adjusters should discuss the damages and come to an agreement regarding how much would be paid from each carrier so that the insured was fully paid for the damage.

Wrap Up

Not all Declarations Pages look like the one discussed here, but all will have the same information. The adjuster must take care to make sure she has the entire policy before adjusting the claim. If the correct form is not used, one word can make a difference between coverage and no coverage, which we will discuss in Chapter 3. It's unlikely an insured would catch the difference unless it were pointed out to him. Even agents and underwriters might not know the difference, which also is discussed in Chapter 3. Therefore, adjusters must use their art to help guide every insurance professional and insured.

When reviewing the policy, adjusters should take care to work with other carriers in order to ensure the insured is fully indemnified and not left with a large gap in coverage. Not only is this good customer service, but it also reduces the chances of being sued for bad faith and a jury determining the amount of damages the carrier will pay.

3

Words Have Consequences

No one really wants to be a claims adjuster. It's not one of those fields where people line up for an opportunity. A colleague and I would tell applicants for adjuster positions, "You get yelled at eight hours a day. If the insured isn't yelling at you, the claimant is. If the claimant isn't yelling at you, the insured is. And if neither are yelling at you, I am because you're not doing your job."

Then there's the fact that the Bean Counters in the Ivory Tower (Home Office) have a belief that the Claims Department only spends money, and they dictate when budget cuts need to happen—well, like in everyday life. The places you spend the most money are where you cut the deepest. So hiring freezes and layoffs tend to occur in the adjuster pool, which means there seems to be twice as much work with fewer bodies to do it. (This is a recipe for bad faith, although that is another topic.)

Who wouldn't sign up for this job?

Agents and underwriters are the fair-haired children of the Bean Counters because they bring in the money. This makes claims adjusters the motorcycle-ridin', leather-jacket-wearin', stayin'-out-past-curfew, tatted-up, red-headed-step-children of the insurance family. *Awesome.*

I love being an adjuster, and if I've not mentioned it before, it is, in my humble opinion, the best part of the insurance industry despite its drawbacks. My mentor, Kevin Quinley, CPCU, ARM, SOB, AIC, LMNOP, AIM ARe,

RPA, XYZ, often says no one becomes an adjuster by choice.[5] I certainly didn't want to become one. My father was an adjuster, and I remember him taking recorded statements at home during the evenings and thinking, "My god, that's boring. I'm never going to become an adjuster."

Fast forward to having graduated from university and working at a car rental facility which paid very little, when my dad, who arranged an interview with Liberty Mutual, said, "I know you don't like it, but just go for an interview."

I got the job, and my supervisors had me read the standard operating procedure book. I remember thinking, "This job is great. I have money. People want money. I can help people. Why don't people sign up for this job?"

It's hard to sell insurance. People already have it and don't want to be bothered about it any further. Insureds just want to pay the very least they can for it, then yell at adjusters when they find out they don't have the correct (or enough) coverage. I know this because I have lured many a risk management student away from becoming an agent into becoming an adjuster. I had two interns who, unfortunately, had to go back to being agents. They hated leaving the adjusting side of the insurance scheme.

I bring this up to point out that being an adjuster is difficult, and I'll talk more about that in later chapters. However, the really great thing about being an adjuster is that you get to help people in their time of need. Folks in the Claims Department are the promise keepers of the insurance industry.

Unfortunately, because people want the least costly insurance and often will allow that fact to outweigh their agent's recommendation (or, god forbid, they purchase insurance online so they have no one advising them) the insureds often receive the *wrong* promise. Then everyone is upset when the adjuster comes along to handle the loss.

Real Life War Story

The insured's house was damaged by a typical spring windstorm. The roof was damaged and there was interior water damage. The building was insured with an HO 00 03 05/11, no special endorsements. The insureds did not live at this house—it was a rental home.

---

5 He's giving me a sweet recommendation for the back of the book and a 5-star review so I can be an "Amazon Best Seller!!!!" in exchange for this mention.

Words have consequences. Use this phrase to remind yourself to review the policy and apply it to the facts surrounding the loss.

The HO 00 03 05/11 states:

SECTION I – PROPERTY COVERAGES

A. Coverage A – Dwelling

    1. We cover:

        a. The dwelling on the "residence premises" shown in the Declarations, including structures attached to the dwelling;

If a word is either in bold or in quotes, it is defined in the policy. Otherwise, the ordinary accepted dictionary definition of a word applies (that, too, becomes important later).

DEFINITIONS

    ...

    11. "Residence premises" means:

        a. The one-family dwelling where you reside;

    ...

    and which is shown as the "residence premises" in the Declarations.

    "Residence premises" also includes other structures and grounds at that location.

For this claim, then, the insureds did not have coverage, because they did not reside at the home. They rented the house to tenants for money. The claim was denied. Both the insureds and the agent were livid, but the agent in this example had made the wrong promise. The adjuster kept the promise the insurer made: to pay a covered loss. This claim wasn't covered because of a failure to read the policy.

It would have been better for the insureds to have a Dwelling Policy, or a DP3. The DP 00 03 12/02 states:

Section I

COVERAGES

This insurance applies to the "Described Location", Coverages for which a Limit of Liability is shown and Perils Insured Against for which a Premium is stated.

A.   Coverage A – Dwelling

1. We cover:

    a. The dwelling on the "Described Location" shown in the Declarations, used principally for dwelling purposes, including structures attached to the dwelling;

As the policy states, the address shown on the Declarations page is the "Described Location." Had this policy been used in the above example, the insureds would have had coverage, and the adjuster would have gone on to the next steps of handling the claim.

Where the Rubber Meets the Road

Things are not always as clear cut as in the situation above. Sometimes the adjuster faces several issues converging at once which create a perfect storm. Marijuana coverage is a good example of this.

The insurance industry and the marijuana industry prefer to call use the term *cannabis*. This makes sense when you think about it. The U.S. Drug Enforcement Administration (DEA) has waged a war on drugs, including marijuana, for decades. Government propaganda calls marijuana a "gateway drug," claiming its use leads to the use of harder and more dangerous drugs.[6] Federally, marijuana is still very much illegal.

Some states have ignored the federal government and legalized marijuana. First and more broadly, medicinally; now, more states are legalizing marijuana for adult use, or "recreational use." So, it seems, marijuana needed a public relations campaign to make it appear less illegal. Enter *cannabis* as a synonym for *marijuana*.[7]

The problem with cannabis begins before the policy is even written. First, marijuana is federally illegal, despite what the states say. But we must go back to Chapter 1 and recall the tenet of insurance that "One Cannot Insure Illegal Things." Because of this doctrine, insurers are hesitant to dip their toes into the marijuana marketplace. However, states mandate insurance for public facing businesses (e.g. liability policies) to protect consumers.

---

6 Fun fact: Marijuana is a Schedule I drug, which means a drug with a high probability for abuse. Cocaine, on the other hand, is a Schedule II drug. Still addictive, but less so than Schedule I drugs, you know, like marijuana, according to the government.

7 This is a tad bit of an oversimplification, but you get the point.

Because of that rule, insurers are required to provide insurance coverage to marijuana, or federally illegal, markets.

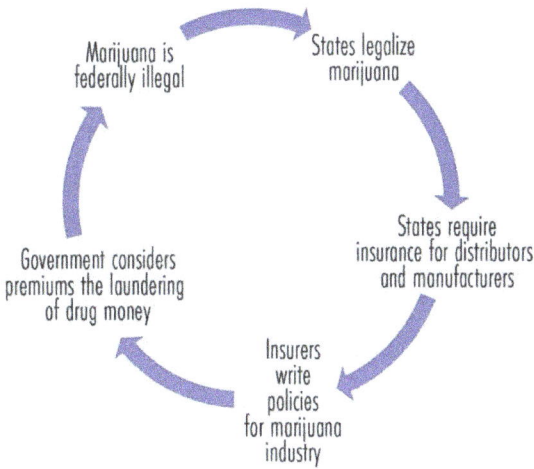

Looking at it from the outside, this PR campaign for marijuana would not seem to be a bad thing. Except that *Words Have Consequences*.

Cannabis is a plant. Contingent on how it's grown, it will either produce hemp-cannabis or marijuana-cannabis. Therefore, referring to "marijuana" as "cannabis" means, when the insurer excludes cannabis, it excludes hemp, too.

Shakespeare said, "A rose by any other name would smell as sweet." He was wrong, of course, because roses, depending on their type, smell differently.

Example

A homeowner has a rose garden consisting of tea roses, climbing roses, knockout roses, and shrub roses. The carrier does not want to insure climbing roses, since these types of roses can be used for a screen or a fence, and children might prick themselves, which could result in a liability claim. Therefore, the insurer has an exclusion for "roses" in the homeowner policy.

A guest is stung by a bee when she leans over to smell one of the knockout roses. Since she is allergic to bee stings, she must go to the hospital for critical care. She files a claim, which is denied because "roses" are excluded—i.e. there is no coverage for any of the flowers in the insured's garden.

This is not what either the insured or the carrier intended, but this is the way the policy was written. Because the word "roses" is used for the exclusion, rather than "climbing roses," the adjuster correctly denied the claim. Had the correct language been used in the exclusion, there would have been coverage, because the injury resulted from the bee on the knockout rose.

It's similar with "cannabis" and "marijuana," and has become more so with the legalization of hemp via the 2018 Farm Bill, which removed hemp with less than 0.3% dried weight of THC from the Schedule I drug list. However, it is difficult for the layperson looking at the photos below to

Image by NickyPe Pixabay

Image by WildØne Pixabay

know which plant is hemp—and legal—and which plant is marijuana—and illegal. It is easier to see why using the word "cannabis" to mean "marijuana" is incorrect. Hemp is as much cannabis as marijuana is.

Insurance in Action

As underwriters and agents sell policies with language they don't understand, this becomes a bigger issue. Especially if the adjuster denies the claim.

For example, the BP 15 33 09/19 is a "Cannabis Liability Exclusion with Hemp Exception." It is written for businessowners in the hemp industry, and it is meant to extend coverage to businesses working in the hemp-cannabis marketplace. It states:

> ### A. The following exclusion is added to Section II –Liability:
>
> *This insurance does not apply to:*
>
> *1. "Bodily injury," "property damage," or "personal and advertising injury" arising out of:*
>
>   *a. The design, cultivation, manufacture, storage, processing, packaging, handling, testing, distribution, sale, serving, furnishing, possession or disposal of "cannabis"; or*
>
>   *b. The actual, alleged, threatened or suspected inhalation, ingestion,*

absorption or consumption of, contact with, exposure to, existence of, or presence of "cannabis";

As mentioned previously, if the words are in quotes or bolded, they have special meaning. The definition to focus on in this example is "cannabis," which is defined as follows:

E. For the purpose of this endorsement, the following definition is added:

"Cannabis":

    1. Means:

        Any good or product that consists of or contains any amount of Tetrahydrocannabinol (THC) or any other cannabinoid, regardless of whether any such THC or cannabinoid is natural or synthetic.

    2. Paragraph E.1. above includes, but is not limited to, any of the following containing such THC or cannabinoid:

        a. Any plant of the genus Cannabis L., or any part thereof, such as seeds, stems, flowers, stalks and roots; or

        b. Any compound, byproduct, extract, derivative, mixture or combination, such as:

            (1) Resin, oil or wax;

            (2) Hash or hemp; or

            (3) Infused liquid or edible cannabis;

            whether or not derived from any plant or part of any plant set forth in Paragraph E.2.a

In order to understand why this definition is problematic, it must be broken down.

Cannabis means *any* product which contains *any* amount of **THC**. The definition of hemp, as defined by the 2018 Farm Bill, is "Hemp is defined as cannabis (Cannabis sativa L), and derivatives of cannabis, with extremely low (not more than 0.3 percent on a dry weight basis) concentrations of THC." This means that hemp, by its very definition, may contain THC. Therefore, if the goal is to provide coverage for hemp, but to exclude marijuana, this definition will lead to ambiguity.

The policy definition goes on to say that "any other cannabinoid, regardless of whether any such THC or cannabinoid is natural or synthetic" is excluded. Taking this exclusion to its extreme, cannabinoids found in the average kitchen, such as cinnamon, black pepper, clove, and anise, are also excluded. This is likely not the intent of the insurance form authors. But in their haste to remain legal in an environment that changes daily, insurers may be accidently excluding their hemp insureds, or they could be inadvertently including coverage for marijuana ventures by using the improper terminology.

Now that the definition of "cannabis" is known, the adjuster can determine whether there is coverage for the insured. In this businessowners' liability policy, the hemp insured cannot design a product consisting of hemp; it cannot cultivate hemp; it cannot manufacture hemp; it cannot store hemp; it cannot process hemp; it cannot package hemp; it can't even handle hemp; it can't test hemp; it cannot distribute hemp; it definitely cannot sell, serve, furnish, or have in its possession hemp. So what exactly does this policy insure, when hemp can contain 0.3 percent THC?

Often cannabis exclusions may not be for a hemp-related business.

EXCLUSION

Attached to and Forming Part of Policy XXXXXX93721-01	Effective Date of Exclusion 12:01 a.m. at the Named Insured address shown on the Declarations	Named Insured: Mom & Pop, Inc.
Additional Premium: N/A	Return Premium: N/A	

Consider a mom-and-pop general store that sells CBD cream. A customer buys the CBD cream and has an allergic reaction. The customer brings suit against the distributor, manufacturer, and Mom and Pop for her bodily injuries.

Mom and Pop have a standard commercial liability policy, but there is an exclusion which reads:

This exclusion modifies insurance provided under the following:

COMMERCIAL LIABILITY COVERAGE

The following exclusions are added to this policy:

1. *This insurance does not apply to any claim or suit for any injury or damage arising directly or indirectly out of related to, or in any way involving the real or alleged emergence, contraction, contribution to, aggravation or exacerbation of any form of adverse health effect, impairment of health, abnormal condition or conditions, disorder, sick-*

ness, ailment, unhealthiness symptom, disease, illness or malady of the human bodily as a result of the use, consumption or exposure to any product that is manufactured, sold, handled or distributed by, for or on behalf of any insured and includes any:

a. *Cannabis sativa, cannabis indica, hemp or marijuana or any of their derivatives;*

.....

Because the CBD cream was formulated from the cannabis plant (even though this particular exclusion specifically mentions hemp and marijuana), the product would not have coverage under Mom and Pop's policy. Because Mom and Pop operate a general store, and did not intend to sell marijuana, they wanted coverage for the products they do sell, such as the CBD cream. Mom and Pop, by the ordinary meaning of the words in the exclusion, "sold, handled or distributed..." a cannabis/hemp product. Due to this exclusion, their adjuster issued a letter of declination.

Further, the insurer will not provide a defense for Mom and Pop because the exclusion specifically states the policy doesn't apply to "any claim or suit..." Therefore, if Mom and Pop are not released from the suit by the plaintiff attorney, they will be forced to hire an attorney to defend them.

"Cannabis" may be too broad of a definition for the insured's business plan.

On the Home Front

But what about the average person who has a "medical marijuana card"? The authors and underwriters of policies have attempted to cover them. To address some of these changes in the insurance landscape, ISO has added the Controlled Substances exclusion to its HO 03. Controlled substances include but are not limited to cocaine, LSD, marijuana, and all narcotic drugs. Consider the HO 00 03 05/11 form which states:

E. Coverage E— Personal Liability and Coverage F— Medical Payments to Others Coverages E and F do not apply to the following:

...

8. *Controlled Substances*

> *"Bodily injury" or "property damage" arising out of the use, sale, manufacture, delivery, transfer or possession by any person of a Controlled Substance as defined by the Federal Food and Drug law at 21 U.S.C.A. Sections 811 and 812. Controlled Substances include but are not limited to cocaine, LSD, marijuana and all narcotic drugs. However, this exclusion does not apply to the legitimate use of prescription drugs by a person following the orders of a licensed physician.*

As the policy states, the exclusion "does not apply to the legitimate use of prescription drugs by a person following the orders of a licensed physician."

Although it is called "medical" marijuana and the public discusses obtaining a "prescription" for marijuana, this is vernacular use of the English language. The American Medical Association (AMA) states in its Resolution 907 (I-16) it "overtly opposes legalization of marijuana and endorses warnings emphasizing its dangers for abuse and misuse (AMA Policies D-95.976 and H-95.995)..." The AMA encourages the federal government to perform "adequate and well-controlled studies of marijuana" in its Cannabis for Medicinal Use H-95.952 document, but states this is not an endorsement of medical marijuana, nor that it "meets the current standards for a prescription drug product." Further, the *AMA Journal of Ethics* reminds doctors it is illegal for physicians to prescribe marijuana because it is a Schedule I drug, which would result in aiding and abetting in an illegal act.

Again, using the common, everyday meaning of words, since doctors cannot "prescribe" marijuana, there is no coverage. Giving the benefit of the doubt to the underwriters and insurers, which would allow for coverage under this part of the policy, what do the insureds in "adult-use" or "recreational" states do if there is a claim? This policy would not cover them because there is no prescription.

Wrap Up

All of this would be a moot point if hemp had no THC levels. However, by the mere fact that hemp comes from the cannabis plant, it contains some THC—just not as much as the marijuana plant.

I hear you.

You're saying, "Chantal, no one is going to say, 'You know? Chantal is right. We should *totally* change all the policies we've already written; the laws already passed; and regulations already enacted because she says so.'"

I get it. I do. Seriously.[8]

The issue is, regardless of whether it's a marijuana policy or any other kind of policy, the wording of the policy is extremely important. It's something all insurance professionals must pay attention to. Otherwise, the policy may be the wrong one for the insured.

Adjusters can only go by the wording of the policy, but due to poor or incomplete wording, the adjuster may deny a claim which is *meant* to be covered. Everyone knows the claim should be covered. Everyone knows what was meant to be covered. If a claim that was meant to be covered is denied due to poor wording, the attorneys get involved and begin debating the meaning of words at $500 an hour. Lawsuits happen. Feelings get hurt. And the courts wind up telling the insurance industry how to define words. Then we *have* to change the wording.

So, given the opportunity, let's get it correct the first time.

---

8 Actually, I don't. If everyone would just elect me Emperor of the Known and Unknown Universe, the world would be a better place.

4

The Claims Handling Process

No matter what any risk management university will tell you, being a claims adjuster is by far the best part of working in insurance. This is where the rubber meets the road; as mentioned earlier, the claims department is the promise keeper of the insurance carrier.

Although written for an adjuster who has approximately 5 or so years under her belt, this book focuses on the Traditional Claims Handling method because young/new adjusters cannot begin their careers without having a strong foundation. The best way to set the foundation is to understand tradition. I am working under the assumption you've got a good foundation, but it never hurts to review things. Even I pick up new tricks on topics I've studied for years when I attend seminars.

There are four claims handling methods:

1. Traditional Handling
2. Fast-Track Handling
3. Virtual Handling
4. Touchless Handling

Fast-Track claims handling is just as it sounds. A claim can fall into this category if there are no coverage disputes and the damages are relatively simple. Virtual and Touchless Handling are becoming more popular with industry disruptors like Lemonade™ and for claims which are easily quantifiable and require little to no verification, such as a windshield replacement claim.

Good Faith Claims Handling

Good faith claims handling is based on the concept of the insured and insurer acting in a transparent manner with one another. I briefly discussed this in Chapter 1 in the sub-caption "Contract of Good Faith." While I would say technically *all* of the book is a lesson in good faith claims handling, and, therefore, you should read and commit the entire book to memory, my editor is making me be nice to you and point out (a) you already have read this information; (b) you skipped it and/or didn't pay attention to the information so you need to read/re-read it; (c) I will discuss it further in Chapter 5 under the sub-caption "Suspicious Claims"; (d) I will discuss it again in Chapter 12 under the sub-caption "Just Like Grandma."

The National Association of Insurance Commissioners (NAIC) is an insurance support network of the insurance commissioners from the 50 states, U.S. territories, and the District of Columbia. Its mission is to help the departments of insurance ensure that best practices and standards are upheld by providing regulatory oversight of the insurers operating in the states, territories, and D.C.

The NAIC has a Model Unfair Claims Settlement Practices Act which lists what the commissioners believe to be the minimum standards for the handling of claims in their states. To be clear, this discussion is only about property and casualty (liability) claims. Many states have codified the act into their laws. A handful have not. As of the publication of this book, the states which have not adopted the Model Unfair Claims Settlement Practices Act are: Alabama, Iowa, Mississippi, and the District of Columbia. However, even in these states this model law is important.

Adjusters should also be aware that this lists the *model* rules, and every state puts its individual twist on the model rules. Therefore, when handling claims it is imperative to know the specific Unfair Claims Settlement Practices Act of the state where the loss occurred. This may not be the state where the adjuster is located.

The NAIC January 1997 Model Laws can be found on the NAIC's website. The rules state it is an unfair claims settlement act to perform an act, or fail to perform an act, with enough repetition or often enough to indicate a general business practice.

Adjusters must inform the insured, and in some cases the claimants, of the relevant policy provisions for the claim. Correspondence must be acknowledged within a certain deadline, depending on the state. Likewise, the adjuster must start the investigation promptly and cannot refuse to pay the claim without a reasonable investigation.

The NAIC states that once the investigation is complete, there is a deadline to pay the claim or let the insured or claimant know why the claim has been denied. Denials should be in writing, citing the applicable policy language.

The Model Unfair Claims Settlement Practices Act is a roadmap for how to handle and dispose of a claim. However, following these rules to a fault still may not be enough to prevent a bad faith lawsuit, but the adjuster who incorporates these guidelines into her claims-handling practice will be better off for it.

First Notice of Loss

How the adjuster receives the claim depends on the type of system the carrier has in place. Sometimes the adjuster receives an email informing her of a new claim she is to begin handling; other times the adjuster is part of the phone tree and takes the claim herself directly from the insured or claimant. Regardless of how the adjuster receives the new claim, she must start by reading and reviewing the First Notice of Loss—the intake information about the claim.

She would then compare the notice of the accident to the coverages. Her next step will be to begin to draft a plan to handle the claim to completion, keeping in mind a denial also brings the file to conclusion.

The adjuster should begin asking herself, even before speaking with anyone involved in the loss, questions about the loss:

- How did this loss occur?
- Did a natural/weather event cause the loss?
  - If not, was someone else responsible for the accident?
- Does the policy offer any coverage for the loss?
  - If not, what is the coverage question?
- What do I need to move the file toward closure?

Reviewing Coverages

The claim handling begins with analyzing the insurance policy to determine the extent of coverage and reviewing how it may apply to the information provided in the First Notice of Loss. This is a good way for the adjuster to become aware of what she may need to discuss with the insured when she calls him.

For example, the loss notice says the insured sustained water damage which had been ongoing for three weeks, and mold is now present. The adjuster knows there is a mold exclusion, as well as no coverage for water leaks which last longer than 14 days. When the adjuster calls the insured to discuss the loss and find out what happened, she can tell him that although there are some policy exclusions, she will still continue her investigation by sending an appraiser, but she's also going to send a Reservation of Rights letter due to the coverage issue.

Reservation of Rights letters will be discussed in more depth in Chapter 5, but the adjuster should also call the retail agent to inform him about the possible coverage issues and copy him on the Reservation of Rights letter. This appendix of this book also has a sample Reservation of Rights letter.

Discussing the Loss with the Insured

As discussed previously, the NAIC devised model guidelines which most states have adopted to bring uniformity to the handling and interpretation of insurance. Several of these regulations pertain to good faith claims handling. One of the most important guidelines is that an adjuster should explain the coverages of the policy to the insured.

The adjuster reviews the loss facts with the insured, then reviews and explains the entire policy, including endorsements and exclusions. The adjuster should make sure she notes the insured has expressed an understanding of the coverages afforded by the policy and inform the insured of the claims handling process.

While the adjuster and insured are speaking, the adjuster should ask the questions she previously noted when reviewing the file upon first receiving it. If she confirms a potential coverage question, she must discuss this with the insured during first contact.

Discussing the Loss with Other Parties

If other parties are involved in the loss, such as witnesses and/or claimants, these should be the next people the adjuster contacts. The insured's coverages are not discussed with the claimant or witnesses since they are not a party to the contract of insurance. But the adjuster should discuss the loss and explain the insurance process to the claimant.

First contact with the claimant and/or witnesses is usually the best time to take a recorded statement from them to preserve evidence of what occurred from their point of view. Since memories fade and are often unreliable, it's best to obtain the information as soon as possible.

Reserves

A reserve is money the insurer sets aside, in reserve, to pay a claim. Therefore, it is of paramount importance the adjuster set reserves as soon as possible.

Reserves are likely one of the most important features in insurance claims, yet adjusters tend to know very little about how they impact the overall health of the company who employs them.

Many insurers have now moved toward automatic reserves, where a computer program sets a standard reserve for the line of business. This has its advantages and disadvantages. Setting a reserve can be an art form which intimidates new adjusters unfamiliar with how much a claim may settle for. In broad terms, the computer reserving program uses past settlements for the type of claim to determine what the reserves should be for the current claim. For example, if the average residential fire claim is settled at $5,500, the reserving program would automatically set the claim's reserves at $5,500 once it has been told the new claim is (a) a homeowner claim and (b) a fire claim.

For newer adjusters, the benefit here is this is one less thing to be concerned with; the problem is all too often, adjusters forget to change the reserves when they receive the estimate. This can leave the claim either over- or under-reserved.

If automatic reserves are not used, the adjuster must rely on her experience (or the experience of her supervisor) to set initial reserves.

Reserves not only encompass the settlement of the claim; they also include potential payment to an independent appraiser, an engineer, medical record/invoice review, or an attorney if a lawsuit is filed.

An adjuster who works in an insurer's office would not set a reserve for the handling of the file, as this expense is already taken into account by the actuaries. An adjuster for a third-party administrator or an independent company handling an insurer's claims would set a claim-handling expense for her work.

In total, all of the expenses for handling a claim are called the "loss adjustment expense" or LAE.

Adjusters often do not realize how reserves touch nearly every portion of the insurer's business. The states' departments of insurance usually mandate a level for total revenue to be held in reserve in order to prevent the insurer becoming insolvent. (Think of this as a mandatory cash cushion in their commercial bank account.) Usually this figure is between 8 percent and 12 percent of the insurance company's total revenues. Further, to remain solvent, an insurer must hold funds which *exceed* the minimum mandatory levels. So, if the claims department routinely under-reserves claims, the insurer will not meet the minimum requirements from the regulators, and thus could become insolvent. If the claims department routinely over-reserves, this would mean there were no funds to invest in the insurer's infrastructure or employees.

Reserves are based on a variety of factors, which I discuss below.

First-Party Reserves

The adjuster needs to look at the type of damage to the physical property and the coverages provided.

Let's say the insured had a fire at his home. In broad, sweeping, generalized terms, the insured's homeowner policy (HO 00 03 05/11) has property (building) coverage, contents (personal property) coverage, and additional living expense (ALE). Depending on the carrier, you, as the adjuster may need to enter 3 reserves (one for the building damage, one for any contents which were damaged as a result of the fire), and room and board if the insured can't live at his house (ALE). Or you may need to get a pencil and paper, add all those figures up and just enter one number into the system and keep it in your head how coverages are split.

Same thing would happen if the insured were a business with a CP 00 10 10/12 policy. He might have property (building) coverage, contents (business personal property) coverage, and business income (also known as business interruption) coverage. You would either enter three reserves for the separate coverages or one reserve for all three coverages.

Just to beat this poor, dead horse and because I want to make sure everyone understands, I'll use the HO3 example below:

Building	$7,500
Contents	$2,000
ALE	$0
Field Appraiser	$150
Defense Attorney	$0

In my mythical example above, our unfortunate insured is able to stay in his house because the loss is a minor kitchen fire. Therefore, there's no need for him to stay at a hotel (although you may find you have to add ALE later because he has to eat out rather than cook because he has no kitchen, but you can discover that later). You've added a reserve for the independent appraiser who will write the estimate, and because there is (currently) no litigation on the file, there is no need for reserves for the defense attorney.

If you were to simply have one reserve for building, contents, and ALE, the reserves would look like this:

Loss Reserves	$9,500
Field Appraiser	$150
Defense Attorney	$0

Third-Party Reserves

A liability claim can have both property damage and bodily injury. Again, depending on the carrier, the adjuster will enter these reserves separately or together.

Let's use the ubiquitous slip and fall accident as an example. The claimant slipped and fell on the insured's property causing him to split his pants and sustain bodily injury (bruised tailbone). The insured's HO3 carrier has accepted liability. Reserves can look like the following:

Property Damage	$75
Bodily Injury	$7,500
Med-Pay	$1,000
Field Appraiser	$150
Defense Attorney	$0

This represents all coverages available to the claimant (we've not discussed Medical Payments, aka Med-Pay, because I'm assuming you know what that is, but if you don't: briefly, it is coverage offered to a claimant regardless of liability).

If you're putting these reserves in one line, it would look like:

Loss Reserves	$8,575
Field Appraiser	$150
Defense Attorney	$0

When considering bodily injury reserves on liability claims, geographic location of the accident will need to be considered as well. Some areas—even within a state—are more likely to award larger jury verdicts to claimants, and this should be considered when setting reserves.

Depending on the circumstances of the loss, there may be a percentage of fault assumed by the claimant, which would reduce the total payment amount and, thus, the reserve amount. This will be discussed more in Chapters 5 and 11.

To drill down more on the above concepts, let's say the insured's 5-year-old vehicle, which had less than 30,000 miles on it, was damaged. The adjuster would need to know the value of a similar vehicle, in that particular geographical location, with the same features as the insured's vehicle. All of these factors will affect the value of the claim. The amount of damage will, of course, also affect the value of the claim. If the insured sustained a minor fender bender, then only the field appraiser's estimate might be needed to help set reserves. However, if the insured was T-boned by a semi, the vehicle would likely be a total loss (meaning the damages are higher than the vehicle is worth), and additional work to discover the value of the vehicle would be needed.

If a claimant slipped and twisted his ankle, the adjuster would set reserves for a soft tissue injury in the geographical area where the loss occurred. Another factor to take into consideration would be the claimant's occupation. Is the claimant a nurse, a job which requires a lot of standing/ walking? Such an injury might mean the claimant would be unable to work for a short period of time, or need to take reduced hours, and thus he would be eligible for reimbursement of lost or reduced wages.

If the same claimant broke an ankle as a result of the slip, this would result in the need for higher reserves, since the claimant would have a higher level of pain and suffering, more significant lost or reduced wages, and longer time for healing.

A new adjuster should not feel intimidated if she doesn't know all the items which should be considered in setting reserves. Her manager should have the skill set to help her, due to their years in the industry, but there are also computer programs which help set these reserves. Such computer programs include:

- Xactimate for estimating building damage

- Jury Verdict Research for reviewing what similar injuries received as awards in previous lawsuits in that particular venue

- Certified Collateral Corporation (CCC), used by many insurers to value a vehicle that is determined to be a total loss

However, these are not the only computer programs which help an adjuster.

Reserves are fluid and change. Because of the impact they have on the overall health of the insurer, it is important the adjuster monitor the reserves frequently. Adjusters should, as a best practice, review reserves once a month and note in the file that they have reviewed the reserves and why the reserves are adequate, or if the reserves change, why the reserves have changed. Yes, this means a lot of work for each adjuster, but it pays off in the long run because it guarantees the money to pay claims is there when it's needed.

Assignment of an Appraiser

If the adjuster is not appraising the damage herself, she will assign an appraiser to estimate the damage. Appraisers have specialized software they use to determine the value of specific damages. They are also accustomed to working with vendors who repair and rebuild damaged property, such as contractors, roofers, and auto repair shops.

Once the damage is appraised, an estimate is written and then submitted to the adjuster. It is the adjuster's duty to review the estimate to make sure only covered items are listed, and, if the estimate is in line, pay the claim.

Often there will be a supplement, or an addition, to the estimate because repair costs are more than expected or there was hidden damage. At this point, the contractor, adjuster, appraiser, and claimant must work together to resolve the disparity. Again, if the additional damage is covered by the policy of insurance, then the adjuster should write a check for payment of the damages.

If the adjuster is not local, she may ask the appraiser to inspect the location of the accident, which is called a locus investigation. This is especially important in liability claims where there is a question regarding who is at fault.

While the Appraiser's Away

Simply because the adjuster has assigned an appraiser to estimate the damages does not mean her job duties are on hold until the estimate comes back with answers.

The adjuster needs to continue to move the file toward conclusion so that once the appraiser's report is received, a decision can be made regarding coverage or liability. The adjuster can review, or assign to a forensic accountant, the insured or claimant's loss of business income documents in order to determine how much income was lost as a result of the claim. The adjuster also can research the costs of contents which were damaged, and if there is a coverage question, the adjuster will need to write a Reservation of Rights letter.

The Next Steps

Once the adjuster receives the appraiser's report, she cannot simply rubber stamp it and either pay the estimate or deny it, based on the recommendations of the appraiser. Because she is the adjuster of record, she is the one to make coverage or liability decisions regarding the cause of the accident, re-analyzing coverage to ensure the policy still would cover the loss; verify the information received is true and correct; review the estimate of damages; negotiate settlement with the insured or claimant; authorize payment or denial of the claim; reduce reserves to nil after all vendors are paid; and close the file.

If the claim cannot be settled, the adjuster would then handle the litigated aspect of the claim by cooperating with defense counsel. She would collect and present the file information, testimony, and reports as evidence in a court of law.

Closing the File

Each insurer will have a different method or timeline for closing the file. Some, for example, want the subrogation (or reimbursement) file to remain open; others would like it closed. Regardless of the insurer's preference, certain steps must be followed.

In the majority of claims, closing documents will be needed in order to close the claim. A first-party claim may require a Sworn (notarized) Proof of Loss. A third-party claim may require a Release of All Claims prior to payment being issued. A claim note should be entered, outlining how the adjuster determined the settlement amount and whether all outstanding issues were resolved.

The adjuster will verify all vendors have been paid and reduce all reserves to zero. The diary will be removed.

Other Handling Issues

Diaries

They (whoever "they" are) say that an adjuster lives and dies by her diary. Being an adjuster is a job driven by deadlines, and the best way to handle these deadlines is through the claim diary. "Diary" being the ubiquitous word for "the computer program which keeps you on task."

Every carrier has a different diary system. At this point in your career, you should be well familiar with the diary, but unless you are fully taking advantage of your diary system and updating it religiously, it is likely working you rather than you working it.

As a brief side note, though, I recommend more than one diary. When I was an adjuster, I would use the carrier's diary system, which told me when to send letters, when to review reserves, etc., but I also made a Microsoft calendar appointment (diary) to remind myself to follow up on certain items. See Chapter 5 for more information about this process.

Correspondence

Adjusters must keep clear, concise, and accurate file notes. These notes represent the factual details of the claim. Inconsistencies in the claim file are often the cause of lawsuits. The adjuster's notes should contain enough information for a reader to reconstruct the insurer's activities relating to the claim. This means the adjuster's notes must be clear enough for someone to understand her thought processes while she was adjusting the claim. See Chapter 9 for more information on documenting the claim file.

Both electronic mail and hard mail (snail mail) are common in today's claim environment. Every relevant document received should be uploaded into the claim file with a note as to the date received and date processed. The adjuster should also comment on any mail received or sent in order to adhere to the expectation that the notes will contain enough information for the reader to reconstruct the file. It is not enough to simply have the letter or email in the file. The adjuster should comment on her impressions or on the requests made.

The state department of insurance has the authority to examine an insurer's claim file. As a side note, while a state department of insurance expects all documents to be in the file, adjusters are, after all, human. Inevitably, the occasionally documents will be misplaced or adjusters will fail to comment on them. That is to be expected. It does, however, create suspicion when the failure to upload or comment on documents becomes a regular practice. It also creates suspicion when documents contrary to the insurer's opinion are missing from the file.

The Model Unfair Claims Settlement Practices Act states that communications should be responded to "promptly." Some states define promptly as within 15 days. The departments of insurance do not want the insurers to dally in settling the claim, either. Once the adjuster has enough information to settle the claim, the adjuster should immediately settle—the NAIC states a standard for prompt settlement as 21 days from receipt of all necessary information.

A denial of coverage could also be a settlement of a claim. In this instance, the denial letter, quoting applicable policy language, needs to be issued within 21 days of receipt of all claim information.

It may be the case that the adjuster has information to settle a part of the claim, but not the entire claim. It is best, then, for the adjuster to issue a partial payment to the insured in good faith. Partial settlement of a third-party claimant's loss is usually not done for reasons that will be discussed in Chapters 11.

Every insurer has claims forms it uses to document the insureds and claimants' losses. These forms include Proofs of Loss, Releases of All Claims, Medical Information Release Forms, and Affidavit of Vehicle Theft Forms, to name just a few. As mentioned previously, the forms which will be used in a claim should be requested from the insurer and mailed to the insured or claimant within 15 days of the loss. Again, it is understandable if the adjuster doesn't learn the insured's vehicle is a total loss until day 17. The adjuster should mail the form to the insured as soon as she has the information.

It is also becoming increasingly common for insurers and adjusters to send blank claims forms when the claim is ready to be settled. The Unfair Claims Settlement Practices require forms be sent to the insured within 15 days of the claim—it's OK, at the beginning of the loss, for the settlement form to be blank. However, sending another blank form (e.g., a Proof of Loss) and the estimate of damages while expecting the insured, a lay person, to know how to fill out the form, is poor customer service.

The settlement practices require the insurer to explain which coverages were used in the settlement of the claim, and in what amount. This explanation should be on the settlement letter and also on the Proof of Loss; the insured would only need to sign and have the document notarized to fulfill his duty.

Insurance Databases

Insurers rely on several databases to reduce fraud and/or comply with government mandates.

Almost all insurers use the ISO ClaimSearch® system, a claims database which contains a person's or business' historical claim information. The information encompasses auto, liability or casualty, and property claims. It is used by insurers, state insurance fraud departments, and law enforcement personnel to detect insurance fraud, which is a crime.

The ISO ClaimSearch® system can also verify the claimant is not on the government's watch list of potential terrorists and/or drug traffickers. That list is known as the Office of Foreign Assets Control Compliance Service, or OFAC. Each insurer and adjuster is responsible for verifying the claimant is not on this list prior to receiving an insurance payment.

If there is an injury claim, the adjuster must verify the claimant is not Medicare eligible. This requires the adjuster to obtain the "Big 5" from the claimant, which include:

1. Claimant's Social Security Number or Medicare Beneficiary Number

2. Claimant's First Name

3. Claimant's Last Name

4. Claimant's Date of Birth

5. Claimant's Gender

The insurer, or its proxy, enters this information into the Centers for Medicare & Medicaid Services (CMS) system. Medicare and Medicaid SCHIP Extension Act (MMSEA) Section 111 Reporting is multifaceted and requires cooperation between the claims department and IT departments. Failure to comply with this government mandate can result in a penalty of up to $1,000/day per claim. This could bankrupt a smaller insurer if it fails to adhere to the procedure of confirming Medicare/Medicaid eligibility.

To make matters worse, CMS will never return an absolute negative on the claimant's eligibility. It is then up to the insurer's IT Department to match the claimant, ensuring compliance. If the claimant is found to be Medicare/Medicaid eligible, CMS will issue an interim recovery amount and a conditional payment letter. The conditional payment amount is considered an interim amount because there may be additional payments while the case is in the process of being settled.

The difficult part to settling a casualty claim with a Medicare/Medicaid-eligible claimant is that the insurer cannot receive a final demand from CMS until after it settles with the claimant. However, insurers are loathed to settle with claimants until all invoices are known; for that matter, claimants do not want to settle without all invoices being accounted for, as they will be required to pay for any unconsidered bills. However, the insurer will not receive a Conditional Payment Notification (CPN) from Medicare/Medicaid until the claim is settled and the release for the claim is received.

Once this is done, the insurer must issue a letter that shows:

1. The date of settlement
2. The settlement amount
3. The amount of any attorney's fees and other costs paid by the claimant

CMS then calculates the final amount owed and the insurer issues payment for that amount. This entire process can take months to determine.

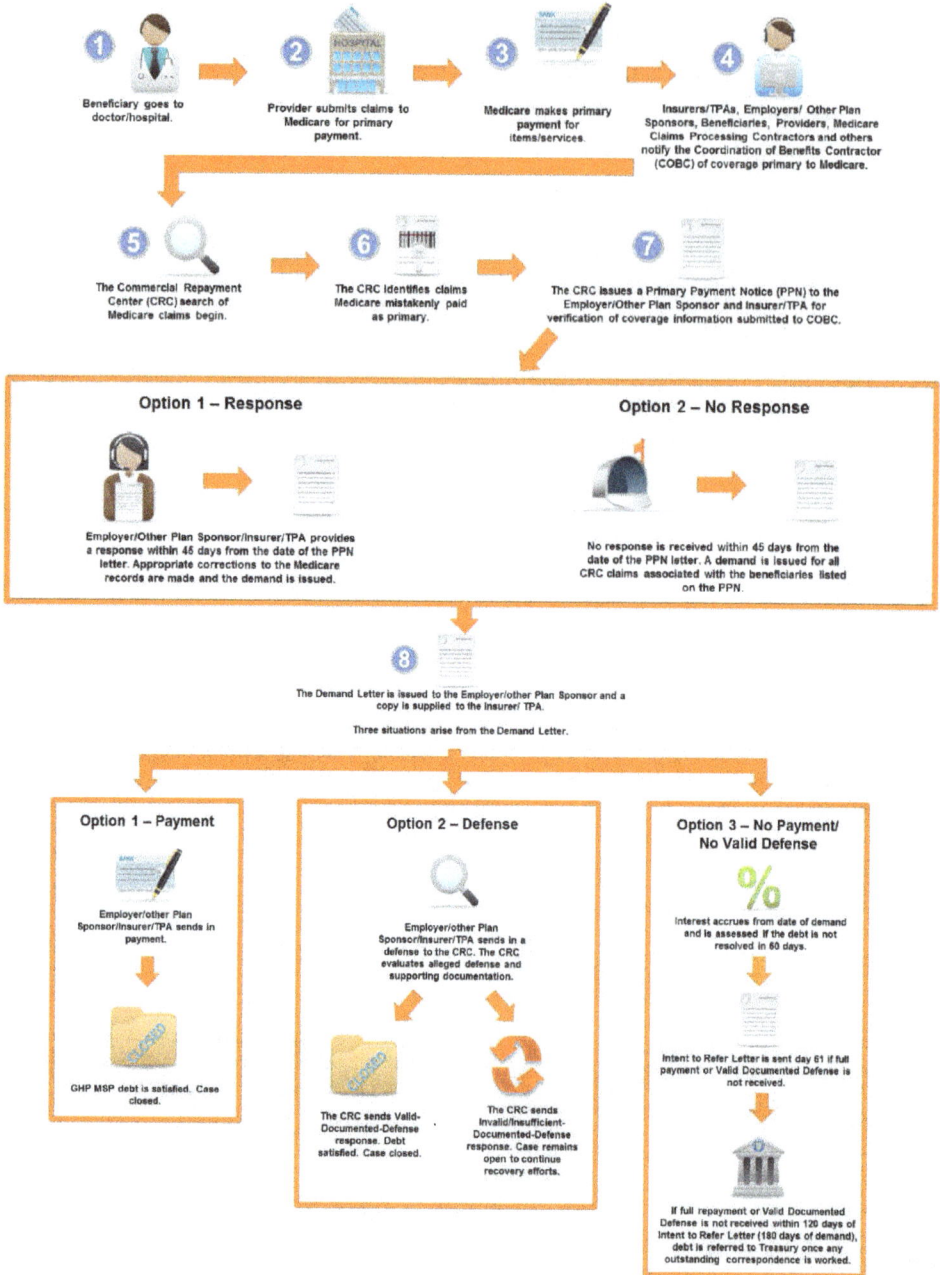

1. Beneficiary goes to doctor/hospital.

2. Provider submits claims to Medicare for primary payment.

3. Medicare makes primary payment for items/services.

4. Insurers/TPAs, Employers/ Other Plan Sponsors, Beneficiaries, Providers, Medicare Claims Processing Contractors and others notify the Coordination of Benefits Contractor (COBC) of coverage primary to Medicare.

5. The Commercial Repayment Center (CRC) search of Medicare claims begin.

6. The CRC identifies claims Medicare mistakenly paid as primary.

7. The CRC issues a Primary Payment Notice (PPN) to the Employer/Other Plan Sponsor and Insurer/TPA for verification of coverage information submitted to COBC.

Option 1 – Response

Employer/Other Plan Sponsor/Insurer/TPA provides a response within 45 days from the date of the PPN letter. Appropriate corrections to the Medicare records are made and the demand is issued.

Option 2 – No Response

No response is received within 45 days from the date of the PPN letter. A demand is issued for all CRC claims associated with the beneficiaries listed on the PPN.

8. The Demand Letter is issued to the Employer/other Plan Sponsor and a copy is supplied to the Insurer/ TPA.

Three situations arise from the Demand Letter.

Option 1 – Payment

Employer/other Plan Sponsor/Insurer/TPA sends in payment.

GHP MSP debt is satisfied. Case closed.

Option 2 – Defense

Employer/other Plan Sponsor/Insurer/TPA sends in a defense to the CRC. The CRC evaluates alleged defense and supporting documentation.

The CRC sends Valid-Documented-Defense response. Debt satisfied. Case closed.

The CRC sends Invalid/Insufficient-Documented-Defense response. Case remains open to continue recovery efforts.

Option 3 – No Payment/ No Valid Defense

Interest accrues from date of demand and is assessed if the debt is not resolved in 60 days.

Intent to Refer Letter is sent day 61 if full payment or Valid Documented Defense is not received.

If full repayment or Valid Documented Defense is not received within 120 days of Intent to Refer Letter (180 days of demand), debt is referred to Treasury once any outstanding correspondence is worked.

The original flowchart of this process can be found at **https://go.cms. gov/3zF1c1W.**

Many attorneys who represent claimants will assure the adjuster their client is not Medicare/Medicaid eligible and there is no need for this information to be obtained. But the government has made it clear the insurer cannot delegate its duty to verify eligibility. Further, if the insurer is the Responsible Reporting Entity (RRE) in the government's eyes, CMS will seek reimbursement from the insurer. The insurer can then seek reimbursement from the claimant or her attorney. Needless to say, this is not an ideal situation. Therefore, it is better to respectfully decline the attorney's offer and follow the government's instructions, even if that means being more assertive than usual.

This section has only discussed reimbursement of costs with no disputes or questions. Naturally, the process becomes more complicated if there is a dispute or a late payment.

Wrap Up

An adjuster performs so many activities that they cannot all fit into one chapter that is still legible and shorter than *War and Peace*. Many of these concepts will be discussed in more detail in upcoming chapters of their own.

There is no better job than being a claims adjuster because it allows you to use your brain to solve puzzles on a daily basis, to help people in their time of need, and to feel like you are contributing to the greater good.

5

The Next Steps

The previous chapter quickly outlined some of the actions the adjuster must take after receipt of the appraiser's estimate or receipt of documentation to move the file toward closure. This chapter will go into more detail regarding some of the steps the adjuster must take in order to determine what amount, if any, needs to be paid to resolve the claim.

Suspicious Claims

Part of investigating a claim is verifying the information the adjuster has received is true. The insured, claimant, and insurer have a duty of good faith dealing to one another—this means that they should be honest, forthright, and truthful when working together regarding the loss. Insurers are only obligated to pay covered claims. The payment made will be "reasonable and customary" for the type of loss.

Fraud is wrongful or criminal deception intended to result in financial or personal gain. Insurance fraud occurs most often when an individual or entity makes a false or exaggerated insurance claim. Fraudulent claims can be as simple as "padding" a contents list with items the insured doesn't own, known as "soft fraud"; or it can be as complex as arson, known as "hard fraud." Soft fraud is more opportunistic and more common; hard fraud is a purposeful act by the claimant or the insured. Regardless, insurance fraud is illegal.

In order to prove a claim of fraud against the insured, an insurer must prove:

1. A false representation of a material fact was made by the insured.
2. The carrier relied on this fact to its detriment.
3. The insured knew or believed that the representation was false.

The insurer relies on the information and documentation the insured or claimant supplies. The carrier has the right to investigate and review the documentation, but for the most part, it is assumed everyone is telling the truth, the representations of which are in the file. So, it follows that a misrepresentation is an untruth.

A material fact is a detail which is directly related to the claim at hand. For example, the insured states its growth facility has a sprinkler system and smoke alarms which alert the fire department in the event of a fire. The insurer will rely upon this information and grant a lower premium due to the decreased risk of fire damage. In reality, the insured has only 10 fire extinguishers to cover a 50,000 sq. ft. grow warehouse, electrical plugs and extension cords sitting in puddles of water, and battery-operated smoke alarms purchased in bulk from a big box retail store.

The possibility of an electrical arc from the plugs and extension cords, coupled with an alarm system that will not alert the fire department and the fact there is no sprinkler system to put out the fire, is a material fact that increases the hazard of fire at the insured's premises. Therefore, when a fire claim is submitted—even if it is a small one—the insurer could void, or cancel, the policy and refuse to pay the claim.

Suppose the same facts applied, but this time a tornado struck the insured's warehouse. There is still a serious misrepresentation, but it is not material to the windstorm damage on the claim.

If some of the claim fact patterns do not fit the alleged damage, the adjuster might suspect the insured or claimant is attempting to defraud the carrier. Adjusters need to know the potential indicators of fraud, which are called "red flags."

Red Flags

- Loss occurs on a Monday
- There is no physical injury
- There are no receipts for stolen/lost items
- Insured or claimant has financial problems
- The item damaged is past its useful life
- Property was over-insured
- Loss occurs immediately after policy start date
- Forms have been redacted or whited-out
- There are no photographs of the stolen/lost items
- There are no witnesses to the accident
- Theft occurred when security system was down
- Insured or claimant has multiple hits on ISO

Of course, claims with red flag indicators can be legitimate. Although it is typical for a fraudulent claim to have more than one red flag, it is possible for there to be only one. If insurance fraud is suspected, the adjuster should report the claim to the insurer's Special Investigation Unit (SIU), which will further investigate the claim. Most states' departments of insurance mandate the insurer to report insurance fraud to the department's fraud division.

In the case of suspicion of fraud, the state fraud department and the carrier's SIU department could be contacted by law enforcement, who might be interested in obtaining the carrier's file. For example, if there is a suspicion of arson, the fire marshal, or the Bureau of Alcohol, Tobacco, and Firearms would likely be interested in obtaining the carrier's file. Remember, these agencies are interested in pursuing the crime related to the fraud. An insurance carrier is not in the business of pursuing or proving an illegal act, such as arson. If an adjuster is contacted by law enforcement, it is wise to refer the agency to the SIU investigator or the manager.

Insurance in Action (Red Flags)

The insured, a medical marijuana dispensary, reports a theft of its product. It has a CP 00 10 10/12 base form policy with a Special Form Cause of Loss, CP 10 30 10/12. The insurer placed a warranty on the policy that the insured would lock its product in a 300-pound safe, which is bolted to the floor, during non-business hours. There was also the requirement of a security system, which would report directly to the police in the event of a burglary.

The thieves were able to circumvent the security system and crack the safe. The theft is believed to be an inside job, particularly since the insured confirms it recently fired two employees caught stealing by the manager. However, the dispensary had not changed the security code for the alarm or the safe combination.

Insurers are obligated to pay for usual and customary damages and to pay for what is lost; therefore, the insured must cooperate with the adjuster's investigation and provide documents to prove it actually owned what it claims was stolen. The adjuster asks for proof the dispensary had the amount of marijuana stolen, which could take the form of a daily product inventory. The insured fails to submit this information.

The adjuster asks three more times, and three more times the dispensary does not submit the requested information. The adjuster informs the insured she will close the file if she does not receive the needed documentation to prove the dispensary had the product prior to it being stolen. Finally, the insured submits sequential, hand-written receipts, with only a first name of the seller. There are no phone numbers, account numbers, credit card numbers, addresses, last names, etc. on the receipts. All the receipts are written in the same handwriting with the same color pen.

Our on-the-ball adjuster notes a few red flags:

1. The receipts are sequential—in the normal course of business, receipts are written for a number of different items. Therefore, it is highly unusual for all of the dispensary's marijuana products to arrive in one shipment on the same day, necessitating receipts in numerical order.

2. Hand-written receipts are not unusual, especially for a small business. However, it is unusual for one person to write all the receipts and for all the receipts to be in the same color pen. Often when delivery occurs, the manager will grab the nearest pen, or if he doesn't have one, he'll borrow the delivery person's pen. Of course, if the business is small and it's one person's job to accept deliveries, this may account for the same handwriting, and perhaps this manager has a favorite pen he

uses. But even in the course of one day, an individual's hand-writing tends to change.

3. It is also highly unusual for the vendor's information to be missing on a receipt. Think about your grocery receipts, gas receipts, or even receipts you receive from a tradesperson, such as a plumber or electrician. These receipts have the company's full name, address, phone number, and more than likely a website and email address. So, for the dispensary's receipts to have nothing but a first name like John, Mark, or Bob, seems to indicate the receipts are fictitious in an effort to supply the information the adjuster requested.

This claim occurred before implementation of the seed to sale[9] tracking method; therefore, a paper trail was all the adjuster and insured had to go on. Recognizing the improbability of several of these items, the adjuster informs the insured she will report this claim to the state department of insurance and the insurer's SIU for fraud.

The insured manager explains that he could not divulge his growers because he fears the insurer might be raided by the federal government, compromising his growers' information. Fortunately, the adjuster listens and realizes the insured's concern. She is able to determine a compromise and obtain the information she needs while still preserving the insured's confidential information.

This is an example of not only recognizing red flags in a claim and further investigation of the red flags, but also an example of how to compromise to resolve the loss to the benefit of all parties.

If fraud is proven in a claim, the policy can be voided *ab initio*, which means from the beginning. This means the claim is not denied because there never was a policy in the first place. This language can be found in the conditions endorsement of the policy. The carrier will refund the entire premium to the insured if this occurs. Likewise, the carrier can simply deny the claim for fraud if it chooses. A letter of declination will need to be issued, quoting

---

9 Seed to Sale is the current method for tracking the cannabis product from "seed" to "sale." Each plant/bud/oil product is assigned a number, and along each stopping point in the manufacturing of the product, the plant is logged in the system. This allows for accountability, in terms of knowing where the plant came from, who had responsibility if something were to go wrong, which batch the plant is from, etc. Previously, dispensaries would work with one or two growers, but nothing was known about the growers' methods.

the applicable policy language. It is always a good idea to have an attorney review the file and the letter prior to issuance due to the possibility of the insured filing a bad faith suit at a later date.

Reviewing Coverages (Again)

Coverage has been discussed briefly a few times, and reviewing coverage is an ongoing event in the life of a claim, much like reviewing reserves is ongoing throughout the claim. As discussed, the first time coverage is reviewed is when the adjuster receives the claim, before the adjuster speaks with the insured. The adjuster will compare the First Notice of Loss to the coverages to see if there are any possible conflicts between the coverage and the loss. The second time is during first contact, when the adjuster and the insured speak and the adjuster obtains more information regarding the loss.

If after speaking to the insured, the adjuster feels there is a conflict between the coverage and the loss—meaning the loss may not be covered by the policy—she must write a reservation of rights (ROR) letter outlining the carrier's position as it relates to coverage and the loss.

A reservation of rights is a notification to the insured by the insurer regarding potential coverage issues and prevents waiver of the insurer's rights to deny coverage under the policy at a later date. Although they both serve the same purpose, there is a difference between a reservation of rights letter and a non-waiver agreement. Usually a reservation of rights letter is a one-way letter, a notification from the carrier to the insured informing the insured of the coverage issue; a non-waiver agreement is signed by both the insurer and the insured, and it acknowledges that there is a coverage question.

Although a reservation of rights letter protects the carrier's interests, it also informs the insured that some parts of his loss may not be covered. The letter also states the insurer will continue to investigate the claim, but in doing so, it does not forego the ability to later deny the claim if coverage is found not to exist. After writing the ROR, the adjuster still must continue the investigation into the loss.

A popular misconception is that a reservation of rights letter is only needed during a lawsuit where the carrier's and insured's interests are in conflict; however, anytime the insurer finds coverage or policy questions is the time to send a reservation of rights letter. Reservation of rights letters preserve the insurer's right to assert defenses if there is a lawsuit at a later date, or if the insurer later denies coverage for the loss. Reservation of rights letters are appropriate in both first- and third-party situations. In order for an insurer to continue to investigate a first party loss without potentially waiving coverage limitations, a reservation of rights is needed. In the context of a third-party claim, an insurer may have coverage of portions of the allegations against the insured, but not all; then, in order to maintain its defenses to coverage, the insurer must issue a reservation of rights and defend the insured "under a reservation of rights."

If after speaking to the insured for first contact, there is no recognized conflict, no ROR is needed. However, if the adjuster recognizes a coverage question after receipt of the appraiser's report, a ROR needs to be issued immediately.

Depending on the outcome of the investigation, the adjuster will either accept the claim and settle the loss, settle a portion of the loss and deny a part of the loss, or deny the entire loss.

There are several parts to a well-written ROR letter, and like other facets of the claim, the state where the loss occurred will govern the rules regarding the ROR letter. In nearly all cases, the ROR letter must be "timely." Timeliness may or may not be defined by the state. The chart below is solely for use as an example. Adjusters must be familiar with the requirements of the states for which they handle claims. In the Appendix, I include charts for things such as deadlines for filing a claim and sample letters.

It should go without saying that the adjuster has up to the deadline of "timeliness" (whatever that may be) to send the ROR, but by no means is it good, standard claims-handling practice to wait until the last minute to write the letter. Further, adjusters should get comfortable calling the insured and discussing the coverage question with the insured prior to the insured receiving the ROR letter. Finally, the adjuster is well advised to also call the insured's retail agent to inform him of the forthcoming ROR letter.

Courts require the ROR letter to fairly and adequately inform the insured of the coverage questions held by the carrier. Despite this, very often neither the agent nor the insured understand the language in an ROR letter; having a simple phone conversation with both parties can alleviate misunderstandings.

An ROR letter should:

1. Be timely

2. State that it is a reservation of rights

3. Identify the applicable policy

4. Identify the correct insurer

5. Specifically discuss the claim and how it relates to the policy in question

6. Chunk the coverage issues into bite-size, easy-to-understand language, accompanied by the relevant policy language

7. Include a general reservation of rights for other defenses as the investigation continues

8. Advise the insured of his right to independent counsel, if necessary

9. Be sent to all insureds

10. Include a right to recoup defense costs, if allowed in the jurisdiction

11. Provide all notices required in the jurisdiction, if any

12. Be updated to provide that the reservations continue or change to a denial of coverage, or issue a withdrawal of the reservation of rights.

A Declination of Coverage Letter or a Letter of Denial should be handled in the same manner as an ROR letter. Once the investigation is complete and it shows there is no coverage for the loss, a denial letter should be issued immediately. Likewise, it is good customer service to call the insured and retail agent and explain the outcome of the investigation.

Many new adjusters are, understandably, intimidated by a decision to deny coverage, as the insured may be extremely unhappy with the news that there is no coverage for the loss. Many insureds will berate and use profanity when receiving bad news. It is important to understand the insured has a loss, and he is likely overwhelmed by what to do next. He may have been counting on the insurer to help him. He may have friends, neighbors, or in-laws who assured him the claim will be covered; he may even have neighbors who had "the same kind of loss" and who received payment from their insurers.

As a side note: adjusters will hear this often. And this very well may be true; the issue is, though, neither the insured nor the adjuster know what kind of policy the neighbors have. The insured might believe it is the same kind of policy, but there might be an endorsement on the neighbor's policy, or it may not have the same exclusion the insured has on his policy. Regardless, what the neighbors' insurers have done is immaterial to the insured's situation.[10]

However, if the adjuster sent an ROR and previously explained the coverage issue, the insured should not be surprised by the declination of coverage.

The declination letter should also invite the insured to submit any further information he feels is important for consideration. If he submits such information, the adjuster must consider the information and respond to the insured, letting him know if the new information has changed the insurer's opinion of coverage. Failure to do so may open the insurer to bad faith allegations.

Reviewing the Damage Assessments

Generally, the word "estimate" is used with property damage to physical items such as cars, houses, and things inside the cars and houses. These claims can be made by a first- or third-party claimant. For bodily injury claims, an adjuster will review medical records and invoices.

The following is a broad overview of how to review an assessment of damages or injuries.

Property Damage

Beginning with property damage, the field appraiser will write an estimate of damage for the physical "thing" that was involved in the accident. Insurers will use standardized estimating software for the most part, such as

---

10 In Chapters 10 and 11, I offer some responses to common questions and phrases the claimant (whether that be the first- or third-party claimant) might say to an adjuster. In this instance, when a claimant says something to the effect that his neighbor's/sister's/best friend's insurer did such and such and they have the same policy (or even are insured by the same carrier), the response is, "That might be so, but I haven't seen your neighbor/sister/best friend's policy. It could have different endorsements or exclusions. I can't speak for the adjuster handling that claim even if it's being handle by (same insurance carrier). I can only speak to your claim and your policy."

Xactimate or Simsol. The generally accepted method for determining insurance policy limits for the value of rebuilding a structure is Marshall Swift; for automobile losses, many insurers use CCC. Remember, not all claims can be assessed through standardized methods, and the best way to learn is by doing. Heavy equipment, for example, is not listed in CCC, so for an adjuster to determine the value of a semi-tractor trailer, she would need to call local vendors to obtain the price of a similar unit with similar features.

An estimate will have a front page with the applicable claim information.

Insured: Property:	John Doe 5555 Main St. Little Rock, AR 72211	Home:	(555) 555-5555
Claim Rep.:	Test Test		
Estimator:	Test Test		

Claim Number: 1111111   **Policy Number:** 2222222/R02   **Type of Loss:** Water Damage

Date Contacted:	2/27/2021 12:00 AM		
Date of Loss:	2/18/2021 12:00 AM	Date Received:	2/27/2021 12:00 AM
Date Inspected:	3/6/2021 12:00 AM	Date Entered:	3/6/2021 12:12 PM
Price List:	TXCS8X_MAR21 Restoration/Service/Remodel		
Estimate:	335595-1		

The blue and red arrows give the adjuster important information. Occasionally, the field appraiser does not see all the damage an insured or claimant may have. The red arrow states the date of the inspection. If an additional inspection is needed, this date will be updated. It is helpful to know when the second inspection occurred or which estimate the adjuster is reviewing, and this is a quick way to determine that.

The blue arrow shows the price list being used by the computer system. This is also very important. Different areas have different prices for the same items. In the aftermath of a catastrophe, prices may raise significantly, due to supply and demand. Therefore, if the insurer is using an out-of-date price list, it will not adequately reimburse the claimant for the damages.

The orange arrow lists the property inspected. The adjuster should verify this is a covered premises and double check with the field appraiser's photographs.

In fact, this estimate has already shown an issue with the pricing list. It is from March 2021 in Texas (TX...MAR21), but our insured lives in Little

Rock, Arkansas. Therefore, the prices will not be accurate for a repair at our insured's location. The prices may be too high (resulting in the carrier paying too much), or too low (resulting in the carrier paying too little).

Next the adjuster will see the estimate itself. This example is a continuation from a previous page discussing the kitchen (gold arrow). The appraiser wrote a line itemization of all the damages she saw. She will also write notes to let the adjuster know why she chose this particular item in the computer estimating system.[11]

Beneath this are two green arrows showing the completion of the estimate of damages for the finished kitchen and the total amount for that room ($4,516.00).

CONTINUED - Kitchen

QUANTITY	UNIT	TAX	O&P	RCV	AGE/LIFE	COND.	DEP %	DEPREC.	ACV
11. Detach & Reset Baseboard - 3 1/4"									
46.74 LF	2.20	0.08	21.61	124.52	0/150 yrs	Avg.	0%	(0.00)	124.52
12. Paint baseboard - one coat									
46.74 LF	0.85	0.31	8.40	48.44	10/15 yrs	Avg.	66.67%	(26.70)	21.74
13. Detach & Reset Cabinetry - lower (base) units									
12.00 LF	53.28	0.00	134.27	773.63	0/50 yrs	Avg.	0%	(0.00)	773.63
14. Material Only Cabinetry - lower (base) units									
3.00 LF	159.42	39.46	108.73	626.45	10/50 yrs	Avg.	20%	(103.54)	522.91
43. Apply anti-microbial agent to the floor									
206.77 SF	0.24	5.52	10.53	65.67	0/NA	Avg.	0%	(0.00)	65.67
Totals: Kitchen		82.92	875.37	5,048.49				532.49	4,516.00
Total: Main Level		82.92	875.37	5,048.49				532.49	4,516.00
Total: Kitchen		82.92	875.37	5,048.49				532.49	4,516.00

Hallway
Main Level

Hallway/Entry	Height: 8'
322.00 SF Walls	90.40 SF Ceiling
412.40 SF Walls & Ceiling	90.40 SF Floor
10.04 SY Flooring	37.33 LF Floor Perimeter
54.83 LF Ceil. Perimeter	

Missing Wall - Goes to Floor	2' 11" X 6' 8"	Opens into Exterior
Missing Wall - Goes to Floor	3' X 6' 8"	Opens into Exterior
Missing Wall - Goes to Floor	2' 7" X 6' 8"	Opens into Exterior

Immediately following the finished kitchen estimate is the hallway. At the beginning of every section in an estimate, the name of the room and its measurements are provided, as well as a small drawing. This helps identify the room, in the event there is a dispute about where damages occurred,

---

11 This is an example from the Xactimate program.

since the appraiser and the policy may refer to the rooms by different names. The appraiser will then list, in a line-by-line fashion, all of the damages in this particular room, finishing it as she did the kitchen above.

One of the last pages is the recap page, which will list each individual trade needed to complete the repairs. This page is important because it will point to overhead and profit, which will be discussed in Chapter 10, and which is a hotly debated topic in the insurance industry currently.

Recap by Category with Depreciation

O&P Items			RCV	Deprec.	ACV
APPLIANCES			**511.68**		**511.68**
Coverage: Above Slab leak	@	100.00% =	511.68		
CABINETRY			**2,032.22**	**95.65**	**1,936.57**
Coverage: Above Slab leak	@	100.00% =	2,032.22		
CONTENT MANIPULATION			**207.92**		**207.92**
Coverage: Above Slab leak	@	100.00% =	207.92		
GENERAL DEMOLITION			**902.47**		**902.47**
Coverage: Above Slab leak	@	90.62% =	817.83		
Coverage: Other Structures	@	9.38% =	84.64		
FLOOR COVERING - WOOD			**2,997.44**	**1,198.98**	**1,798.46**
Coverage: Above Slab leak	@	100.00% =	2,997.44		
FENCING			**476.48**	**397.07**	**79.41**
Coverage: Other Structures	@	100.00% =	476.48		
FINISH CARPENTRY / TRIMWORK			**449.52**		**449.52**
Coverage: Above Slab leak	@	100.00% =	449.52		
PLUMBING			**225.10**	**38.92**	**186.18**
Coverage: Above Slab leak	@	100.00% =	225.10		
PAINTING			**173.69**	**115.80**	**57.89**
Coverage: Above Slab leak	@	100.00% =	173.69		
WATER EXTRACTION & REMEDIATION			**170.87**		**170.87**
Coverage: Above Slab leak	@	100.00% =	170.87		
O&P Items Subtotal			**8,147.39**	**1,846.42**	**6,300.97**
Material Sales Tax			190.44	78.93	111.51
Coverage: Above Slab leak	@	87.51% =	166.65		
Coverage: Other Structures	@	12.49% =	23.79		
Cleaning Mtl Tax			1.76		1.76
Coverage: Above Slab leak	@	100.00% =	1.76		
Overhead			834.01		834.01
Coverage: Above Slab leak	@	92.99% =	775.52		
Coverage: Other Structures	@	7.01% =	58.49		
Profit			917.43		917.43
Coverage: Above Slab leak	@	92.99% =	853.09		
Coverage: Other Structures	@	7.01% =	64.34		
Cleaning Sales Tax			17.23		17.23
Coverage: Above Slab leak	@	100.00% =	17.23		
Total			**10,108.26**	**1,925.35**	**8,182.91**

The final page will be the summary for the estimate.

Summary for Above Slab leak

Line Item Total	7,586.27
Material Sales Tax	166.65
Cleaning Mtl Tax	1.76
Subtotal	7,754.68
Overhead	775.52
Profit	853.09
Cleaning Sales Tax	17.23
Replacement Cost Value	**$9,400.52**
Less Depreciation	(1,508.45)
Actual Cash Value	**$7,892.07**
Less Deductible	(4,590.00)
Less Amount Over Limit(s)	(802.07)
Net Claim	**$2,500.00**
Total Depreciation	1,508.45
Less Residual Amount Over Limit(s)	(1,508.45)
Total Recoverable Depreciation	0.00

This will list the depreciation, if any, which is subtracted, as well as the deductible.

The insurer should be fair and reasonably accurate in its analysis of applicable coverages and the scope of damage, and provide the claimant with the money to repair the damages. The claim file must be documented thoroughly to reflect the thought process of the adjuster and management on any decision material to the claim. If there is a question regarding coverage, the undisputed amount of money related to the claim should be surrendered immediately to the claimant in order to avoid bad faith allegations at a later date.

Liability

In order to move on to a bodily injury damage assessment, the adjuster must be familiar with medical terminology and have the ability to read and understand medical records, charts, and invoices. This is discussed in greater detail later in this chapter.

The most complete form of medical information is the HICA ICD-10 form which has the Big 5 (listed in Chapter 4 and needed to run a Medicare/Medicaid eligibility check on the claimant). This is the form medical offices use to submit their invoices to health insurers. The claimant is likely unfamiliar with this form, so care should be taken when explaining what is needed in order to move his file toward resolution.

In the following pages, I will break down the key components of the HICA ICD-10 form.

HEALTH INSURANCE CLAIM FORM

APPROVED BY NATIONAL UNIFORM CLAIM COMMITTEE (NUCC) 02/12

PICA

1. MEDICARE	MEDICAID	TRICARE	CHAMPVA	GROUP HEALTH PLAN	FECA BLK LUNG	OTHER
(Medicare#)	(Medicaid#)	(ID#/DoD#)	(Member ID#)	(ID#)	(ID#)	(ID#)

1. This indicates the type of healthcare the claimant has or will be paying with; this is a good clue about whether there will be a lien—another (third?) party who will seek reimbursement from the carrier for their payments.

2. Here is the claimant's name, address, phone number, etc. on the health form which helps fill out the Big 5.

> 2. PATIENT'S NAME (Last Name, First Name, Middle Initial)
>
> 5. PATIENT'S ADDRESS (No., Street)
>
> CITY | STATE
>
> ZIP CODE | TELEPHONE (Include Area Code) ( )

3. The claimant's date of birth is another key piece of information you need to adjust the claim.

> 3. PATIENT'S BIRTH DATE MM DD YY | SEX M F

4. 1.a. can give the policy number or the claimant's social security number to the health care carrier.

> PICA
>
> 1a. INSURED'S I.D. NUMBER (For Program in Item 1)
>
> 4. INSURED'S NAME (Last Name, First Name, Middle Initial)
>
> 7. INSURED'S ADDRESS (No., Street)
>
> CITY | STATE
>
> ZIP CODE | TELEPHONE (Include Area Code) ( )
>
> 11. INSURED'S POLICY GROUP OR FECA NUMBER
>
> a. INSURED'S DATE OF BIRTH MM DD YY | SEX M F
>
> b. OTHER CLAIM ID (Designated by NUCC)
>
> c. INSURANCE PLAN NAME OR PROGRAM NAME
>
> d. IS THERE ANOTHER HEALTH BENEFIT PLAN? YES NO If yes, complete items 9, 9a, and 9d.
>
> 13. INSURED'S OR AUTHORIZED PERSON'S SIGNATURE I authorize payment of medical benefits to the undersigned physician or supplier for services described below.
>
> SIGNED

CARRIER

PATIENT AND INSURED INFORMATION

5. Number 10 offers a good clue regarding what the claimant initially told the medical provider as to how the accident occurred.

10. IS PATIENT'S CONDITION RELATED TO:
a. EMPLOYMENT? (Current or Previous)
☐ YES   ☐ NO
b. AUTO ACCIDENT?   PLACE (State)
☐ YES   ☐ NO
c. OTHER ACCIDENT?
☐ YES   ☐ NO
10d. CLAIM CODES (Designated by NUCC)

14. DATE OF CURRENT ILLNESS, INJURY, or PREGNANCY (LMP) MM DD YY QUAL.	15. OTHER DATE QUAL. MM DD YY	16. DATES PATIENT UNABLE TO WORK IN CURRENT MM DD YY MM FROM TO
17. NAME OF REFERRING PROVIDER OR OTHER SOURCE	17a. / 17b. NPI	18. HOSPITALIZATION DATES RELATED TO CURRENT MM DD YY MM FROM TO

6. The date that should correspond with the date of the loss is 14. Number 16 shows the date the claimant must be off work (an adjuster would need this information in order to reimburse for diminished salary). A clue as to how the claimant came to the medical provider is number 17. If the claimant has an attorney, and the attorney is listed here, this may cause some concern regarding either the validity of the injury, treatment, or potential bias of the medical provider.

21. DIAGNOSIS OR NATURE OF ILLNESS OR INJURY Relate A-L to service line below (24E) ICD Ind.				22. RESUBMISSION CODE	ORIGINAL REF. NO.
A. B. C. D.					
E. F. G. H.				23. PRIOR AUTHORIZATION NUMBER	
I. J. K. L.					

24. A. DATE(S) OF SERVICE From MM DD YY To MM DD YY	B. PLACE OF SERVICE	C. EMG	D. PROCEDURES, SERVICES, OR SUPPLIES (Explain Unusual Circumstances) CPT/HCPCS MODIFIER	E. DIAGNOSIS POINTER	F. $ CHARGES	G. DAYS OR UNITS	H. EPSDT Family Plan	I. ID QUAL	J. RENDERING PROVIDER ID. #
1									NPI
2									NPI
3									NPI
4									NPI
5									NPI
6									NPI

25. FEDERAL TAX I.D. NUMBER	SSN EIN ☐ ☐	26. PATIENT'S ACCOUNT NO.	27. ACCEPT ASSIGNMENT? (For govt. claims, see back) ☐ YES ☐ NO	28. TOTAL CHARGE $	29. AMOUNT PAID $	30. Rsvd for NUCC

7. Number 21 lists the specific injuries the claimant has in a numeral format and is good information to have. The adjuster can research the numbers to ensure the injuries correspond with the type of loss. The list of treatment dates, what was done (CPT codes), how much it cost, and who did the treatment is

listed as 24. The adjuster should double check the treatment did not occur on weekends or holidays if the invoice is not from a hospital or medical provider who specifically works on these days. An invoice showing treatment on a holiday could be an indication of fraud. Numbers 28 and 29 show the amount charged and the amount paid. 29 could be important if the claimant is being funded by another source (the attorney perhaps or medical health insurance).

31. SIGNATURE OF PHYSICIAN OR SUPPLIER INCLUDING DEGREES OR CREDENTIALS (I certify that the statements on the reverse apply to this bill and are made a part thereof.)	32. SERVICE FACILITY LOCATION INFORMATION		33. BILLING PROVIDER INFO & PH # ( )	
SIGNED DATE	a.	b.	a.	b.

NUCC Instruction Manual available at: www.nucc.org   *PLEASE PRINT OR TYPE*   APPROVED OMB-0938-1197 FORM 1500 (02-12)

8. Finally, 32 and 33 show the address and the location of services. You can obtain the medical records from the provider.

Invoices will change from provider to provider, but all will have similar blanks to be completed; some will be printed from the practitioner's computer system. Every invoice should contain the proper information to allow an independent review of the treatment by the adjuster.

The invoices and records must be reviewed in order to determine the injuries suffered by the claimant and to arrive at a settlement figure.

Adjusters will also need to learn how to read and understand medical information. This example is redacted to protect the actual patient's medical information. It is also an adjuster's duty to protect the information she receives. The below example contains the discharge paperwork and MRI findings after the claimant had a two-week hospital stay due to a motor vehicle accident. The adjuster does not have to be a medical doctor to understand all the terms, but she must become familiar enough with them to be able to handle the claim effectively and efficiently.

Paul ▮▮ MD, Dr
▮▮ LA 70403-▮▮   MRN: ▮▮ DOB: ▮▮ , Sex: M
Acct #: ▮▮
Adm: 10/11/▮▮   D/C: 10/31/▮▮

Discharge Summary (continued)

Discharge Summary by ▮▮ Aaron ▮▮ at 10/31/▮▮ 1400 (continued)   Version 1 of 1

Procedure	Component	Value	Ref Range	Date/Time

Additional findings: The urinary bladder is not distended.

IMPRESSION:
1. Bilateral renal cortical thinning/atrophy.
2. No ureteral obstruction or urinary retention.

Electronically signed by John ▮▮ MD on 10/17/▮▮ 3:35 PM

MRI Cervical Spine WO Contrast [5238977257]   Collected: 10/12/▮▮ 1418
                                                         Updated: 10/12/▮▮ 1434

Narrative:
REASON FOR EXAM: mva

TECHNICAL FACTORS: Sagittal T2, sagittal T1, sagittal STIR, axial T2 and axial 2-D MERGE sequences were obtained of the cervical spine without administration of intravenous contrast.

COMPARISON: CT cervical spine 10/11/▮▮

FINDINGS: There is reversal of the normal lordotic curvature of the cervical spine unchanged from previous CT. Bone marrow signal is unremarkable aside from degenerative changes, with no abnormal bone marrow edema appreciated. Ossification of the
posterior longitudinal ligament is noted in the upper cervical spine better defined on prior CT. Postoperative changes of decompressive laminectomy and posterolateral fusion are again noted at the C2-T1 levels. A small 6 mm fluid collection of doubtful
significance is noted along the cephalad aspect of the decompressive laminectomy site at the C2-3 level. A second small, linear fluid collection of doubtful significance is noted at the decompressive laminectomy site at the C3 level. Blooming artifacts
are noted from metallic fixation devices. The bilateral T1 transpedicular screw fractures noted on prior CT are not well visualized by MRI. The cord is normal in caliber and signal intensity. Vertebral body and intervertebral disc heights are maintained.
Mild to moderate disc dehydration is noted throughout the cervical spine. There is no significant spinal or foraminal stenosis noted. Visualized ligamentous structures are generally unremarkable. Extensive scarring is noted in the subcutaneous tissues
at and just below the decompressive laminectomy site.

IMPRESSION:
1. Postoperative and degenerative changes as discussed above.
2. There is no evidence of recent significant traumatic injury to the cervical spine or cervical cord appreciated.

Electronically signed by Robert ▮▮ MD on 10/12/▮▮ 2:31 PM

CT Ankle Left WO Contrast [5238977246]   Collected: 10/12/▮▮ 1338
                                                    Updated: 10/12/▮▮ 1429

Narrative:
EXAM: CT ANKLE LEFT WO CONTRAST

CLINICAL HISTORY: Left ankle pain and swelling.

COMPARISON: None available

After the documents are received and reviewed, it is time for the adjuster to authorize payment or denial of the claim. Payment may involve negotiating a settlement, which is most often seen in liability claims.

It is important to note the adjuster cannot simply sit back and wait for the information to come to her or wait until she has all the information. There is no such thing as a perfect claim file—there will always be one more piece of information needed, but waiting for it must be weighed against the insurer's duty to its insured that it will fully investigate a claim against the insured and the fiduciary duty it has to protect its insured in the case of a liability claim. In the real world, the more appropriate yardstick is what is reasonable, given all the circumstances.

Further along this thought, although claims departments are often short staffed and adjusters are overworked, adjusters must actively pursue the documents they need to move the file toward resolution. There is a school of thought that the claimant (or insured) must prove his claim, and to do that the claimant should submit all relevant documents. This is a valid method of handling a claim. However, the majority of claimants and insureds are lay people who do not understand how an insurance claim is handled, are overwhelmed by the sheer number of documents they must procure, and are frustrated by a seeming lack of concern by the harried and frantic adjuster.

It is better, therefore, when discussing the claim with the claimant or insured to explain in detail what is needed upfront; explain you will send documents/authorizations for the claimant to sign, notarize and return to you (be sure to explain what these documents are and what they are used for); and what the adjuster will do to attempt to obtain the documents.

When I handled bodily injury claims, I would tell the claimant he had to prove his claim, but I would attempt to help him. I would let him know I would send several forms to him: a lost wage form, a medical authorization form, a list of providers, and a document which would help me verify whether he was Medicare/Medicaid eligible (despite the fact he just told me he was not in his recorded statement—I would explain again, as I did in the recorded statement, that CMS will fine an insurer $1,000/day/file if a claimant was found to be eligible and not reported).

I asked the claimant to sign and return the documents to me. Sending them via email was fine (in fact, I would often send the documents to the claimant via email in order to speed the handling of the file). I explained I would contact the claimant's employer for his wage information, and if coverage and liability were in order, I could reimburse him for the reasonable time he was off work due to the injury. I explained I would need the doctor's note for him to be off work and for me to consider this portion of the claim. Without both, I would be unable to consider the lost wage claim.

I explained to the claimant I would reach out to the providers for their medical records and invoices, but as an insurer, providers often put my requests at the bottom of the pile. If he wanted to obtain these, he was welcome to try, as he might be able to obtain his information faster than I could. I also let him know there could be a charge for the copying of his medical records and invoices. If that was the case, he should pay that and send me the invoice for consideration.

When I received the authorizations and the notice the claimant had finished treatment, I would then send letters to the providers asking for the medical invoices and records. As a side note: if the claimant went to the hospital and then to other treatment, such as a chiropractor, I would not wait until the claimant finished the chiropractor treatment to request information from the hospital. Hopefully, the claimant would only go to the hospital once; therefore, he'd be finished with that treatment, and it would be safe to obtain that information. The benefit of this is that hospitals generally take longer to send the requested information, and this would be one less piece of information to wait on when you're trying to settle the claim.

Most importantly, I made a calendar diary to follow up with these providers in three weeks to see if I had received these documents. Remember, the NAIC model uniform claims settlement practices do not permit an adjuster to allow a file to languish—the file must be pushed to conclusion. If I had received nothing in 3 weeks, I would follow up with a second request letter to the provider.

Again, get in the habit of *setting a diary for three weeks to follow up and make sure you receive this information*. If you do not do this, you very likely will forget and let the file languish until it comes back to your diary.

By letting a file languish, the file is working you rather than you working the file.

You may feel that putting it off will allow you get to other things, but in reality, creating this habit of procrastination means you will always be on the defensive, never caught up, always harried and stressed.

Also remember the model practices encourage communication every 30 days as to why a claim cannot be settled. In most cases, this communication is solely to the insured, but in some states like California, it is also for a claimant, who could be a third party to the claim. It is best to get in the habit of updating both the claimant and the insured, since this demonstrates good faith claims settlement practices on the adjuster's part.

By the time the 30-day letter requirement for my client came, a week after my second request, I could report to the claimant and insured that I had sent off for information, received nothing, and made a second request. Approximately 45 days from the date the claimant told me he had completed treatment, if I still had nothing, I would ask for his assistance. This is when I called the claimant to let him know which providers had not sent me the information I needed and asked him to obtain it for me.

While this may seem like more work on the front end (I assure you it is), that is the point. It is incessantly better to spend 5 minutes marking a letter "Second Request" and remailing it than spending 15 minutes with an irate claimant who does not believe you are helping resolve his claim. Further, if it takes 5 minutes to speak with the claimant and explain you've asked twice for his medical invoices and records but received nothing, and you need his help getting these documents in order to avoid a lawsuit, that is time better spent doing so now than dealing with an escalation of the situation later.

Insurance in Action (Reviewing Damage Assessments)

As mentioned previously, once all the documents are received and reviewed, it is time to move the file toward payment, partial payment and partial denial, or full denial. This is when an ROR and a Letter of Declination would come into play, although one hopes the ROR would have already been issued if the adjuster knew about the coverage question.

However for our example, let's say the adjuster did not know about the coverage question, and while reviewing the estimate, she saw this line-item charge:

CONTINUED - Kitchen

QUANTITY	UNIT	TAX	O&P	RCV	AGE/LIFE	COND.	DEP %	DEPREC.	ACV
11. Detach & Reset Baseboard - 3 1/4"									
46.74 LF	2.20	0.08	21.61	124.52	0/150 yrs	Avg.	0%	(0.00)	124.52
12. Paint baseboard - one coat									
46.74 LF	0.85	0.31	8.40	48.44	10/15 yrs	Avg.	66.67%	(26.70)	21.74
13. Detach & Reset Cabinetry - lower (base) units									
12.00 LF	53.28	0.00	134.27	773.63	0/50 yrs	Avg.	0%	(0.00)	773.63
14. Material Only Cabinetry - lower (base) units									
3.00 LF	159.42	39.46	108.73	626.45	10/50 yrs	Avg.	20%	(103.54)	522.91
43. Apply anti-microbial agent to the floor									
206.77 SF	0.24	5.52	10.53	65.67	0/NA	Avg.	0%	(0.00)	65.67
Totals: Kitchen		82.92	875.37	5,048.49				532.49	4,516.00
Total: Main Level		82.92	875.37	5,048.49				532.49	4,516.00
Total: Kitchen		82.92	875.37	5,048.49				532.49	4,516.00

Hallway

Main Level

Hallway/Entry   Height: 8'

322.00 SF Walls	90.40 SF Ceiling
412.40 SF Walls & Ceiling	90.40 SF Floor
10.04 SY Flooring	37.33 LF Floor Perimeter
54.83 LF Ceil. Perimeter	

Missing Wall - Goes to Floor	2' 11" X 6' 8"	Opens into Exterior
Missing Wall - Goes to Floor	3' X 6' 8"	Opens into Exterior
Missing Wall - Goes to Floor	2' 7" X 6' 8"	Opens into Exterior

The blue arrow points to #43 of the kitchen, which states the contractor should apply an antimicrobial agent to the floor. The adjuster knows the insured has an absolute mold exclusion in the policy. This means there is no coverage for mold or the cleanup of mold; therefore, the insurer cannot pay the $65.67 charge for the antimicrobial application.

There are a few things the adjuster can do at this point.

First, and most importantly, the adjuster needs to issue an ROR to the insured, explaining that mold and the cleaning of mold may not be covered. The adjuster needs to call the retail agent and then the insured to let both of them know the letter will be forthcoming.

Second, the adjuster can then audit the estimate herself by deducting the $65.67 anti-microbial application charge (she will need to remember to deduct it from the final settlement, which will also affect the overhead and profit amounts) or she can ask the appraiser to remove it from the estimate so that the estimate is clean, meaning there is no difference between the total amount settled per the estimate and the total amount of the insurer's check.

There are pros and cons to both methods.

If the adjuster keeps the original estimate, deducts the antimicrobial application charge, and retallies the total settlement figures, including that math with her ROR letter, the insured can clearly see how his settlement was determined and clearly link the amount/charges that are not covered. However, this can confuse the insured, since it does not make sense to have something included on the written estimate if it will not be honored by the insurance carrier.

If the adjuster asks for a clean copy of the estimate, this will delay the settlement of the loss, since she will then have to wait for the appraiser to remove the uncovered items, and the insured may already have a copy of the appraiser's original estimate. This can create confusion, although the clean (i.e., updated) estimate is easier for the insured to read and understand. The adjuster will still need to send an ROR regarding the antimicrobial cleaning as soon as she becomes aware of it.

Make no mistake, the insured will need to have the cleaning done, but the carrier cannot pay for it, due to the exclusion.

Despite the coverage issue, a proof of loss needs to be issued if the carrier requires one and a check issued for the covered loss (which in this case is the total amount, less the antimicrobial cleaning).

Then a Declination of Coverage letter should be issued to the insured concerning the antimicrobial cleaning amount.

There is a school of thought that says if an ROR is issued for a coverage issue, yet the claim is paid, there is no need to further complicate matters by issuing a letter of declination for the uncovered coverage matter. The model uniform claim settlement practices do not agree. The adjuster should check with the state where the loss occurred, but if there is no coverage for something the insured has made a claim for, and the insurer is not paying for that damage, a declination letter must be issued.

Disagreements with the Damage Assessments

Although everyone would prefer them not to be, insurance claims can be adversarial. Very often the two parties, either the insured or claimant and the carrier, disagree on the damages sustained by the injured party.

There are specific methods for both property and liability to address these issues, but we will discuss the 10,000-foot view. The specific methods will be discussed in upcoming chapters.

If there is a disagreement regarding an estimate of damages, whether that be physical or bodily injuries, the first step would be for the insured or claimant to contact the adjuster handling the file and explain why they disagree. There must be a logical reason for the adjuster to reconsider the amount offered. It cannot be "Because I said so," or "Because I want more money." Or because the contractor said it will cost more money—in such a case, the contractor would need to demonstrate why it will cost more. Usually this is done by providing the adjuster with the contractor's receipts to show the materials used are the same as what the insured had before the loss and that those same materials cost more than what was originally estimated.

I should also mention that regardless of the reason offered by the insured—even if the reason seems, on its face, ridiculous—the adjuster must always *consider* a demand for more money submitted by the claimant. Failure to do so opens the door to bad faith claims handling by not promptly investigating the claim. Let's say, for example, the insured or claimant calls the adjuster and says, "I won't settle for this amount, because I need more money." The adjuster must drill down to find out why the claimant believes he needs more money, even if the claimant's belief is, ultimately, because "I said so."

Aggravating? Sure. But this must be addressed. Again, failing to investigate this is usually against the state insurance department regulations. Best practices are to issue a letter asking for concrete reasons why the claimant believes what he believes. Then set a diary to follow up in two to three weeks to see if you have that information. If not, send a second request.

The reasons should be supported by documentation or other relevant information. For example, the adjuster might have missed an invoice; the cost of construction could have increased based on scarcity of a particular item; or the adjuster may not have understood a provider's medical note.

The claimant should explain this to the adjuster, and when presented with new information, the adjuster must take it under consideration.

After considering the information, the adjuster can either increase the offer or deny the request. This procedure occurs whether the claimant is a first- or third-party claimant. Remember, if this is a first-party claim, the adjuster needs to send an ROR quoting policy language, and then a declination of coverage letter formally denying the request.

Subrogation

I often called subrogation "a fancy insurance term for reimbursement," while speaking with insureds. Subrogation occurs when another party is at fault for the accident, but the insured's carrier pays for the loss. The insured's carrier then "seeks reimbursement from" the at-fault party's insurer or the at-fault party him/herself if there is no insurance.

Both the policy and common law establish that when an insurer pays for damage suffered by the insured, the carrier steps into the shoes of the insured and has all the rights the insured would if he were going to seek payment of the claim from the at-fault party. I will, for the sake of brevity, simply use the term "at-fault party," though it should be understood that I mean both the person who caused the damage or accident and his/her insurer, if there is one.

One of the most important parts of a subrogation claim is to obtain information pertaining to the at-fault party as soon as possible. The reason for this is to preserve the insured's and carrier's right for subrogation and to allow the at-fault party to conduct its own investigation. The at-fault party has a right and duty to investigate the claim made against its insured, just as our adjuster has the right and duty to investigate our insured's claim.

The first notice of subrogation should be sent to the at-fault party within 30 days of the accident. If the adjuster does not know who the at-fault carrier is, the letter should be sent to the at-fault individual. If neither the carrier nor the individual responds, a second request should be sent in another 30 days (60 days into the life of the claim). We hope by this time, the amount of damages will be known so that a formal reimbursement demand can be made.

If the at-fault party continues to ignore the subrogation demand, disagrees with the adjuster's liability analysis, or disagrees with the adjuster's estimate of damages, remedies are available, including mediation and arbitration between insurance companies. These methods are usually used rather than the carriers filing suit against one another.

Mediation takes place when an impartial third-party acts as a go-between for the two disagreeing parties and attempts to settle the case. Usually, mediation is not binding—meaning if one party does not wish to abide by the agreement the mediator reaches, it does not have to.

Arbitration, on the other hand, occurs when an impartial third-party is chosen by the disagreeing parties. Like mediation, arbitration Forums, Inc. provides a venue for insurers to settle the claim without need for litigation. Before sending a claim to arbitration, the adjuster should know if the at-fault carrier is a "subscribing member" or a "signatory member" of the arbitration process. Arbitration differs from mediation in that both parties agree to be bound by the decision of the arbitrator, who acts more like a judge than a go-between. This means both carriers agree to accept the arbitration decision, rules, and procedures.

Most carriers have a department that handles subrogation on behalf of the adjusters, but the adjuster would do well to remember she is the first point of contact, and she is responsible for obtaining all the information to make recovery of the carrier's payment successful. The subrogation adjuster's duties do not involve obtaining documents to support his "file." (I put "file" in quotes because there is only one file—that is the insurer's file, and every adjuster is responsible for the information in it, but it is the responsibility of the main adjuster to obtain information needed for subrogation.) In fact, the very information he needs is the same information the main adjuster must have to handle her claim:

- Estimate of damages/injuries
- Police accident reports/fire reports/weather reports
- Recorded statements
- Photographs of damages/photographs of the scene
- Reasoning why the at-fault party is legally liable or negligent
- The statute of limitations

The subrogation letter to the at-fault party should include the estimate of damages, any photographs of damages, accident or fire reports, reasonings why the at-fault party is legally liable, a demand for settlement, and a demand for the insured's deductible.

As the first-party carrier, the insurer will not pay the entire loss. It will pay the loss, less the deductible. It should, as a courtesy to its insured, ask for the insured's deductible from the at-fault party. Sometimes when the at-fault party's carrier receives the subrogation notice (and receives it early enough), the at-fault carrier asks to take over the handling of the file. This is allowable, but the adjuster should continue to follow up with the insured to make sure he is paid. This is not the time to simply close the file because someone else is picking up the check. Doing so is akin to leaving your Best Gal at the dance with your Number 1 Rival—you're not really sure he's going to take care of her the way you can.

The adjuster's duty to keep the insured informed continues, even through the subrogation process. As such, 30-day letters must be sent advising the insured of the recovery status; in the event the subrogation adjuster decides not to pursue reimbursement, the insured needs to be made aware of this, as well.

Upon settlement, if the at-fault party sends the insured's deductible to the insured's carrier, the subrogation adjuster will issue a check to the insured for his deductible. Care should be taken here.

It is possible for the at-fault carrier to believe its insured is not 100 percent responsible for the loss, so it will not completely reimburse the subrogating carrier. Most states require the insured be made 100 percent whole before the insurer is reimbursed the settlement funds it paid.

> For example, if Pay-Em Insurance Company indemnified its insured, Insured Works, Inc., $900 for its automobile accident, it would send a subrogation demand in the total amount of for $1,000 to Not At Fault Insurers.

Total Loss and Damage to Insured Works, Inc. Auto	$1,000
Mr. Smith's Deductible	$100
Total Pay-Em Ins. Co.'s Settlement	**$900**

Not At Fault's adjuster believes Mr. Smith is 45 percent at fault because he pulled out in front of its insured, but Not At Fault's adjuster acknowledges its insured had the last clear chance to avoid the collision. Therefore, Not At Fault's adjuster deducts 45 percent of Pay-Em's settlement and sends a check for $550.

Total Subrogation Demand from Pay-Em	$1,000
Not At Fault's Liability Determination	55% fault for its insured 45% IWI fault
Not At Fault's Reimbursement Determination	$1,000 x 55%
Not At Fault's Reimbursement	**$550**

Depending on the laws and rules of the state where Pay-Em Insurance Company is located, it may or may not split the percentage of the deductible with Smith. If Pay-Em is in a "made whole" state, Pay-Em must reimburse Insured Work, Inc. the $100 deductible in full. If the state allows Pay-Em to share a portion of the settlement from Not At Fault with the insured, the settlement for the deductible would be $55.

Not At Fault's Reimbursement	$550
Smith's Deductible	$100
Pay-Em's Portion of Smith's Deductible	$100 x 55%
Pay-Em's Additional Payment to Smith	**$55**

If this occurs, the subrogation adjuster should call the insured and explain the partial settlement, and then follow up the phone call with a letter.

Salvage

Salvage is a method of recovering value in lightly damaged or non-damaged parts of physical items. Insureds and claimants usually hear about salvage when dealing with automobiles which are total losses (the damage to the vehicle is more than the worth of the vehicle). Some portion of these vehicles usually is undamaged or lightly damaged, so it can be removed and sold for parts.

Besides automobiles, salvage can apply to a homeowner's contents, cargo, and commercial/warehouse contents. Like subrogation, it is important to act swiftly in order to secure the highest value for the undamaged/lightly damaged property. (For the sake of brevity, I will refer only to "undamaged" property, but it should be understood that I mean both undamaged or lightly damaged items.)

Salvage is determined by receiving bids from salvors who wish to buy the undamaged property. The bids operate much like any bidding or auction procedure: the salvor will submit a blind bid on the property, and whoever submits the highest bid wins the property. Depending on the type of property that is damaged, there may be charges against the property, usually referred to as storage charges. Towing companies usually charge a storage fee to hold the undamaged items on their premises until the high bidder retrieves its winnings.

The hope is that the bid is more than the storage charges. In this case, the salvor issues a check to the insurer for the difference. These funds help reduce the overall incurred loss for the insurer.

At times, the insured or claimant may wish to retain possession of the property. This is allowable, and in that instance, the adjuster still must obtain bids from salvors, then "sell" the property to the insured/claimant for the high bid amount. As a courtesy, the property owner need not submit a higher bid, à la *The Price Is Right*.

Finally, if the damaged item(s) will change hands due to the salvor taking possession of the property, and some form of ownership documentation exists—such as an automobile title—the ownership documents will need to reflect the new owners. The carrier may have a total loss department which handles changing a regular title to a salvage title in the name of the new owner.

Wrap Up

Upon receipt of the field adjuster's report and estimate (i.e, field appraiser), the desk adjuster must take several steps. Most importantly, the adjuster cannot simply rest on her laurels. She must continuously review coverage, continuously review the claim for suspicious activities, actively review the estimate and medical records, and quickly pursue recovery actions, such as subrogation and salvage.

6

Introduction to Litigation

> ## The goal of the claims department is to *NOT* Pay Claims.

At least this is what policyholder attorneys, most insureds, some agents, pretty much every claimant and trial attorney, and the general public believe. And this is what leads to numerous lawsuits—the delay of and the refusal to pay claims.

Almost all of this can be avoided with a properly staffed claims department, properly trained adjusters, and a properly educated buying public. However, I could tilt at windmills till the cows come home, yet none of these things will ever come to fruition—which is outside this particular chapter's purview.

Usually, the adjuster will know a lawsuit is coming down the pike because the attempt to settle the claim is derailing, or the insured or claimant has threatened suit. There are three types of lawsuits:

- First-party lawsuit, brought by the policyholder, who will usually allege bad faith claims settlement practices
- Third-party lawsuit, brought by the claimant of a liability policy, who will sue the insured in order to achieve settlement
- Third-party lawsuit, brought by the claimant of a liability poli-

cy, who will sue the insured in order to reach the insurer's defense dollars

A few states are "direct action" states[12] regarding third-party lawsuits. According to the fundamentals of contract law, only the people (insured and insurer) to whom the contract (policy) applies directly have the ability (standing) in the policy to file suit to ensure the contract provisions are enforced.

The liability policy covers the insured for injuring or damaging a third party, the claimant, who has no standing in the policy. Because the claimant does not have the ability to file suit directly against the carrier, he may file suit against the insured—which is why the policy provides a defense to the policyholder. However, some states have special statutes allowing claimants to directly sue the carrier. There are some requirements for the claimant before such a suit is allowed, and it's beyond the scope of this chapter to go into detail about that. If the adjuster is working in a state where direct action is allowed, it is her duty to know the prerequisites for a direct action.

Finally, before getting into the meat of litigation, I'll briefly describe another scenario the adjuster may encounter with a lawsuit: the Mary Carter agreement. The original case, from a Florida state court, involved multiple defendants. One defendant engaged in a secret pact with the plaintiff which did not involve the other defendants. The pact was an agreement that the original defendant would stay in the suit, but his liability would diminish while the liability of his codefendants would increase.

A traditional Mary Carter agreement absolves the settling defendant of joint and several liability and removes a possible payment from non-settling codefendants.

Mary Carter agreements may be called by other names in other states, but in practice, the insured may stop defending himself and allow the plaintiff to assume his rights to sue the insurer directly in exchange for releasing him from the claim. In simple terms, the claimant now becomes the insured. Usually for this to occur, the original liability suit must go through to ver-

---

12 See Appendix, page 221.

dict where an excess verdict is assessed against the policyholder. The plaintiff will then file suit on behalf of the insured.

Threat of Litigation

As mentioned, often the adjuster knows a lawsuit is coming. If the insured or claimant (or their respective attorneys) threatens a lawsuit, it is a good practice to denote the file:

This file is being handled in anticipation of litigation.

The reason is this: during the normal handling and investigation of a claim file, everything is discoverable. However, if a claim is being investigated or handled for litigation, the file may not be discoverable (or parts of the file may not be discoverable).

I've discussed use of this cautionary phrase with many defense attorneys, most of whom poo-poo the phrase and tell me it does not offer any protection at all. In my experience, it offers a delineating line between when there was not litigation and when at least the threat of litigation begins. Besides, it can't hurt.

Sources of the Law

The United States has three sources of law:

- **Common Law:** the unwritten decisions developed by judges through the process of litigating lawsuits. It is based on English Common Law, brought by the Colonists and outlines the rules regarding the ownership and use of property, as well as a person's code of conduct and duties towards others. Judges rely on the doctrine of *stare decisis*, or legal precedent, which state that once a court has decided an issue concerning a certain set of facts, it will rule in the same manner in all future cases, provided that the facts are generally the same.

- **Statutory Law:** contrary to common law, statutory law is written and is the law created by legislatures. The legislature can enact laws which may enhance or reduce the rules, conduct, and duties found in common law. If there is a conflict between the two, statutory law is superior, unless it is found to be unconstitutional.

- **Civil Code:** the only place where civil code is found is Louisiana, due to its colonial heritage. Here, judges are not bound by *stare decisis* and are given the authority to interpret the law's intent relating to the facts of the individual case.

Introduction to Litigation

One of the first parts of a lawsuit is the ***pleadings***. This is the plaintiff's formal statement regarding the suit. The pleadings will have the individual causes of actions which contain the allegations against the ***defendant***. The

```
              IN THE DISTRICT COURT OF COUNTY, STATE

PLAINTIFF NAME, Individually, and    )
CO-PLAINTIFF, (if applicable)        )
     Plaintiff,                      )
                                     )      ELECTRONICALLY FILED
vs.                                  )      YYYY MONTH DAY TIME
                                     )
DEFENDANT NAME, Individually, and    )      COURT CLERK
INSURANCE COMPANY (probably),        )      CASE FILE #:
     Defendant.                      )
_____)

                           PETITION
              (PURSUANT TO STATE CHAPTER/LAW/STATUTE)
```

causes of actions are usually enumerated. The ***petition***, or complaint, is a formulaic manner of listing the plaintiff's claim and the facts on which he is relying to support the demand. The petition has a set form which should become recognizable to all adjusters, whether they handle lawsuits or not. This is especially important if the adjuster does not handle suits. If she sees something like the image below, she must notify her supervisor immediately.

The suit can also be filed in Federal Court, in which case the header would indicate this. Regardless, quick action should be taken when notice of a suit arrives.

Coupled with the petition is the ***service of process*** which is the notification by the court to the defendant that a suit has been filed. Below is an example.

```
                     NOTICE

    You have been sued in court. If you wish to
    defend against the claims set forth in the
    following pages, you must take action within
    XX days after the complaint and notice are
    served, by entering a written appearance per-
    sonally or by attorney and filing in writing
    with the court your defenses or objections to
            the claims set forth against you.
```

It is important for the adjuster to know when the defendant was served because there are strict timelines regarding the answering of the lawsuit. Often the adjuster or defense counsel can obtain permission from the plaintiff attorney for an extension to answer the pleadings. This extension must *always* be confirmed in writing. When an extension is obtained, the adjuster should ensure the extension will not waive any affirmative defense to the claim.

If the suit is not answered in time, it is presumed by the court the defendant agrees with the plaintiff's allegations, and a ***default judgment*** occurs. This should not be confused with a declaratory judgment, which will be discussed later.

When the defendant—usually the insured—is served, the adjuster should obtain a copy of the suit and forward it to the attorney the insurer assigns to defend the policyholder against the allegations of the lawsuit.

The defense attorney will file an ***appearance*** and an ***answer***, which is the defendant's response to the suit. It, too, is usually prescribed in form.

Often with pleadings, the plaintiff will attach the ***discovery*** proceedings, which is the way both parties to the suit uncover (or discover) the factual basis for the claim and defense of same. The purpose of the discovery process is to lay all the cards on the table so each party can arrive at the decision that one should either settle the claim and accept the offer/demand, or defend the claim and reject the offer/demand.

Within the discovery process, there are several sub-steps, including ***depositions***. Depositions are usually oral testimony under oath, obtained using a question-and-answer format. The process is usually recorded both by a court reporter and a videographer.

Interrogatories are the written questions to the parties involved in the lawsuit, and they are written under oath; *request for admissions* is a demand the other party admit an alleged fact is correct. These are quite stylized. Below is an example of a first-party discovery process:[13]

INSURANCE COMPANY'S
FIRST SET OF INTERROGATORIES AND
REQUESTS FOR ADMISSION TO PLAINTIFF

Pursuant to Federal Rule of Civil Procedure 26(a)(1), Defendant Insurance Company ("Insurer"), through its undersigned counsel, hereby serves its first set of discovery requests to Plaintiff Office, LLC ("Plaintiff").

INSTRUCTIONS

1. Produce all requested documents within your possession, custody, or control, or within the possession, custody, or control of any of your agents, representatives, and/or attorneys, or anyone acting on your behalf.

2. In responding to this discovery, please use the definitions provided below.

3. In responding to this discovery, Insurer requests that Plaintiff restate verbatim the discovery request to which the response is directed immediately prior to each response.

4. Wherever appropriate, the singular form of a word should be interpreted in the plural.

.....

DEFINITIONS

1. "Insurer" means Defendant Insurance Company.

2. "Plaintiff," "you," "your," or "Insured"

---

13 Keep in mind that the insured can be sued by the third-party claimant (where the interrogatories and admissions would sound a little different) or that the insurer can be sued by the insured (first-party, usually bad faith allegations, which is what these are examples of).

means Plaintiff Office, LLC, legal counsel for Plaintiff Office, LLC, and all agents, employees, and representatives of Plaintiff Office, LLC, including but not limited to Mr. Insured Contact and Mrs. Insured Contact, employees of Plaintiff Attorney Law, PC, and employees of Independent Adjusting, Inc.

3. "Communication" means all occasions on which information was conveyed from one person to another either by means of a written communication or orally, including but not limited to emails, correspondence, memoranda, notes, instant messages, text messages, telephone messages, and voice mail.

...

INTERROGATORIES

INTERROGATORY NO. 1:

Identify each of your representatives, employees, agents, officers, or directors, who has had substantive involvement in your decision-making regarding the Subject Claim, including but not limited to Mr. Insured Contact and Mrs. Insured Contact, and, for each, please provide a description of that person's involvement.

INTERROGATORY NO. 2:

Beginning 10 years prior to the date you made the Subject Claim to the present, describe any construction, repairs, maintenance, changes, replacements, or modifications made to the Subject Property, including, but not limited to, (a) a description of each construction, repair, maintenance, change, replacement, or modification; (b) the identity of all persons who performed each construction, repair, maintenance, change, replacement, or modification; (c) the dates on which each construction, repair, maintenance, change, replace-

```
ment, or modification was made; and (d) the
total cost of construction, repair, mainte-
nance, change, replacement, or modification.
```

...

REQUESTS FOR ADMISSION

REQUEST FOR ADMISSION NO. 1:

```
Admit that the proposal from Heating and Cool-
ing was not submitted to Insurer as part of
the Subject Claim.
```

REQUEST FOR ADMISSION NO. 2:

```
Admit that you are not seeking any damages
based on the proposal from Heating and Cool-
ing.
```

REQUEST FOR ADMISSION NO. 3:

```
Admit that you did not report the Subject
Claim to Insurer until Date of Reporting.
```

REQUEST FOR ADMISSION NO. 4:

```
Admit that the only sworn statement in proof
of loss that you submitted is dated Date of
Submission.
```

...

Everything in a lawsuit, just like in claims handling, is driven by due dates. This is why it's extremely important to find out when the defendant received service, because that's when the clock starts ticking to answer the suit and avoid going into default and receiving a ***default judgment***.

Looking at this process from the carrier side, if the suit is not answered in time, it is presumed by the court the defendant agrees with the plaintiff's allegations, and a default judgment occurs. A default judgment is actually a two-step process. First comes the default, when the plaintiff asks the court clerk to enter the default. This is an administrative act which formally establishes that the defendant is in default. Once in default, the defendant cannot answer or respond to the complaint.

This should not be confused with a ***declaratory judgment*** or ***DEC Action***, which is a binding judgment from the court usually before a lawsuit begins. The declaratory judgment is utilized by both the policyholder and the insurer regarding coverage issues. It is a legal motion to determine the obligations, rights, and responsibilities of both parties. It also helps eliminate potential bad faith claims handling allegations because the judge has determined coverage for the loss.

Here's an important thing for adjusters to understand: often plaintiff attorneys will submit the written discovery with the lawsuit. In other words, the insured may not only receive the actual ***complaint*** but also receive the discovery paperwork. When assigning the lawsuit to defense counsel, the adjuster also needs to give her the discovery paperwork from the plaintiff counsel. The defense counsel will write the answers to the discovery (the ***answers to interrogatories*** and ***answers to request for admissions*** as seen below) and then submit them to the court and opposing counsel. I have heard of lawsuits going very wrong for insurers because the adjuster didn't forward all the information to defense counsel. Like failing to respond to the lawsuit, if the insured (through his insurer through its attorney) fails to answer discovery, the insured has admitted to everything being alleged by the plaintiff.

A good rule of thumb is to forward everything to defense counsel.

Now that I scared you, I will also say, "There. There. Don't worry." Defense counsel should have your back and double check there's not outstanding interrogatories or discovery.

You should also realize attorneys think they are paid by the word, and answers will be long with a lot of "here afore to mentioned" and "notwithstanding the contrary" and "just checking to see if you're still reading this." The attorneys may have several rounds of discovery; so, it's not uncommon to see ***second*** (or Third or Fourth) ***set of interrogatories*** along with the corresponding ***second*** (ad nauseum) ***responses to written discovery***.

It is your responsibility to help defense counsel answer the Answers, although, if the lawsuit is a third-party claim, the attorney may seek answers from the insured.

The answers to interrogatories are the written answers to the questions and are also under oath. Answers to request for admissions are the written answers to the request, and they, too, are written in a formulaic way. The following is an example of a first-party lawsuit discovery request:

DEFENDANT INSURANCE COMPANY'S RESPONSES AND OBJECTIONS TO PLAINTIFF'S SECOND SET OF WRITTEN DISCOVERY

Defendant Insurance Company ("Insurer"), by and through its undersigned counsel, hereby submits the following responses and objections to Plaintiff's Second Set of Written Discovery ("Discovery Requests").

PRELIMINARY STATEMENT AND GENERAL OBJECTIONS

Insurer has made a reasonable and good faith effort to respond to those Discovery Requests that are intelligible in the context of this case and are not otherwise objectionable. Insurer has not yet completed its investigation of the facts related to this case, interviewed all witnesses in connection with this case, or completed its discovery or preparation of the factual and legal issues in this case. Each of the following responses, therefore, is based upon information known to Insurer at this time and specifically known to it after a reasonable inquiry.

Insurer objects to Definition (a), which purports to define "Defendant," "you," "your," and "yourself." Definition (a) is overly broad and vague, as it includes "any other person or entity acting on behalf of [Insurer]." Any Discovery Requests using this definition would be unduly burdensome to comply with and not proportional to the needs of the case by requesting of Insurer information or documents which are not reasonably within its possession, custody, or control, and by requesting information or documents that are privileged or constitute protected work product. Unless otherwise stated, Insurer is responding on behalf of the named Defendant, Insurer, only.

...

RESPONSES AND OBJECTIONS TO INTERROGATORIES

RESPONSE TO INTERROGATORY NO. 1:

To the extent Plaintiff seeks additional information, Insurer objects to this interrogatory on the basis that it contains numerous discrete subparts, each of which must be counted separately. (Attorneys will generally insert a case or ruling in the interrogatories to support their arguments). Subject to, limited by, and without waiving the objections stated below and preliminary objections above, Insurer's representatives are: Claim Adjuster, Supervisor, and Team Leader. Each representative handled the claim and reviewed coverage.

RESPONSE TO INTERROGATORY NO. 2:

Insurer objects to the interrogatory as it is overly broad and unduly burdensome to the extent it purports to require Insurer to perform any unreasonable additional search or inquiry for documents or information. Insurer will undertake: (a) a reasonable and thorough search for documents or information maintained in its possession, custody, or control, in locations where documents or information responsive to the interrogatory are most likely to be found; and (b) a reasonable and thorough inquiry of those persons reasonably available to Insurer who are most likely to have knowledge of documents or information responsive to the interrogatory.

Insurer further objects to interrogatory no. 2 because each request for production that seeks "all," "any," "any and all" documents or an "entire" category of documents is overly broad, seeks information that is duplicative or cumulative of other documents that might contain some information related in some way to the topic, or found in a location within the company that would not be expected to maintain documents or information relevant to this matter, and on those bases, is unduly burdensome and not proportional to the needs of the case.

...

RESPONSES AND OBJECTIONS TO REQUEST FOR ADMISSION

RESPONSE TO REQUEST FOR ADMISSION NO. 1:

Subject to, limited by, and without waiving the objections stated below and preliminary objections above, Insurer states as follows:

DENIAL OF REQUEST FOR ADMISSION NO. 1:

The Policy requires Plaintiff to cooperate with Insurer in the investigation of its claim. The facts indicate that Plaintiff violated its duty to cooperate with Insurer in the investigation of this claim by failing to submit a sworn proof of loss and other requested documentation, among other breaches. In the absence of such materials, Insurer cannot ascertain what Plaintiff asserts are "claimed property damages" in order to perform a meaningful re-inspection.

DENIAL OF REQUEST FOR ADMISSION NO. 2:

Plaintiff's failure to provide a sworn proof of loss was a breach of the Policy. Plaintiff's failure to timely provide an accurate, sworn proof of loss obstructed Insurer's adjustment of the claim, particularly because of information learned from documents withheld by Plaintiff and testimony by Plaintiff's agents revealed that Plaintiff and its agents repeatedly submitted inflated and misleading estimates as to the amount of damages it claimed.

Requests for production are a request for the opposing party to produce documents so the other side may examine them. This is part of making sure everyone has the same pieces of information. The following is an example:

DEFENDANT'S FIRST REQUEST FOR PRODUCTION TO PLAINTIFF

Pursuant to STATE STATUTE, Defendant requests that Plaintiff produce for inspection and copying at the offices of Defendant's attorney's office within thirty (30) days of service hereof, the following:

1. Any and all medical bills and medical expenses incurred as a result of this alleged accident.

2. Any and all hospital, x-rays, laboratory and doctors' reports, notes and summaries made in connection with PLAINTIFF'S alleged injuries.

3. Any and all statements from any alleged witnesses to the accident in question.

4. Any and all photographs taken by anyone at the scene of the accident, PLAINTIFF'S alleged injuries, or any other object material to the issues in this lawsuit.

This discovery process may be called different things in different states. For example, New York calls interrogatories a "bill of particulars." Like interrogatories, the bill of particulars will have similar admissions, denials, or requests for productions, but it may be organized differently.

Subpoenas may be issued in a suit; a subpoena is the court's order for an event to occur—documents to be produced, a witness to appear, testimony to be given.

There may be various *motions* through the discovery process. A motion is an effort by one of the parties to preclude evidence or ask the judge to rule on a matter the plaintiff and defense attorney cannot agree upon.

One motion an adjuster hears quite often is a *motion for summary judgment*, also known as an *MSJ*. This is usually filed by a party who hopes the discovery shows enough evidence for the judge to rule in the party's favor without having to go through trial. However, if there is a question of fact or an interpretation of the evidence needed, that will be reserved for a jury and the motion will be denied.

Cases go through a *pretrial conference*. The conference is a meeting with the judge and all parties prior to the *trial*. It is a time to discuss the status of discovery and to see if any other discovery should be completed so the trial can continue without delay. The judge may facilitate settlement negotiations to assist resolution prior to trial. Once discovery is complete, the trial date is set. Because courts are overburdened, the judge may order a *settlement conference* in another attempt to have the parties arrive at a settlement. The reason is to once again discuss coverages, liability/negligence, and damages among the parties in an effort to settle the claim outside of litigation.

A *jury* is chosen from a jury pool once discovery is complete. It should go without saying that both the defense and the plaintiff are looking for jury members who will be sympathetic to their side. In order to weed out some biases, both attorneys go through *voire dire*, which is questioning of the potential jury members regarding their thoughts or beliefs.

Trial is not necessarily portrayed correctly on TV. There are *opening statements* by each party, or parties if there are multiple defendants. The plaintiff presents his case first. Unlike TV, the defense can immediately question the witnesses rather than having the plaintiff rest and then "recalling" a person to the court. This helps streamline the process. Also, because of the in-depth discovery and settlement conferences, there is very rarely a "bombshell" uncovered in the trial, the likes of which make for such dramatic cinema in Hollywood. After all parties have given their evidence, each side will issue a *closing statement*, or a summary of the trial.

Adjusters have likely heard some version of Dale Carnegie's quote: "Tell the audience what you are going to say; say it; then tell the audience what you said." This is the flow of the trial proceedings.

Most people who watch court dramas are familiar with jury *deliberations*—when the jury steps outside the court and to debate and discuss with the goal of reaching a decision regarding the claim. *Verdict* is when the jury reaches an agreement and delivers its decision to the court; *judgment* is the final order of the court.

If a monetary judgment is rendered, the defendant has a time limit to pay the judgment. The defendant will pay up to the policy limits in the event of a liability suit, or it may have to pay in excess of that if it is a bad faith suit. *Prejudgment interest*, interest that accumulates on the award from the time of injury to the time of judgment, may apply. Adjusters need to know their states' statutes and understand that prejudgment interest can apply to property damage claims, too. Since it usually takes several years for a case to reach the courtroom, the interest can add a significant cost to the settlement of the case. Post-judgment interest is added when the insurer does not pay the award timely, plus prejudgment interest.

This chapter will not go into litigation procedures in the appeals process.

Litigation Management

Claims departments have robust litigation management guidelines for adjusters. It is important that adjusters are familiar with these guidelines in order to effectively handle lawsuits.

When an adjuster receives a new lawsuit or other legal papers, she should immediately review them and discuss them with her manager. The documents should be scanned into the claim file and detailed in the claim notes. If it is a liability claim, the adjuster will contact the insured to determine the details of service. If it is a first-party claim, contact with the insured is prohibited, as the policyholder will be represented by an attorney. Adjusters are not allowed to contact an individual who is represented by an attorney due to the contract between the attorney and that individual.

As mentioned previously, it is a good idea to mark the file: ***"This file is being handled in anticipation of litigation."*** Again, this delineates portions of the file as pre-litigation and post-litigation.

The adjuster provides effective control of the litigation process by assigning defense counsel. Whether it is a first-party or third-party lawsuit, the handling of litigation remains the same. The adjuster should first contact defense counsel and discuss the file and the allegations in the lawsuit with him. The adjuster will then send a copy of the lawsuit to defense counsel for so he can file an appearance and answer. Again, it is important to do this in a timely manner so as to avoid a default judgment.

There are certain items the adjuster should send to the defense counsel so that counsel can efficiently and properly defend either the policyholder or the insurance carrier:

- Copies of the lawsuit
- Copies of the claim file
- Details concerning service;
- Details concerning any extension or time to answer, if obtained by the adjuster
- Court and venue
- Name of the insured and contact person, as well as any additional named insureds if applicable
- Name of the persons intended to be defended or indemnified
- Full and complete copy of the policy

While discussing the policy, it is important for defense counsel to have a certified copy of the policy. This simply means that the defense counsel has a true and correct copy of the policy and nothing is missing.

Defense counsel and the adjuster have a symbiotic relationship. The handling adjuster should provide her liability analysis and damage evaluation to defense counsel. Defense counsel should provide copies of responses to interrogatories, responses to requests for production, and answers to the lawsuit for the adjuster's file.

After review of the lawsuit and some initial discovery has taken place, the defense counsel should provide a report to the adjuster for the file. The report should outline the defense counsel's thoughts regarding liability, coverage, and ability to settle the lawsuit. If the insurer does not feel the claim should be settled, defense counsel will continue with discovery, as described above. Generally, every step the defense counsel makes must be approved by the insurance carrier through the adjuster.

Adjusters should be aware not only of the time sensitivity of handling legal documents, but also the venues and jurisdictions where the lawsuits have been filed. Venues and jurisdictions have a direct impact on the value of a claim's settlement. Generally, federal courts are seen as more conservative, and therefore verdicts tend to be lower. Areas where verdicts are outside of the norm and where large judgments are usually received are known pejoratively as "judicial hellholes." An adjuster must be aware of these areas, as plaintiffs will often "venue shop" in order to find more liberal judges and juries who may be inclined decide in their favor.

Finally, when a lawsuit is received, the adjuster should note what the *prayer* requests. This term may vary in jurisdictions, but it means what the plaintiff wants, and usually it is a monetary amount. If there is no monetary amount listed—the prayer may say something to the effect of "whatever the Court wishes to grant"— an *excess letter* must immediately be sent to the insured in the event of a third-party claim.

The excess letter is a letter informing the insured there is a possibility the judgment may exceed policy limits, and if the policyholder has an excess (or umbrella) carrier, that carrier should immediately be placed on notice of the claim. Failure to perform this step may open the insurer up to a bad faith claim by the policyholder, who can claim that had he known of the potential for an excess verdict, he would have instructed the adjuster to settle within policy limits.

Choosing Defense Counsel

Insurers are in a constant tug-of-war to offer the best insurance product for the lowest price. Unfortunately, this affects personnel and vendor relationships. Depending on the insurance carrier, defense counsel will either be an in-house or an outside attorney.

An in-house attorney is an attorney who is employed by the insurer. It is his responsibility to handle all litigation for the carrier. Having an internal attorney has cost benefits for the insurer. Since the attorney is an employee, adjusters can approach the attorney for information like quick legal research, coverage opinions, and jury verdict research that shows how juries in a particular jurisdiction have awarded similar injuries or damages to plaintiffs, with no surprise legal invoices. Insurers also know, within reason, what their litigated expenses will be for a given year.

Outside counsel, on the other hand, can lead to improved service, since the litigation work would be spread among several different firms. Carriers generally do not hire only one attorney. They hire the entire firm, which gives them access to several attorneys at a single location. The disadvantage to using outside counsel is that the carrier does not control expenses. While the insurer can ask for a budget and negotiate a fee arrangement with the law firm, there still may be a fluctuation in legal fees from an outside vendor.

Often the choice of which attorney to use is made by the home office, as the lawsuit will either go to the in-house counsel or an independent attorney firm which has been preapproved and listed on a vendor panel.

Many insurers use a legal billing review service to check (outside) defense counsel's invoices. The invoices must reflect an itemization of work done by anyone who handles the file. This usually is done in segments of a tenth of an hour (or 6 minutes). The use of billing review services for counsel invoices is a contentious issue. Defense counsel, in the case of a third-party lawsuit, represents the policyholder, not the insurer. This is known as a "tripartite" relationship. Defense counsel may believe that cutting his invoices hampers his ability to provide a vigorous defense for the insured. In such an instance, the adjuster and the insurance carrier must recognize this issue and be flexible regarding billing matters. The insurer's duty is a fiduciary one to the insured and one in which the insurer must place the insured's interests at least as high (if not higher) than its own.

In the event of a first-party claim, where the defense counsel is defending the insurance carrier, there would be no conflict of interest between ensuring legal bills are properly reviewed by an outside vendor.

The parties in the tripartite relationship are the insured, the insurer, and defense counsel. To be plain, defense counsel's duty is to the insured, even if he reports what is happening in the lawsuit to the adjuster. This is an important concept to understand.

Defense counsel cannot (and should not) consider coverage; he must focus only on defending the policyholder. He is not beholden to the insurer to let the adjuster know if he finds a coverage issue. However, if the adjuster discovers a coverage issue while litigation is ongoing, she must immediately notify her supervisor.

If the adjuster discovers a coverage issue during the course of the lawsuit, the claim file will be bifurcated (split into two parts). The original adjuster should at that point become the coverage adjuster, since she now has knowledge of the coverage issue. A new file will be set up that will become the defense file. Defense counsel will then begin reporting to the defense adjuster.

The original adjuster, now the coverage adjuster, will assign another attorney—known as a coverage attorney—to review coverage. He may intervene (a legal motion) in the lawsuit, or he may file a DEC Action in order to determine coverage.

The claim file is bifurcated because *the duty to defend is broader than the duty to indemnify*, a phrase which all adjusters should become familiar with. The defense team should solely focus on defense and pay no attention to coverage. They should not be allowed to look at the coverage file to avoid becoming biased; the coverage team, however, is allowed to review the defense file since coverage impacts everything in the claim, going forward.

Once the file has been bifurcated and a Reservation of Rights letter has been issued, the insurer may owe the insured a *second*, independent attorney, sometimes called *Cumis* Counsel or *Moeller* Counsel, depending on the jurisdiction.[14]

In plain English, the insurance carrier can be paying for a total of *three* attorneys to file an appearance in one lawsuit if there is a coverage issue and the carrier has reserved its rights regarding coverage.

Like everything, there is an exception to the rule. Simply sending a Reservation of Rights letter regarding a coverage issue does not automatically invoke the right to independent counsel to protect the policyholder. The carrier's reservation of its rights must create a conflict between it and the insured for this to occur. Let's review the following example.

> The insured was tardy in reporting a claim. Three weeks ago, he received service, and an answer is due Friday at 5 p.m.—it is presently 3:30 p.m. on Thursday. The plaintiff attorney cannot be reached to obtain an extension for answering. Therefore, the adjuster must assign defense counsel, who must immediately file an Appearance and a general Answer.
>
> In discussing the lawsuit with the insured, the adjuster discovers that while the policyholder was late in reporting the claim (in conflict with the policy provision that insureds report claims as soon as practical), no real harm was done, as the carrier has not been prejudiced by the late notice. The adjuster can still investigate the alleged damage.
>
> The adjuster pens a Reservation of Rights letter, alerting the insured to this coverage issue, but there is no conflict between the carrier and the policyholder; therefore, independent counsel (the third attorney) may not be needed.

Compare, for example, if the delay in reporting the claim had been one year. By that time, a judgment might have been entered against the insured,

---

14 See Appendix, page 225.

who tried to defend the claim himself because he thought it was fraudulent. He now wants to appeal the verdict and sends the lawsuit paperwork to his carrier. The alleged damage has been repaired or discarded, and there is no possibility for the insurer to inspect the damages. This creates several conflicts between the carrier and the policyholder; therefore, the independent counsel may be appropriate, pending a DEC Action by the insurer's coverage attorney.

States recognizing the need for independent counsel when a conflict arises are California, Florida, New Jersey, Mississippi, Missouri, Texas, and Wisconsin. As always, the adjuster should confirm this with coverage counsel and/or the supervisor and know the jurisdictional rules where she is working.

Small Nuggets of Litigation Wisdom

What does the maxim "The duty to defend is broader than the duty to indemnify" actually mean?

Plaintiff attorneys are familiar with insurance policies and what is and is not covered. They are also familiar with the adage about defense and indemnification. Therefore, they will fashion their pleadings so there is at least one method to hook the insurer into the lawsuit. This is called "pleading to coverages."

Pollution, in most policies, is not a covered cause of loss. However, a plaintiff attorney who pleads to coverage will allege the insured negligently hired, trained, and supervised its employees, which led to the accident causing the pollution.

Negligence in hiring, training, and supervising employees may be covered; therefore, the attorney has "hooked" the policyholder into the suit. The insured will turn the pleadings over to its insurance carrier, who will now provide a defense for what appears, on the surface, to be an uncovered claim.

Both the carrier and the plaintiff attorney know this scintilla of an allegation is a veiled attempt to obtain "defense dollars." This is the dirty underside of litigation no other insurance books discuss. The plaintiff attorney is attempting to force the insurer to decide if it wants to defend a lawsuit—which is costly and which the carrier (really the policyholder) may lose—or if it wants to settle the claim by "giving" the money it had allocated for the defense attorney to the plaintiff in exchange for a dismissal and a signed release.

Insurers are risk averse. After all, that is literally the carriers' job—to avoid or minimize risk. Therefore, many insurers, once a suit is filed, will attempt to settle a previously denied claim by throwing defense dollars at the plaintiff. Unfortunately, these actions have become so ubiquitous that there is almost an abuse of the court system now with lawsuits in an effort to obtain these settlements.

The opposite of throwing defense dollars at the plaintiff is the "scorched earth" method, in which one side, usually the defense, will fight every allegation and suit. This method is extremely expensive, as it entails generating a great deal of paperwork. The goal is to have the plaintiff spend as much money as possible, which makes any settlement obtained a matter of diminishing returns. Plaintiff attorneys will be familiar with firms that regularly employ the scorched earth method and be less enthusiastic about filing suit. The defense hope is that this method will discourage lawsuits.

I am writing this in 2021, when *diversity* is a popular concept which many companies want to be associated with. Insurers and plaintiffs, being ahead of the game, have always focused on diversity, but in this case the definition is different.

When filing a lawsuit, the suit should be brought in the venue closest to where the loss occurred. In most cases, all parties to the suit are local. Think, for example, of neighbors who file suit against each other about a fence. They would both be subject to the same local rules. The insurance company might not be local, however. Its home office could be in another state, and the desk adjuster might be in yet a third state. When there is a "diversity" of parties, meaning several states' jurisdictions and/or laws might be involved, the suit is usually moved to federal court.

As mentioned previously, federal court is generally more conservative; therefore, the plaintiff attorney who wants to "defeat diversity" will often name the adjuster (if the desk adjuster is in the same state as the loss) or the field appraiser as a defendant to the suit in order to keep the lawsuit in state court. Again, the plaintiff attorney hopes the state court will give him a "home court" advantage (yep, pun most definitely intended).

Another nugget of litigation wisdom for the insurance adjuster:

You will be sued.

It may or may not be justified—I'm hoping if you're reading this book that being named in a lawsuit will be unjustified.

While we're at it, though it's not necessarily related to litigation, this also should be discussed:

You will have a Department of Insurance complaint filed against you.

I would love to say this means that you, as an adjuster, are doing a good job, following the policy, protecting the fiduciary interests of the carrier, as well as the insured (who filed the complaint) and the other policyholders insured by the carrier. I would love to say the insurance department complaint against you is false and a weak attempt by the insured to force you to cave on the policy interpretation and pay additional sums. I would love to say this is just another arrow in everyone's quiver as we battle it out, much like venue shopping or pleading to coverage.

But I can't.

Mostly because there are, as in any industry, those adjusters/insurance carriers who make the rest of us look bad.[15] And there are times when only a complaint to the state department of insurance or a lawsuit can induce a carrier to move off center and reevaluate the claim.

So, these are things to be prepared for during your career as an adjuster.

The thing to remember in these instances is that everyone has a point of view, and someone thinks you're not doing your job properly. The onset of a lawsuit or insurance department complaint is a good time to review the file—perhaps with another adjuster or your supervisor—to get a fresh take on it and see if there is a way to resolve the claim.

Finally, the insurance policy lists the time by which the insured must file suit to protect his interest in the claim. There are also statutes governing both first- and third-party claimants' deadlines—called statutes of limitations, or prescription periods in some jurisdictions—for filing a lawsuit. Some states have regulations regarding informing an unrepresented insured or claimant about an impending statute of limitations. While this may seem counterintuitive, the reason is departments of insurance and regulators want

---

15 Yeah, I'm looking at you, health insurers.

to level the playing field between the insurers, who have knowledge of the limitations, and a layperson who does not.

Wrap Up

To a new(er) adjuster, litigation proceedings can appear frighting, alien, and intimidating. However, there are several people, including the adjuster's supervisor and defense counsel, who can help walk the adjuster through the thicket of the next phase of the claim's life.

The adjuster must be aware of deadlines, the jurisdiction, and legal costs when taking into consideration the settlement or denial of a claim. Adjusters use this information to know when to settle claims. Litigation is an expensive endeavor and is never a sure thing, which places additional pressure to settle the claim.

7

Adjuster Ethics

I was going to start this chapter out with a funny adjuster ethics joke. Something similar to an attorney ethics joke. Because all of us know attorneys and adjusters don't have ethics, right? We're right up there with used car salespeople for most distrusted professions in the U.S.

Fortunately for you (and me?), I didn't find any such jokes, and better yet, we weren't listed among the most distrusted professions (used car salespersons and attorneys were on the list, though—right up there with nurses and high school principals?!?!?).

Morals and Ethics

Most treaties on ethics spend a paragraph or a chapter or entire books on the difference between "morals" and "ethics." Morals are the overarching guiding principles in a society, and ethics are the specific rules and actions within a specific segment of the society. Most people believe the words are interchangeable, and perhaps they are.

So, morally, it's an overarching guiding principle not to murder someone, but if you were a member of the International Contract Killers Association (ICK), it'd be unethical *not* to murder your target because your industry's ethical code of conduct dictates the way you behave.[16]

---

16 This is a good example of how morals and ethics are not interchangeable. I use it to illustrate a point. I certainly hope ICK does not exist, but if it does, please don't kill me because I discussed your code of ethics. I don't think you're like Fight Club, about which I also know

Adjusters must behave ethically while handling claims.

The adjuster ethical code of conduct is set by either the state department of insurance, insurance organizations, or both.

State Departments of Insurance

If your state requires a license to be an adjuster, you must take a certain amount of continuing education courses to satisfy the ethics requirement. The NAIC model guidelines for independent adjuster licensing, which most states follow, recommend 24 hours of continuing education, with three of those hours spent studying ethics.

Several states do not require adjusters to have licenses to handle claims—Colorado, Kansas, and Missouri among them. This does not mean that adjusters have a license to act unethically (*hilarious pun intended*). Adjusters must still uphold the ethics of their career field.

Most states regulate adjuster ethics, as discussed in Chapter 4 under the Unfair Claims Practices and defined by the NAIC. Departments of insurance have done this as a result of too many instances of improper claims handling by adjusters and insurers.

Organizational Ethics

Many insurance organizations have creeds outlining their ethical standards. These apply to agents, underwriters, and adjusters.

The Society of Registered Professional Adjusters (RPA) and the National Association of Independent Insurance Adjusters (NAIIA), under whose umbrella RPA falls, both have codes of ethics.

Some of the ethical codes encountered in these organizations are:

- Acting in a manner which will inspire trust, confidence, and respect for the claims adjuster profession
- Acting in a manner of fairness toward all parties in a claim
- Acting in a courteous, respectful, and understanding manner with both insureds and claimants while handling the claim
- Assisting insureds and claimants in documenting their losses
- Avoiding discrimination in thought or action

---

nothing. And even if I did, I certainly know better than to discuss it.

- Avoiding conflicts of interest or the appearance of a conflict of interest
- Obeying all laws and regulations related to handling claims
- Possessing the technical competence to handle the loss
- Seeking alternative resolutions for the quick, efficient settlement of claims

The Institutes is a group of insurance professionals who are in the process of or who have earned the Chartered Property Casualty Underwriter (CPCU) designation. It promotes excellence through ethical behavior and continuing education through its Code of Professional Conduct, which includes not only the items listed above but also aspects such as:

- Improving public understanding of insurance and risk management
- Maintaining and improving its members' professional knowledge, skills, and competence
- Stressing that its members should place the public interest above the members' own interests

Insurance in Action

Below are some ethical scenarios an adjuster is likely to encounter.

Example 1

Adjuster Brenda Ewing is handling Jude Greene's bodily injury claim. Jude is frustrated by the time frame for settling the loss and believes Brenda is offering him less than the full value of his claim. Despite her best efforts, Brenda has lost Jude's trust. In the middle of their negotiations for settlement, Jude states he will retain an attorney.

What should Brenda do now?

It would be unethical for Brenda to inform Jude that he is not allowed to hire an attorney because it would be a lie; anyone at any point in time can retain an attorney and/or file suit. Brenda's ethical code of conduct states she must place Jude's interests above the carrier's. We, as adjusters, don't really like it when a claimant sues, but this is something the first- or third-party claimant can do. Second, and check your state's regulations on this, but advising a person not to hire an attorney may be illegal.

Perhaps speaking with and retaining an attorney would be beneficial for Jude. An attorney, whom Jude would presumably trust since he is paying to retain that person, could explain that Brenda is acting in Jude's best interest and that he should settle. Just as probable, however, the attorney could attempt to rack up Jude's medical bills by sending his client to an additional physician or other practitioners in an effort to increase the claim cost (and hopefully increase the settlement offer). The attorney might then attempt in the lawsuit to obtain the cost of defense.

If Brenda would like to retain control of the file, she could inform Jude that should he retain an attorney, the attorney would most likely take, at minimum, one-quarter of his settlement. And if a suit were filed, the attorney percentage would likely climb to one-third of the total settlement. In other words, if Jude hired an attorney and was offered $100 to settle his claim without a lawsuit, the attorney would take $25; the attorney would take $33.34 of the $100 (plus expenses, depending on the contract) if it took a lawsuit to settle the claim. All of which means that Jude will wind up receiving less money, even though he may not realize this at the outset.

Ethically, Brenda might say, "I understand your frustration, Jude. I can't tell you *not* to retain an attorney. I want to inform you that if you retain an attorney, I will not be able to speak with you any longer due to attorney-client privilege.

"I will need a Letter of Representation from your attorney.

"I also want to let you know an attorney may take one-quarter of your settlement if no lawsuit is filed. If a lawsuit is filed, the attorney could take one-third of the settlement.

"So, please talk with an attorney and let me know what you decide. I will follow up in a letter."

Then Brenda should follow up their conversation in a letter.

> *Dear Jude:*
>
> *I understand you want to speak with an attorney concerning your settlement. I have offered $100 to settle your claim.*
>
> *Should you retain an attorney, I will need a letter of representation from his or her office in order to continue the handling of your loss.*
>
> *Please let me know if you have any questions or concerns.*

Sincerely,

Your Ethical Claims Adjuster Brenda

Brenda then will diary the claim for two weeks to see if she hears from an attorney or Jude. If she has received no contact from either, she might call Jude to discuss the claim further.

Example 2

> Maci Phelps is the adjuster for Jordon Savage's water damage claim. Jordon is the owner of a tenant-occupied structure. Without notifying Jordon, the tenant broke his lease and moved out of the building on December 18, 2020. The tenant turned off the electricity and gas/heat to the structure, and on December 22, 2020, a pipe froze and burst. Jordon was not aware of the loss until he received a call from a neighbor on December 28, 2020.
>
> Maci investigated the claim. She assigned an appraiser to inspect Jordan's building damage, but she did not attempt to locate the tenant. She did not review the lease agreement, which states the tenant is responsible for heating the building. She was unaware, or did not understand, the tenant broke his lease. Maci denied the claim stating there was no coverage for the loss because Jordon did not do his best to "maintain heat in the building," or "turn off the water to the building" if there was no heat to the building. She also denied the loss for a "continuous repeated leakage."

Did Maci act ethically?

The answer may not be as clear cut as Brenda's case above. There could be extraneous circumstances to explain Maci's behavior.

Consider the possibility that two adjusters have just quit, doubling Maci's workload and making her unable to adequately investigate every claim assigned to her. This is an issue Maci should address with her supervisor, since she cannot keep up with the work, which is why she failed to fully and thoroughly investigate the claim, leading to the quick denial.

Or, perhaps Maci is a new adjuster, lacking the experience to handle this type of loss. This, too, could be an ethical issue, since adjusters are supposed to have the technical experience to handle the losses assigned to them. We'll put aside the "chicken-and-egg" debate regarding how an adjuster gets the experience without handling the claim. The quick answer that is Maci can handle the claim without the proper experience, but only with close monitoring and guidance from her supervisor.

Did Maci look for a way to deny the claim versus a way to find coverage? This, too, may be an ethical concern. The policy requires Jordon to do his best to maintain heat to the building and/or turn off the water. If Jordan's lease requires his tenant to heat the building, and Jordan does not know (and has no reason to expect) that the tenant vacated the premises and turned off the electricity/gas/heat, has Jordon done "his best"? Some attorneys—and adjusters—would argue "yes, Jordon has done his best to maintain heat in the building." He was relying on the tenant to do this, pursuant to their lease contract.

Surely Jordan would have assumed the utilities had he known the tenant was moving out. And had he had done that the pipe would not have burst.

Example 3

> Maria's insured, Danny Lynch, was involved in an automobile accident which resulted in the death of the claimant driver, Jenny Snyder. Maria investigated the loss by obtaining a recorded statement from Danny; obtaining statements from the witnesses listed on the police report; obtaining photographs of Danny's vehicle; and obtaining the police report. Maria did not contact the claimant driver's spouse, Joe Snyder, despite having his phone number and address from the police report.
>
> Maria hoped if she deliberately failed to contact Joe, the claimant's widower would not know the name of Danny's insurance carrier and would be unable to make a claim. Maria also hoped Joe would simply file through his own insurance company and then let the matter rest.

Has Maria acted ethically?

It is unethical for Maria to intentionally avoid contacting the claimant's family in the hopes they will not file a claim; it is also unethical to force the claimant's family to file with their insurer; finally, it is a breach of good faith claims handling practices to expose Danny to a lawsuit by not investigating the claim thoroughly and adequately.

As uncomfortable as it this situation might be, Maria must make contact with the widower and the family to determine what exposure Danny might have.

It occurs to me that a newer adjuster might not know what to say to the spouse of a deceased person (or the parent of a deceased child—I've had to do that unpleasant task as well). You can't, at this time, admit liability for the accident because the investigation is still ongoing, but what, exactly, do you say to the survivor?

Ethically, Maria's call might sound something like:

> "Mr. Snyder, I'm Maria, the insurance adjuster for the other car involved in your wife's accident. I want to express my condolences for your loss. Do you have time to speak with me about this insurance claim? I need to get some information about Jenny in order to conclude my investigation."

Hopefully Joe will say he has time; if he doesn't, Maria will acknowledge his response, give her name, number, and the claim number, and tell Joe she'll send a letter. (Spoiler alert: Maria will send a letter after the following phone call anyway.)

> "Thank you for speaking with me. I know this is a difficult time. You might want to get a pen and some paper ready so I can give you my name, claim number, and email address so you can keep in contact me with. I am not with your insurance company; I am with the insurance company for the other vehicle.[17] I have to ask you some questions about Jenny as part of my investigation. For example, Medicare requires I determine she is not a beneficiary; to do this, I need what's called her 'Big 5.' I will send you a letter outlining this information when we get off the phone. I can email it to you if you give me your email address.
>
> "I also need to take a look at your vehicle. Have you filed a claim with your auto insurer? Who is your insurer and adjuster? I can coordinate with them for this inspection.
>
> "Did Jenny work? OK, I'll need some information about her job, and, again, I'll send you the paperwork for this information later. What about any children living with you? Again, my condolences. I know this must be hard.
>
> "Mr. Snyder, I've not completed my investigation yet, and I cannot accept liability, meaning I can't accept responsibility on behalf of my insured. I encourage you to continue to work

---

17 This is important to let the claimant know. Often people don't understand how many insurance companies can be involved in an auto accident.

with (or I encourage you to file a claim with) your insurer. However, I am able to offer you the Medical Payments (aka MedPay) limits of $1,000. This coverage is available to you for Jenny's medical invoices. I understand she was transported to the hospital after the accident. The MedPay coverage is available regardless of liability. Again, I've not accepted liability right now. I am just working to complete my investigation.[18]

"Mr. Snyder, I know I've given you a lot of information right now. Here's how to contact me. I will recap our conversation in a letter. If you have any questions, please reach out to me."

As is often the case, well-meaning people will tell Joe he shouldn't speak to Maria, as she is the opposing adjuster. There is a deep-seated mistrust of insurance companies. The problem for Joe is that if Maria doesn't speak to him and obtain information about Jenny, Maria cannot determine liability because she doesn't have permission to inspect the vehicle or determine the amount of damages if she accepts liability. This should be explained to him.

If Joe doesn't want to immediately speak to Maria, in her letter, Maria will tell him this. The claims investigation process is not a State Secret. The claims process works better when everyone knows what's going on and what is expected of them. If Joe understands it's in his best interest to cooperate, then he will likely cooperate. *Demanding* that he cooperate will only justify his fear that Maria is out to take advantage of him while he is in a vulnerable state.

Because Joe is, understandably, traumatized (he just lost his wife), he may not understand all that is being said to him. Put yourself in his shoes—there'd be a lot going through your mind and it would be hard to concentrate. Joe might ask if Maria could speak to a friend or colleague on his behalf.

The answer is "no."

That being said, I have had a friend or colleague sit in on the call (I'm old enough to say "the friend was on the other phone or extension." Nowadays, I think it'd work if Joe simply had the call on speaker). This is a judgment call. I want to make Joe comfortable, and if it makes him comfortable to have a friend there who can listen to what I'm saying and take notes, fine. I don't have a problem with that. If that friend tried to insert himself into

---

18 You may think I'm repeating myself here in this imagined conversation. I am. But it's important to do this. Joe has lost his wife. He may not "hear" everything you have said, which is also why it's important to put all of this in a letter.

Joe's claim, that would be another story. The friend doesn't have an interest in the claim, meaning a financial interest. Even if were Joe's father-in-law (Jenny's father), there's no financial interest. Jenny was married. Her spouse is the one who would settle her claim. (If she had no spouse and was an adult, Maria would deal with Jenny's estate.)

If the friend were to get a bit aggressive in the initial phone call with Joe, I'd politely inform Joe that I'm having the friend on as a courtesy, but I must deal with him. Not the friend. And if the friend continued to interrupt, I would be forced to cut the call short. But Joe should never fear, because I would be sending a letter outlining everything that is needed.

If the friend began calling me to ask about the status of the claim or my investigation, I'd politely inform the friend they had no standing in the claim, and I would no longer speak to them. I would then send a letter to Joe letting him know what I said to the friend. (Are you sensing a theme here?)

At the end of her conversation with Joe, Maria would send a letter recapping the conversation. She would then reach out to the other insurance company.

This is the ethical way to handle a very uncomfortable claim. You should be prepared for Joe to be very upset. He might understandably blame Danny for the death of his wife. He may be angry you're not automatically accepting liability. He will probably be angry that on top of planning a funeral, he's got to give you a bunch of documents like her work/salary information, the Big 5, etc. Be prepared for him to yell at you. If he doesn't, terrific. Also, as a side note, if you can get the information from your counterpart at the other insurance company, try. They may not be able to give you personal identifying info, but you can ask.

And for goodness sakes record in the claim file the steps you've taken.

Wrap Up

Determining whether there is an ethics violation is sometimes difficult. There are a few truisms which can help the adjuster determine whether her behavior is ethical:

- If I saw this action on the front page of a newspaper, would I be embarrassed?

- ◆ I suppose the current equivalent of this would be: if this story were trending (or went viral), would I be embarrassed?

- Is this the way I would want an adjuster to treat my grandmother?

  - ◆ If I have to ask myself these questions, this behavior is probably unethical.

8

Claims Will Always Be Adversarial

A lways" is a strong word. Surely, not every claim will be a fight and a battle.

No, of course not.

But Why *Are Claims Adversarial?*

There are several reasons, all of which influence one another. First and foremost, claims **should not be** an adversarial process. Claims departments are the Promise Keepers of the insurer industry. The policy is the Promise, and the Promise states that a claim will be paid in the event of a loss.*

The problem is that virtually no one reads past the *.

The asterisks, fine print, or however those parts no one reads are referred to, are all the bits and bobs that are *not covered* in a policy. I write this during the COVID pandemic, and there is still much debate about whether a policy can cover a virus. The words "all-risk policy" continue to be bandied about in articles, even though as I stated in Chapter 2 there is no such thing as an all-risk policy.

Let that sink in.

> ## There is no such thing as an All-Risk Policy.

Secondly, and this is not a ding on the agents who sell policies, there is little to no consumer education about insurance. This is the fault of the insurers themselves. During the pandemic, insurers have discounted auto rates and have given rebates because people aren't driving as much. Good. This is the right thing to do, but the industry is missing a golden opportunity to bombard the public (possibly on the streaming media channels) à la *School House Rock* about what insurance is (transfer of risk); about what policies cover; about what policies *don't* cover; and about which policies would be considered basic for businesses / homeowners / renters. Instead, the insurance buying public is asked to go with the Flo(w) and be a good neighbor by saving an equal amount of time and money because the insurer has seen a thing or three.

Put another way, here we are in Chapter 8, and I've not even discussed specific types of policies or claims yet. Insurance is not something that can be easily comparison-shopped, like looking at grocery store sales for red apples. There is big a difference, but the consumer doesn't know that.

And that's the industry's fault.

To be fair, no one wants to study insurance. I don't want to study insurance, and I *love* insurance.

Another reason claims will always be adversarial is that the general public does not understand the claims process, and neither the industry nor the adjusters do anything to reverse this lack of education. Again, that's on us. However, adjusters barely have the time.

Insurers do not consider the claims department to be the Promise Keeper; they consider it to be the Money Pit. Money flows out of insurers' pocketbooks through the claims department. It does not come in. While this may technically be true, it is incredibly short-sighted for a variety of reasons. First, adjusters *adjust* claims. They do not automatically pay whatever comes across their desks—if a charge is unreasonable, the cost is adjusted. That is a "savings."[19] Subrogation, or recouping payment made from the at-fault party, is a "savings." Even a justifiable denial is a "savings." The Bean Counters in the Ivory Tower do not see it that way, probably because they don't keep track of the adjustments. Regardless, the people who do bring in

---

19 I place "savings" in quotes because a plaintiff/trial attorney will attempt to argue that this is an example of an insurer attempting to shortchange the policyholder and increase its profit by not paying an entire claim. I am a claims adjuster, not a wordsmith, but I know from experience that almost any word or phrase or sentence can be twisted into meaning any number of things. So, stop it. Just stop it.

money are the underwriters and the agents; therefore, when it comes time to tighten the belt, who is the first to feel it?

As with any household budget, the highest expense is usually going to be the one to get cut first—in the insurance business, this is the claims department. An insurance company needs to put its budget on a diet, so a hiring freeze will go into effect. Adjusters will receive more and more claims to process, and because of this, they will leave. The departing adjusters' claims then go to the remaining adjusters, who begin to buckle under the strain of working 2.5 people's desks. Then those adjusters will leave.

The remaining adjusters, just to keep their heads above water, will pay claims just to close them. To save time, they will not investigate, and claim payments will increase. Bean Counters now have created the self-fulfilled prophecy that money goes out of the claims department.

Because the adjusters do not have time for lunch, let alone to catch their collective breaths, they do not attend continuing education classes unless required for renewal of their licenses. And because some continuing education classes cost money, most claims adjusters are not independently wealthy, and the insurer is attempting to save money, adjusters don't attend continuing education classes. Therefore, adjusters are less skilled at handling their chosen profession.

Because adjusters are bending under the massive claims load, they also do not have time to respond to all the mail and demands for settlement as they come in. So they miss deadlines because they are running behind. This places the insurer behind the eight ball. Claimants are angry because they are tired of waiting for money to repair their homes, pay medical invoices, fix their automobiles, etc. So, they file suit. Or the insured files suit for bad faith. Again, this is a self-fulfilling prophecy and a vicious circle which could be alleviated by hiring more adjusters and properly training them.

A final word, trial attorneys like to make a big deal that if a claim becomes adversarial, that is proof of bad faith claims handling. My mentor, Kevin Quinley, discussed this in his podcast, *The Claims Coach*.[20] People in the insurance industry will always argue, but it's not necessarily a sign of bad faith if the claim is adversarial.

---

20 If you are not listening to insurance podcasts, reading insurance periodicals, or watching insurance vlogs, you need to develop this habit. You don't have to do all three, but at least do one. It's the best way to stay on top of the industry.

Wrap Up

Claims are adversarial for two main reasons:

1. Insurers have not properly trained their customer base. They treat policies as something that can be compared as buyers do grocery when shopping.

2. Insurers overwork and undertrain their adjusters. A more robust and better trained claims department would lower indemnity payments and customer complaints/suits.

In short, the industry has shot itself in its own foot.

9

Claim Notes

The adjuster's file notes are one of the most important pieces of a claim file. The mantra of every claims manager is:

If it's not written down, it didn't happen.

This means that an adjuster must document *everything* that occurs in the life of a file. Should she fail to do so, any reader of the file can only assume that a conversation, agreement, or other relevant action *didn't happen*, absent some other piece of information.

Don't let the above fool you into thinking that actions will never slip between the cracks. Adjusters are human, and at some point they will fail to put something into the file. It happens. There is no such thing as a perfect claim file, either in terms of investigation or claim notes. However, the notes should be complete enough to recreate the adjuster's thought process while working the claim.

File Documentation

Documenting the claim file with notes is essential to managing the claims process.

All claim file correspondence (including electronic and snail mail) should be uploaded into the "document" section of the file. This also includes discussions and emails between the adjuster and management. See below for my thoughts regarding "cutting and pasting" emails into the claim file.

Anything relating to the file, should be uploaded. If an adjuster happens to make handwritten notes while investigating the insured's property onsite, those handwritten notes need to be scanned and uploaded.

Writing File Notes

State departments of insurance require file notes to be complete enough to recreate the thinking of the adjuster; so the notes should be fairly robust, but they do not have to be a word-for-word or blow-by-blow transcript of a conversation. There should also be little abbreviation of words, since an outside auditor would likely be unfamiliar with industry or company short-hand. The goal, again, is for the file to stand on its own feet if it ever were to be seen by a jury.

Take the following examples.

> P/C to NI about P1 dx; disc. I/A will call tomorrow; disc. cov. NI ack.

What does this mean? Unless another adjuster were reading this note, it likely could not be translated into English.

> Called Named Insd. about premises 1 damage; informed insd. I/A will call tomorrow; discussed coverage; insd ack.

This is better, but allow me to tell a story.

I wrote a note similar to this when I was a new adjuster. A few days later my supervisor received a call from the insured who was angry because I had not contacted him about the loss. My supervisor read my note and stated I had contacted the insured and recapped our conversation. The insured insisted he never spoke with me. My supervisor stated she would investigate his complaint and call him back.

When asked about the note, I confirmed I spoke with the insured, who was a woman. Turns out I spoke with the insured's wife, who had failed to tell her husband she had spoken with me. Therefore, best practices for this kind of note are:

> Called Mrs. Insd at 213-555-1232 about the p/d at loc. 1, 9876 Main St., Anywhere, TX. I told her the I/A will contact her tomorrow, but if not, she should call me. I confirmed coverages and Mrs. Insd. Ack.

There are still abbreviations in the note (I/A, p/d). These are fairly standard in the insurance claims industry.

Insd= insured	I/A= independent appraiser
clmt= claimant	p/d= property damage
d/atty= defense attorney	b/i= bodily injury or business income (depending on the type of claim)
PA= public adjuster	

If the second set of notes had been what I recorded and Mr. Insured called complaining he hadn't been contacted, my supervisor could not only have told him whom I spoke with, but at what number. If a manager was contacted, his/her name should be listed for the same reason. If the number is not working, that should be memorialized.

> Attempted to contact Mr. insd. at 213-555-1232 but received recording the number was invalid. Sending letter to insd. asking him to contact me.

If you double-checked the loss notice or contacted the agent to make sure the number was correct, that should be entered as well. The reason is that the department of insurance requires the insurer to make contact within a certain number of days. The adjuster should demonstrate she did all she could to reach the insured, because if the note is not in the file, the jury in a bad faith lawsuit will assume she did not contact the insured.

> Attempted to contact Mr. insd. at 213-555-1232 but received recording the number was invalid. Looked at the underwriting file and loss notice but the numbers listed were the same. Contacted retail agent and s/w Susan, the CSR. She does not have any other numbers for the named insd. Sending letter to insd. asking him to contact me.

The above note indicates the adjuster did everything possible to reach the insured. And it only took an additional five minutes, if that, of work. That small extra effort will save the adjuster and the insurer massive headaches in the future against bad faith claims regarding lack of contact.

In addition to being specific about whom the adjuster spoke with and which number was called, if there is math in the claim (and there almost always is math in a claim), this should be written down and explained. Claim settlement figures must be clearly outlined.

> Rec'd est for insd. veh. repair $3,582.91; sending check to NI for $3,332.91.

Wait. Where'd we get $3,332.91 if the estimate is $3,582.91? What is the estimate for? What does it entail? Has the deductible been applied? How can the jury in a bad faith lawsuit be assured the adjuster reviewed the estimate and coverages to pay what is owed?

> Rec'd est. for insd. veh. repair $3,582.91. This is for rt. front end damage with LKQ parts. The damages fit with the accident. OK to pay. Also paying $250 for rental. Allowing $25/ day for rental; shop states it will take them 10 days to repair insd. veh.

Auto Estimate	$3,582.91
Deductible	($500.00)
Rental $25/day * 10 days	$250.00
Total Payment to Insd.	$3,332.91

This note shows the adjuster looked at the estimate and confirmed there was right side damage, which is what the photos showed and what the insured reported. An auditor can see that the deductible was applied and the additional payment is for a rental vehicle. The note even demonstrates how the rental amount was determined.

There are still plenty of abbreviations, but if an adjuster handles this particular book of business, then the acronyms LKQ (Like Kind Quality) and OEM (Original Equipment Manufacturer) are familiar.

If there are negotiations for settlement, which is common in liability claims, the file notes should recap the demands and offers discussed during the settlement conversations with the claimant.

> I discussed case with TL (team leader) and received auth. to settle claim up to $6k inclusive of meds.

This is a slip-and-fall accident. Mr. Clmt. slipped on ice in front of the insd. business. The insd. is responsible for snow and ice removal, per his lease. This is a non-delegable duty. Liability and coverage are clear.

Mr. Clmt. went to 3 weeks of physical therapy for a sprain/strain of his neck and a bruised tail bone. This consisted of hot packs, chiro. manipulation, massage, and electro-therapy. Reviewed meds and they are reasonable.

He missed approximately 3 hours of work 3/wk; his lost wages are $1,000, which have been verified with his employer. There is not a need for a doctor's note as the clmt. went to PT during his lunch break. The addt'l time is for traveling to and from PT and work. Mileage is owed for this. Mr. Clmt. sent in his mileage sheets (total $55.32) and I uploaded them into the documents section of the file.

Medicare/Medicaid has been run and the clmt. is NOT eligible. OK to settle. There are no currently known liens.

This is a plaintiff-oriented venue with high verdict results despite minor injuries.

I s/w Mr. Clmt. at 212-555-1212 about settling his injury claim. I offered him $5,000 + meds for a total settlement of $5,380.64. This was determined in the following amount:

Pain/suffering, future medical costs, loss of consortium (Mrs. Clmt & children)	$4,000.00
Mileage to and from P/T	$53.22
Lost Wages	$1,000.00
Medical Invoices	$327.42
Total Settlement	$5,380.64

Mr. Clmt. stated this did not accurately reflect his future medical costs and demanded $15,000. I asked for additional documentation to support the future medical invoices. Mr. Clmt. stated he would send to me.

I will follow up my offer with a letter.

Offer	Demand
$5,380.64	$15,000.00

> Sent letter to Named Insured to let him know of offer and demand.

Shortly before or after this note from the adjuster should be a note from the supervisor:

> S/W CMR concerning settlement of claim. Authorized total of $6,000 inclusive of medical invoices to settle.

Both of these notes are important for a variety of reasons.

1. The adjuster notes recap liability and coverage and makes it clear that the insured is responsible for the loss, and the insurer is paying per the policy.

2. The adjuster states how she obtained her figures:

    a. Number of times the claimant went to physical therapy; the kinds of physical therapy he received; whether the therapy costs were reasonable

    b. Lost wages, which were verified by claimant's employer

    c. Mileage and the documentation are noted in the file

3. The adjuster is aware of the type of venue and verdicts rendered in said venue. This has an effect on settlement, and she has not only acknowledged it, but also put it in the settlement note so that another adjuster can understand the status of the claim and the reasoning behind the offer.

    a. As a side note, let's say that $4,000 is too low for the general damages, and the insured, having been sued, has a large verdict filed against him. He then files a bad faith claim against the insurer for not settling the claim in a timely manner. Adjusters are allowed to be wrong. The $4,000 may be the wrong number, but the adjuster and her supervisor clearly thought things through. Their reasoning is discussed in the note. It would be hard to find they acted in bad faith. However, if they had "hidden the ball" and didn't discuss how they came up with the number, the jury could assume the adjuster and supervisor pulled the figure out of the air with no thought about protecting the insured and settling the claim.

4. The adjuster discusses Medicare/Medicaid and other liens. She has made sure the settlement is free from any other issues.

5. The adjuster shows the math in the note.

6. The adjuster states her authority in the note.

7. The adjuster documents her conversation with the claimant and what he demanded.

8. The adjuster documents her next steps.

9. The supervisor documents his authority for the adjuster.

    a. This is a step that most supervisors seem to miss. It is important that supervisors document their conversations with the adjusters, as well. It shows there is proper supervision of the adjuster and there has been another set of eyes on the file.

File notes should be clear and understandable to someone else who would pick up the reins of the file. They should accurately portray the adjuster's thought process.

Getting Personal

Adjusters should be personable with the insured and claimants, but they should not get personal with them. The claim notes definitely should not reflect any personal comments or thoughts.

The adjuster must walk a tight line between adequately reporting what happened in the interaction with the insured or claimant and keeping the notes neutral, even though she may actually be upset or angry. It helps to think of the claim file as a newspaper—reporting the facts, and only the facts. There is no Op-Ed section of a claim file.

Take this scenario and the note the adjuster wrote memorializing the conversation:

> Received call from Mr. Clmt. He was upset at the amount of time it is taking to settle the claim. He asked if I was a "fucking retard" and couldn't read. I ignored him, but instead stated I was waiting for the medical records from the hospital. I had followed up for them last week to no avail. I suggested he may be able to obtain them more quickly, since they are his records. Mr. Clmt. began cussing me out calling me a "bitch"

> and a "motherfucker." I told him I would not listen to him if he continued to call me names and it showed that he was unable to communicate effectively. I then hung up on him before he could reply. I told Sean what happened in case this moron calls and complains about me.

This closely resembles the actual phone call. The adjuster's file note is probably a good blow by blow, but there is no reason to put the profanity in the file. And there is definitely no reason to call the claimant any names (moron) even if he's calling you names. We can't control the actions of others, but we can control our (re)actions.

Newer adjusters may not know how to walk the tightrope between accurately reporting what was said and embarrassing themselves with "keeping it real." Below is an example of how this type of interaction should be recorded.

> Received call from Mr. Clmt. He was upset at the amount of time it is taking to settle the claim. He asked if I had the mental capability to review the documents. I did not respond to this, but instead stated I was waiting for the medical records from the hospital. I had followed up for them last week to no avail. I suggested he may be able to obtain them quicker since they are his records. Mr. Clmt. began to use profanity. I stated I would be unable to speak with him while he continued to speak to me in this manner. I terminated the call and notified my supervisor.

In this claim note, there are almost no abbreviations. This is because it is a note which will not come up often, but it needs to accurately reflect the actions taken by all parties. It does not need to be so accurate that it will cause embarrassment if shown to a jury.

While the first example is accurate—nothing is left to the imagination—it is not professional.

Insurance in Action

Likewise, personal opinions should be kept out of the file, which is a professional document. Consider the following:

> Inspected the insd's veh. It is a POS and will be a TL. I will run an ACV on it.

There's an urban legend about an appraiser who wrote "POS" on the insured's estimate. Somehow, the insured received a copy of the estimate with the "POS" note written on it. A suit was filed for bad faith, with allegations that the insurer had a preconceived opinion about the insured and was lowballing the settlement.

The insured's attorney asked the appraiser, in court, what "POS" meant. The appraiser replied, "piece of shit."

"What is a 'piece of shit,' Mr. Appraiser?" inquired the attorney.

"The insured's car," admitted the appraiser.

The jury awarded the insured vast sums of money as the scrawled "POS" note demonstrated the insurance company was biased against him.

The moral of the story is to keep your opinions to yourself.

Because adjusters have it drilled into them from the management team, adjusters document everything, but sometimes there are items which should not be itemized such as a legal strategy or the conversation of a roundtable if adverse to the insured.

Therefore, the dutiful adjuster will simply write "Roundtable with management" as her note. This is a red flag to plaintiff attorneys. It is akin to a bookmark for the adjuster. In other words, this note is saying, "I had a conversation with my manager and we discussed how we think the insured is a fraud (or whatever may be the case). We discussed that we will hire coverage counsel to file a DJ (declaratory judgment) against the insured so we do not owe anything."

Naturally, the latter comment, spelling everything out, would be incendiary if blown up in front of a jury. The former comment, short and sweet, is a signal that something is up, but the policyholder attorney might not know what, and would therefore need to keep digging.

What is the fine line that the adjuster must walk? How does she document the discussion, recap what is said, but not waive any rights the insurer may have?

> Roundtable with supervisor concerning claim and cause of loss. She suggested hiring coverage counsel to review file.

Remember personal opinions (the insured is a fraud) must be kept out of the file. Further, coverage counsel may suggest paying the claim; so, the latter note suggests the insurer has already made up its mind and will not investigate the claim. It is better to say you're waiting on coverage counsel's opinion.

I recognize some will read the above and think adjusters are being disingenuous in the documentation of the file. This is not the case at all. Adjusters are akin to reporters—they must report the facts. Not what they want to be the facts. Not what they hope will be the facts. But the facts.

Some insurers prefer adjusters cut and paste emails into the claim notes. If that is company policy, then that is what the adjuster should do. However, if that's not company policy, I'd encourage the adjuster not to do this. First, it does not accurately portray the adjuster's thought process. The email must be uploaded into the file regardless; so, there is no reason to cut and paste the email. Further, it's awkward because the adjuster still must respond to the email. Where does the email get cut off if the message shows a string of emails between the adjuster and recipient? Does the entire email get copied every time? Even the parts that have been entered into the claim notes before? If the adjuster decides to only cut and paste the new part of the email, is that arbitrary? What happens if the adjuster misses an email (as can happen when emails are tacked together in a long thread) and doesn't cut and paste that section?

It is standard procedure to simply recap the email, and if there is an error in the email, mention that in the claim note.

> Rec. email from Mr. Insd. who stated it's been 3 weeks since he heard from me and wanted to know when he would receive his check.

> I reviewed the file and see Mr. Insd. and I discussed the claim via telephone on XX/XX/XX. I told him then I was waiting for the I/A report; I have not received the report to date.

The next action from the adjuster should be to call the appraiser and find out the status of the estimate, and then the adjuster should note:

> Called the I/A and s/w manager. Asked for status of estimate, as it's been 3 weeks since date of loss. Manager said he would research the file and call me back.

> Called Mr. Insd. at 217-555-1232 and left message stating I rec'd his email and I was sending him a reply via email. Stated he could call me if he had any questions.

Naturally, the adjuster should call the appraiser and the insured, and then reply to the email.

Emailed Mr. Insd. (mrinsured@gmail.com) and stated we spoke last week on XX/XX/XX. I said I was waiting on the appraiser estimate. I am waiting for the manager to call back with a status.

For the sake of brevity, I'm not writing it here, but it should be obvious to email the appraiser and his/her manager confirming the conversation that the manager will call back regarding the status of the estimate. Again, if it's not written down, it didn't happen. And if the insured sues for bad faith, a paper trail showing the adjuster oversaw the appraiser and pushed the file toward resolution is helpful to defeat this allegation.

Again, it should be obvious that all these emails should be dragged & dropped or uploaded (however the system works) into the claim file document section. If the emails aren't in the file, how does the jury know the adjuster actually sent them? Otherwise, the claim notes could be nothing more than a self-serving statement by the insurer that it is doing what is required to move the file towards conclusion.

Wrap Up

Claim documentation and file notes are some of the most important parts of the claims process. They help recreate the thought processes and actions of the adjuster and insurer. The notes should be clear and precise. Detailed information such as name and number should be used in order to avoid confusion at a later date. When there is a suit against an insurer or insured, the suit usually occurs several years after the events of the file; therefore, a good file with proper documentation will help the insurer defend itself or its insured.

Property Coverage Unwritten Claims Rules Written Down

As mentioned previously, this book has gone through several iterations, and I finally settled on making it an intermediate book for adjusters, the things adjusters usually learn in years 5 through 10 of their careers. Though that is the specific purpose of this and the following chapters, there is no way to cover every situation. Mostly because I continue to learn and expand my knowledge of this topic, and also because I can't possibly guarantee that I've remembered to include everything I know or have learned.

Virtually every profession develops unwritten rules or tricks of the trade. A professional learns many, if not most, of them on the job *because* they are unwritten. There's no reason to learn them until you encounter the specific scenario in your hands-on work and your mentor/supervisor helps you through the issue based on her past experience. In this chapter, I've tried to capture the unwritten rules for handling property damage claims.

There are three methods for determining and measuring actual cash value (ACV): Market Value, Broad Evidence, and the mathematical formula listed above. As with everything in claims, jurisdictions determine which test will be used. For example, Texas law states, "the term 'actual cash value' in a commercial property insurance policy is synonymous with 'fair market value'..." which is the price a buyer would pay to purchase a property from a seller in a free market.

When the policy or state law does not define actual cash value, a majority of states use the broad evidence rule which includes replacement less depreciation, purchase price, condition of the item, reproduction of the item, obsolescence of the item, and the item's fair market value. Depreciation includes the devaluation of an item due to wear, tear, and its condition. Many courts are now expanding the definition of ACV to mean the broad evidence rule. The reason is that simply using the mathematic formula of RCV less depreciation can be unequable when old buildings are damaged. The depreciation on an old structure may be so high that the insured ends up with very little ACV to begin repairs.

Insurers argue that the insured will receive the recoverable depreciation once repairs are complete (in a RCV policy), but the insured may not have enough "seed money" to begin repairs if a high depreciation is assessed based on a straight mathematical formula. This is where the broad evidence rule kicks in.

Why am I bringing this up? The valuations of structures (and contents, for that matter) can lead to the insured being a co-insurer of his loss, when, in fact he should not be. So, as an adjuster, you must know your jurisdiction and the rules for determining ACV.

RCV and Coinsurance

There is a little-known commercial policy interpretation involving RCV and coinsurance adjustments. I will explain it in plain English, then give all the policy language for it.

First, everything (building/contents) should be assessed to make sure it is compliant with its coinsurance requirement. If the insured has an RCV policy, the valuation should be at replacement cost; if the insured has an ACV policy, the valuation will be at actual cost.

Second, the commercial policy allows the insured to chose between receiving replacement cost settlement or actual cash value settlement. Now, I have never seen an insured say, "You know what? I think I *will* take less money than what you're offering, thankyouverymuch." Everyone knows the insured will take replacement cost if he has the option on his policy. So, this is the way the claim is adjusted.

Third, the policy dictates that if the insured has RCV, and the settlement is more than $2,500, the insurer can first settle on an ACV basis until the insured repairs or replaces the property. Then the insurer will pay the recoverable depreciation in the amount the insured spent, up to the holdback amount or the policy limits, whichever is less.

Fourth, coinsurance applies to the RCV settlement.

Notice that there was no comment about coinsurance applying to the ACV settlement. The first ACV settlement. The one where the insured chooses to take less money. Not the one where the insurer is giving "seed money" to start repairs (which is ACV to begin with, but since the insured will get the rest once repairs are done, technically it's RCV).

Ready? OK. Here's the fun part: if the coinsurance adjustment in an RCV policy means that settlement will be less than the ACV without the coinsurance adjustment, then the insured gets to take the ACV settlement (without adjustment for coinsurance).

I'll wait right here while you reread that paragraph three more times in an attempt to understand. Don't worry. There will be an example later.

Don't believe me because "no one has ever done it that way"? I'll divulge one of my sources.[21] First, Google *Wetmore v. Unigard Ins. Co.*, 125 Wash. App. 938, 107 P.3d 123 (2005). It will take you a few articles. You can also look up *Buddy Bean Lumber Co. v. Axis Surplus Ins. Co.*, 715 F.3d 695 (8th Cir. 2013).

I'll wait.

All good?

See, the point here is to give the insured the full benefit of the policy. This is the policy's job. This is the insurer's job. And it is the adjuster's job to tell the insured, "Um, so, you're going to get more money going with Option B. I'm going to assume that's what you want to do even though it means you won't be able to obtain your recoverable depreciation under the RCV option (Option A). Let me know if I have that wrong."

It is *not* the job of the insured to know about this little-known interpretation of the policy and then challenge the adjuster who is working on autopilot.

Just for the sake of clarity (not because I want to thoroughly mess with your brain) before I move on to the policy language and give you an example, I will tell you that this rule only applies to the replacement cost option. If the policy is only valued at actual cash and the insured has a coinsurance issue, then the insured is up a creek without a paddle. He will receive an adjustment in his final settlement. There is no Option B.

---

21 I told you in the Author's Notes I had sources. I just didn't want to reference them all the time, but thank you for thinking I knew all of this stuff up to Chapter 10.

Also, up to this point, I've only been talking about commercial policies. The court decisions only reference commercial policies. Now let's compare the homeowner policy with the commercial policy.

First, the HO 00 03 05/11 states:

SECTION I – CONDITIONS

D. Loss Settlement

In this Condition D., the terms "cost to repair or replace" and "replacement cost" do not include the increased costs incurred to comply with the enforcement of any ordinance or law, except to the extent that coverage for these increased costs is provided in E.11. Ordinance Or Law under Section I – Property Coverages. Covered property losses are settled as follows:

...

2. *Buildings covered under Coverage A or B at replacement cost without deduction for depreciation, subject to the following:*

   a. *If, at the time of loss, the amount of insurance in this policy on the damaged building is 80% or more of the full replacement cost of the building immediately before the loss, we will pay the cost to repair or replace, without deduction for depreciation, but not more than the least of the following amounts:*

      ...

      (2) *The replacement cost of that part of the building damaged with material of like kind and quality and for like use;*

         ...

   b. *If, at the time of loss, the amount of insurance in this policy on the damaged building is less than 80% of the full replacement cost of the building immediately before the loss, we will pay the greater of the following amounts, but not more than the limit of liability under this policy that applies to the building:*

      (1) *The actual cash value of that part of the building damaged;*

         ...

   e. *You may disregard the replacement cost loss settlement provisions and make claim under this policy for loss to buildings on an actual cash value basis. You may then make claim for any additional liability according to the provisions of this Condition D. Loss Settle-*

ment, provided you notify us, within 180 days after the date of loss, of your intent to repair or replace the damaged building.

Here's the commercial policy CP 00 10 10/12 which states:

E. Loss Conditions

The following conditions apply in addition to the Common Policy Conditions and the Commercial Property Conditions:

...

> 7. *Valuation*
>
> *We will determine the value of Covered Property in the event of loss or damage as follows:*
>
> > a. *At actual cash value as of the time of loss or damage, except as provided in b., c., d. and e. below.*
> >
> > *...*

F. Additional Conditions

The following conditions apply in addition to the Common Policy Conditions and the Commercial Property Conditions:

> 1. *Coinsurance*
>
> *If a Coinsurance percentage is shown in the Declarations, the following condition applies:*
>
> > a. *We will not pay the full amount of any loss if the value of Covered Property at the time of loss times the Coinsurance percentage shown for it in the Declarations is greater than the Limit of Insurance for the property.*
> >
> > *...*

G. Optional Coverages

If shown as applicable in the Declarations, the following Optional Coverages apply separately to each item:

...

> 3. *Replacement Cost*
>
> *...*
>
> > c. *You may make a claim for loss or damage covered by this insurance*

on an actual cash value basis instead of on a replacement cost basis. In the event you elect to have loss or damage settled on an actual cash value basis, you may still make a claim for the additional coverage this Optional Coverage provides if you notify us of your intent to do so within 180 days after the loss or damage.

The two policies sound very similar; therefore, I bet dollars to donuts the concept of allowing the insured to choose ACV if it gives him more money would apply to the homeowners policy as well as the commercial policy.

Insurance in Action (Coinsurance)

The insured has a commercial policy with the RCV option. He sustains a covered loss.

The building policy limit is $7; the RCV is $10. Coinsurance requirement is 80%. The insured is under-insured and will sustain a coinsurance adjustment in the settlement of his claim if he chooses the replacement option.

The total damage is $5 and the deductible is $1. The depreciated settlement is $3.50.

Coinsurance adjustment is:
$7 ÷ $8 = 0.875 (88%)
$3.50 - $1.00 = $2.50
$2.50 × 88% = $2.20

The insured would receive a total of $2.20, which is less than the ACV settlement of $3.50. With this newly learned rule, though, we'd offer the insured $2.50 ($3.50 - $1.00 = $2.50) because that is more than the coinsurance settlement.

Another Insurance in Action Example (Coinsurance)

In another example, say the insured had a policy with the actual cash value option. Then the coinsurance adjustment would apply to the actual cash value.

$$\left(\frac{Did}{Should} - Deductible \right) \times Loss$$

The building policy limit is $6; the ACV is $9. Coinsurance require-ment is 80%. The insured is under-insured and will sustain a coinsurance adjustment in the settlement of his claim.

The total damage is $5 and the deductible is $1. The depreciated settle-ment is $3.50.

$$\left(\frac{Did}{Should} \times Loss \right) - Deductible$$

$6 \div $7.20 = 0.77 (83\%)$
$3.50 - $1.00 = 2.50
$2.50 \times 83\% = 2.08

Finally, notice that I took the deductible before I adjusted for coinsur-ance. If you're old school, like I am, you were taught the formula was:

But if you take the deductible first, you reduce the amount that is ap-plied to coinsurance, which gives him more money (I know. I just contra-dicted myself). This is the new-fangled way to compute coinsurance.

Here are the old-fashioned figures:

RCV: $5 \times 88\% = 4.40
$4.40 - $1.00 = 3.40
ACV: $2.50 - $1.00 = 1.50
$1.50 \times 83\% = 1.25

You're also supposed to take the deductible from the whole loss when the estimate exceeds policy limits. Put another way, you do not take the de-ductible from the policy limits. All of this is, of course, dependent on policy language, the state you're in, and the company rules.

And get off my lawn.

Depreciation of Labor

There is another hotbed of drama in the insurance world, which is the depreciation of labor. Who knew insurance could be so intense?

Everyone knows and understands the materials of which an item is comprised—whether they be a car part or part of a house—suffer from use and obsolescence. This wear and tear of items is what causes depreciation. What is not agreed upon is whether the labor to install or repair these items can be depreciated.

Many carriers are now depreciating labor. This is mostly seen in home-owner claims. The thought of depreciating labor seems illogical. How does labor depreciate when the labor that installed the item (car part, shingle, door, etc.) is still in use? For that matter, the car part, shingle, and door are still in use, but they are a little worse for wear due to being, well, worn and torn.

Some courts have argued the insured does not buy two policies: one ACV for the material and one RCV for the labor. To *not* depreciate labor would be unjustly enriching the first- or third-party claimant. Other courts, as recently as March 2020, chastised insurers for depreciating labor if it was not specifically stated in the policy they would do so.

The moral of the story is if the policy doesn't have an endorsement to that effect, don't depreciate labor. Again, the goal is to put the first-party claimant back to where they were before the accident.

But Wait! There's More!

In addition to depreciating labor, the policy can allow for depreciation of general overhead, profit, and sales tax.

Let that sink in for a moment.

If the insurer writes an endorsement that allows it to take a percentage off the taxes that go to the government, the adjuster does that.

Is that moral, ethical, or correct? I have my personal opinion, but my professional one is that if it's in the policy and the courts support it, then yes, the adjuster can do that.

I strongly urge the adjuster to forewarn the insured that this will happen in order to avoid unpleasant phone calls later.

Overhead and Profit

Somewhere along the way, overhead and profit (abbreviated O&P) appears to have gotten a dirty reputation. Insurers are loathe to pay O&P until repairs have been completed. Many have begun to issue endorsements stating that O&P will not be paid until the expenses are incurred.

Giving insurers the benefit of the doubt, perhaps this is meant to prod the insured along in the repairs of the property rather than allowing the property to sit in disrepair. Perhaps this is similar to including the mortgage holder on the check—it ensures that repairs actually get completed. Unfortunately, like all good plans, this process can sometimes go awry. Sometimes, insureds do not receive full payment for their loss, which is contrary to the insurer's duty.

The question becomes whether the O&P is a part of the damaged property. "Repair" and "replacement" costs tend not to be defined in the policy, and insurers do not contest that labor is part of the repair and replacement of a damaged building. The part most insurers question has to do with the general contractor's O&P (abbreviated GCOP).

This concept is directly related to the Three Trade "Rule," listed below.

Say a general contractor oversees the repair of a damaged building. It is his job to hire the necessary subcontractors, such as the carpenter, plumber, and electrician. Repairing the building can be a complex issue that involves coordinating which trade begins work before another can start. For example, the plumber and the electrician cannot replace parts if the carpenter has not first put a stud wall in place. Likewise, it would be foolish to bring in the drywall technicians before the plumber and electrician, who need access to the wall's cavities to run pipes and wires. General contractors are also the ones who research city zoning requirements and obtain necessary permits for the reconstruction.

Very few lay people have the skillset to do all of these detail-oriented tasks, along with their "normal" 9-to-5 job.

General contractors, like anyone else in the industry, have the right to make a profit, which is what GCOP covers. Some examples of a general contractor's overhead include:

- general & administrative expenses
- licenses
- costs of project materials
- office supplies for the project
- salaries for project personnel (foreman, etc.)
- temporary office buildings (on site)

The "rule" is that GCOP equals 20 percent of the total estimate of damages. The 20 is the total of 10 percent overhead, plus 10 percent profit. Notice, I have put "rule" in quotes. There is not a specific rule stating that

GCOP must be 20 percent or is always broken down into 10 and 10. This is what is commonly done; it's an accepted method, but there is no rule. In fact, there may be times when the GCOP is 25 to 35 percent. The only "rule" is that the adjuster must review the documentation the general contractor submits and determine whether the requested amount is reasonable.

The insurer owes the insured for the reasonable cost of repair.

Is it reasonable for a general contractor to submit an invoice marked up for 500 percent profit? I would likely argue, "No." Can the contractor support this mark-up? Perhaps the item is rare, had to be imported, incurred several fees and surcharges to enter the United States and move onto the repair site, etc. Then perhaps the answer could be "Yes." But again, the contractor would have to prove this charge because an average mark-up is about 10 percent.

The point is that the adjuster must *adjust* the claim. That is her job, even though there are very few hard and fast rules.

The majority of courts agree with the interpretation that O&P is owed as part of the actual cash value (ACV) payment if the insured has a replacement cost policy. Indeed, some courts have gone so far as to say that even if the insured doesn't have a replacement cost policy, he will still receive GCOP. However, because this is becoming more of an issue as insurers attempt to control indemnity expenses, state departments of insurance have begun wading in with bulletins.

Bulletins are neither laws nor regulations, but they are departments' interpretations of how a claim should be handled. For example, Texas states in B-0045-98:

> ### Re: Calculation of Actual Cash Value Under the Texas Standard Homeowner's Policy - Form B
>
> ...
>
> *The insurers are interpreting the following Loss Settlement provision of the Texas Homeowners Policy - Form B:*
>
> *We will pay only the actual cash value of the damaged building structure(s) until repair or replacement is completed.*
>
> ...
>
> *The Department's position is based on the following:*
>
> *Indemnity is the basis and foundation of insurance coverage. The objective is that the insured should neither reap economic gain nor incur a loss if adequately insured. This objective requires that the insured receive a payment equal to*

THE ART OF ADJUSTING

that of the covered loss so that the insured will be restored to the same position after the loss as before the loss. The calculation of this payment results in under-compensation if an insurer deducts prospective contractors' overhead and profit and sales tax in determining the actual cash value under a replacement cost policy. Conversely, **the inclusion of contractor's overhead and profit and sales tax on building materials does not over-compensate an insured for the amount of the loss because these items represent part of the insured's loss.** (emphasis mine)

In bulletin number B-5.1, Colorado states:

> **Calculation of Actual Cash Value: Prohibition Against Deducting Contractors' Overhead and Profit from Replacement Cost Where Repairs Are Not Made**
>
> ...
>
> *I. Background and Purpose*
>
> ...
>
> *Bulletins are the Division's interpretations of existing insurance law or general statements of Division policy. Bulletins themselves establish neither binding norms nor finally determine issues or rights.*
>
> ...
>
> *III. Division Position*
>
> **Insurers shall be prohibited from deducting contractors' overhead and profit in addition to depreciation when policyholders do not repair or replace the structure.** (emphasis mine)
>
>> *The relevant policy language states:*
>>
>>> *"We will pay the actual cash value of the damage to the buildings, up to the policy limit, until actual repair or replacement is completed."*
>>
>> *The Division of Insurance has learned that one or more insurers have interpreted this language, or substantially similar language, to permit deduction for contractors' overhead and profit, in addition to depreciation, from replacement cost in calculating actual cash value.*
>>
>> **The position of the Division of Insurance is that the actual cash value of a structure under a replacement cost policy, when the policyholder does not repair or replace the structure, is the full replacement cost with proper deduction for**

> *depreciation. Deduction of contractors' overhead and profit, in addition to depreciation, is not consistent with the definition of actual cash value.* (emphasis mine)

Florida goes a step further and states in Bulletin 92-036:

> *The payment of a partial loss on real property must be handled in a manner consistent with existing statutes and case law.*
>
> ...
>
> *The Florida Supreme Court, in Sperling v. Liberty Mutual So2d 297 (Fla 1973), held that the "actual amount of such loss" is the cost of placing the building in as nearly as possible the same condition that it was before the loss, without allowing depreciation for the materials used.*
>
> *This authority is specifically applicable to the practice by insurers of imposing a "holdback" of insurance proceeds greater than actual cash value until replacement has taken place.*
>
> ...
>
> *Insurers who have been applying "holdbacks" in claims for partial loss on real property should pay the actual amount of the loss. **The best indicator of actual loss is the contract for repair entered into by the insured.** Once an actual amount of loss is determined by contract, the full loss payment should be made with no hold back applied. This arrangement satisfies the public policy interests both in timely and sufficient claim payments, and in encouraging rebuilding. **In instances where a holdback is currently being applied and a repair contract has been executed, the holdback should be released.*** (emphasis mine)

All three states have "suggested" payment of the full cost, which will include GCOP; therefore, to avoid stricter regulations, insurers should stop nickel-and-diming their policyholders and pay what is owed.

Three Trade "Rule"

Adjusters are familiar with the rule of thumb that when three or more trades will be involved int the repair (e.g., carpentry, electrical, and plumbing), a general contractor is required and, as discussed above, GCOP therefore will be needed. This is presented as an industry standard because, for the most part, it is.

The phrase Three Trade Guideline, though perhaps more accurate, doesn't have the same authoritative ring. I am going to continue to call it a "rule" because that's how it is known in the industry. It should be noted this is not a hard and fast rule to be obeyed every time three trades appear (or don't appear) in a loss.

To my knowledge and research, no state law has regulated the three trade rule. In 2013, the Florida Supreme Court stated GCOP must be paid where "it is reasonably likely a general contractor would be needed." *Trinidad v. Fla. Peninsula Ins. Co.*, 121 So. 23 439. "Reasonably likely" is a broad term open to interpretation.

Take the example of a residential home which sustained roof damage as a result of wind. Only a roofer is needed to repair it. That is one trade. Would a general contractor be needed? Generally, no. Therefore, there would be no O&P or GCOP included in the estimate.

But if an apartment complex of 20 buildings sustained wind damage to its roofs, would a general contractor be needed for the repair?

- Is it reasonable to believe a roofing company would work on only one building at a time?

- Is it reasonable to believe the residents' safety would be at risk of flying debris from the roof as workers removed shingles and tossed to the Dumpster below?

- Is it reasonable to believe there would be construction debris (e.g., nails, cut shingles, etc.) the residents could step on, possibly injuring themselves?

- Is it reasonable to tape the buildings off or allow only one way to enter and exit to protect residents from the construction?

If the answer to all of these questions—and others like them—were "no," I'd argue the adjuster was unfamiliar with construction processes for a large loss. Additional oversight would absolutely be required at the loss location in order to control the construction site and protect residents from injury. Perhaps the roofer could hire a safety person to oversee safety issues, and that cost would show up in the roofer's invoice. But more than likely, a scenario like this would necessitate a general contractor My point is that inclusion of only one trade for the repair does *not* mean insurers should automatically eliminate GCOP.

Adjusters should adjust the claim. Examine the reasons the vendor is asking for the money. If the ask is reasonable, pay the claim.

Making a Profit from Insurance Claims

It is a fundamental maxim of insurance that a claimant, neither first- nor third-party, can profit from an insurance claim. If the claimant does make a profit, or attempts to make a profit from the claim, the claimant has engaged in insurance fraud. In some states, fraud is a felony; in every state, it is illegal.

In theory, the insurance policy is a method to put the claimant back to where he was prior to the accident. In reality—and you will never see this written anywhere else—it is possible for a claimant to make a profit from the insurance policy.

Legions of insurance tomes will tell you that the first- or third-party claimant must not profit from a loss, as this will increase incidents of moral/ morale hazards, and indeed, promote the risk of lax property upkeep.

People—and insurance companies—like things to be black and white. Unfortunately, nothing in life is ever so clear cut. Insurers call the ability to earn a profit from an insurance claim "betterment," because the insured comes out of the claim in a better position than he was previously. We do see betterment more with first-party claimants (insureds).

Take the following example.

> A Texas policyholder suffers hail damage to his 10-year-old asphalt shingles. The insurer pays to have them replaced, since the insured has a Replacement Cost Policy. During the tear-off of the damaged shingles, the contractor finds an additional two layers of old shingles under the damaged shingles. The carrier refuses to pay for the removal of these layers, stating they were not damaged by the current storm.

> First, the insured is already "profiting" from the insurance claim by receiving a new roof. His roof was used, and he is obtaining new shingles. But remember, we call this "betterment."

> Second, the insurer has run afoul of the Texas Department of Insurance, which stated in a June 11, 1993, bulletin, and reiterated on August 10, 1994:

"...where roof damage occurs due to a covered cause of loss and there are multiple overlays of roof coverings, the cost to remove all layers of roof coverings is part of the covered loss, and in accordance with the valuation clause contained in the policy, the settlement of any claim for damage to a roof with multiple overlays of roof coverings should include the cost to remove those multiple layers of roof coverings."

The department of insurance reminds the carrier that it must act "pursuant to the Unfair Claim Settlement Practices Act (Article 21.21-2, Insurance Code)."

In this example, the policyholder has not only "profited" from obtaining a new roof, but his roof is "better" because there is now only one layer of new shingles, rather than an overlay of new over old.

This is not to say that adjusters can, will, and do pay without regard to the policy and industry standards. It is insurance industry standards to pay for "reasonable" costs. If it is reasonable to pay for one slope of a roof, rather than the entire roof, then that is what the policy will pay.

The betterment in a claim only applies to replacement cost policies. If the insured has an actual cash policy and receives a new roof, television, clothes, etc., the adjuster will depreciate the damaged item. Third-party claimant losses are almost always settled on actual cash value (depreciated value); they may attempt to "profit" in other ways, which may or may not be legal.

Insurance in Action (Depreciation)

The insured sustains damage to his appliances due to an electrical surge caused by lightning. His 54" television, bought in 2015 at a cost of approximately $720 new, is damaged. The insured has an RCV endorsement for contents on his homeowners policy.

The easiest way to depreciate an item is straight line depreciation, which assumes an item depreciates evenly over its useful life. An adjuster may use this for a quick and dirty method to figure recoverable/holdback depreciation and get a check out the door for the insured. There are several ways to depreciate items, but we'll stick to our quick method here for the sake of the example.

A television may only have a lifespan of 5 years, based on technology advances, before it becomes obsolete.

Year 1	$720 ÷ 5 years = $144	$720 - $144 = $576
Year 2	$576 - $144	$432
Year 3	$432 - $144	$288
Year 4	$288 - $144	$144
Year 5	$144 - $144	$0

Therefore, if the loss occurs in 2021, the insured's television is, technically, worthless even if the TV was working the night before lightning struck.[22] The concept of something being virtually worthless but still being useful is not a foreign one. See the section below on rolling totals.

The insured, having a replacement cost endorsement on his HO 00 03 05/11 policy, buys a new 55" 4K smart TV for $500. Does the adjuster owe $720? No. Has the insured "profited" from the claim? Yes.

How can this be?

The unendorsed homeowner policy states Coverage C (contents) is at actual cash value. The endorsed policy allows for replacement cost of contents. RCV policies will pay for ACV until the insured has repaired or replaced the damaged goods, but the TV is past its useful life. How much money would the adjuster allow for ACV, and how much is held back?

There are a few ways to approach this.

1. If the insured has already bought the replacement TV, the adjuster can pay the entire $500.

2. If the insured needs the ACV payment to purchase the TV, the adjuster can offer an amount which would allow this to occur (say $350), then hold the other $350 back pending proof of purchase from the insured. *(I'm deliberately ignoring the likelihood of a deductible.)*

3. The adjuster could state the original TV has no value and thus she'd will pay only the salvage value for it. I wouldn't recommend this, although it is technically correct. This alienates the insured, who has suffered a loss. The insurer appears to be

---

22 Almost nothing is worthless. The TV can be sold for salvage or scrap parts. The insurer could take credit for the money it obtains for the scrapped TV, but it would likely cost more to scrap the TV than it would to find someone to buy the TV for salvage. So, in this scenario and in real life, you usually just let the insured throw the TV away.

penny-pinching. The job of an adjuster is to help the insured in his time of need. While we're only focusing on a TV for this example (in order to keep things simple), if this were a true claim, the insured might have incurred damage to several TVs, along with computers, phones, and other devices plugged into the outlets of the house. In other words, the insured is looking at a larger bill than buying just one TV set, and nickel-and-diming here or there is not keeping the policy's promise.

4. OK, so how has the insured profited from this loss, then? He is receiving new appliances without any depreciation. This is a betterment of his position. He's bought a nicer, newer TV than he had. That's a profit.

Samsung Electronics UN55J6201AFXZA 54.6" 1080p Smart LED TV *PARTS ONLY*

Condition: **For parts or not working**
"*Buy for "parts only", not working / no sound*"
Ended: Mar 24, 2021, 9:42AM

Winning bid: **US $75.00** [1 bid]

Shipping: Free Local Pickup | See details
Item location: East Hampton, New York, United States
Ships to: Local pick-up only

Delivery: Varies

Payments: PayPal VISA Mastercard Amex Disc/Visa
PayPal CREDIT
Special financing available. | See terms and apply now

Returns: Seller does not accept returns | See details

Example of a broken TV which still has some value; can be used for parts

5. Profit is not only padding medical invoices in attempt to receive a larger settlement, which is clearly fraud. It would clearly be fraud if the insured deliberately fried the electrical components of the TV in order to receive money for a new and improved TV. It is not fraud to receive a new TV from a fortuitous loss.

Making Repairs...Or Not

People buy insurance in order to receive money to repair damages they incur as the result of an accident. Most people want to repair or replace the damage.

An insured can choose *not* to repair or replace the damaged property.

Again, some would argue this is profiting from insurance. Perhaps it is. That is the rationale behind the depreciation of labor, overhead and profit, and taxes. If the insured has a loss, for example, on the right front fender of his car, receives payment to repair it, but does not repair the vehicle, that is fine. Later, if the insured were in an accident which damaged the entire front fender, the adjuster would not pay for the right front fender again. That would be considered pre-existing damage, and she would deduct the prior payment from the current claim. If the adjuster did pay for the right front fender a second time, the insured would have profited from his insurance policy.

By contrast, if the insured had repaired the damage from the first accident before the second accident, the adjuster would pay the entire second loss, without deducting the original damage. Because the insured would have repaired the damage, he'd have spent his insurance proceeds and would not have profited from the accident.

Line of Sight Repairs

"Line of sight" means that any area in a direct line of sight must have a uniform appearance once repairs are completed. Line of sight may also be referred to as "matching," as in the repairs/replacement must match the original materials which are not being repaired or replaced. If the new materials (the repaired/replaced materials) do not match the original materials, then the carrier should, according to policyholder advocates, replace the entire item—damaged and non-damaged—in order to achieve uniformity in sight (or matching). This ties back to the thought that insurance places the insured back into his pre-loss position, and the entire item was uniformly worn; therefore, the insured is not placed into his pre-loss condition if part of the item is worn (because it was not damaged) and the other part is new (because it was damaged and has been repaired/replaced).

This is a hotly debated topic in the insurance industry, and state departments of insurance often wade in to tell insurers how to interpret their policies. So although I am going to briefly discuss this and industry standards, the adjuster should be aware of what the applicable state's department of insurance thinks. These guidelines are usually found in the departments' bulletins. There may also be case law rulings or legislative regulations on the topic.

For example, Ohio regulation states an insurer must replace as much of the item as necessary to reach a uniform appearance:

> *[If]...an interior or exterior loss requires replacement of an item and the replaced item does not match the quality, color, or size of the item suffering the loss, the insurer shall replace as much of the item as to result in a reasonably comparable appearance. O.A.C. § 3901-1-54(I)*

Regulation in Kentucky mandates in the 906 Ky. Admin. Regs. § 12:095:

> *Section 9. Standards for Prompt, Fair, and Equitable Settlements Applicable to Fire and Extended Coverage Type Policies with Replacement Cost Coverage.*
>
> *(1) If the policy, contract, or certificate authorizes the adjustment and settlement of first party losses based on replacement cost, the following shall apply:*
>
> *...*
>
> *(b) If a loss requires replacement of items and the replaced items do not reasonably match in quality, color, or size, the insurer shall replace all items in the area so as to conform to a reasonably uniform appearance. This applies to interior and exterior losses. The insured shall not bear any cost over the applicable deductible.*

As always, the decision comes down to definitions. What constitutes a "reasonable match in quality, color, and size"? Replacement cost coverage in homeowners policies compensates insureds for the value of replacing the damaged property without deduction for depreciation such as deterioration or obsolescence of the property's value. The policy states, however, the insurer will pay for the repair/replacement of damaged property with "material of like kind and quality."

Is replacing/repairing with "similar" materials acceptable?

The carriers' position is that replacing/repairing the entire item (damaged and non-damage) results in a profit to the policyholder (see above about this issue). There are vendors who specialize in finding discontinued items. For example, if the insured's special imported Brazilian hardwood floor is damaged, there are vendors who know how to locate additional boxes of the same make and model flooring so the carrier can purchase it and replace the damaged wood.[23]

Another issue with line-of-sight repairs is determining where the carrier can stop the replacement. Suppose the insured suffers a burst pipe, resulting in water damage to his hardwood floors. Does the insurer owe for replacement of the stairs and landing floors? Is it within the line of sight, or can the insurer say, "No, we're drawing the line here. This is where we'd stop because there is a break in the continuity."?

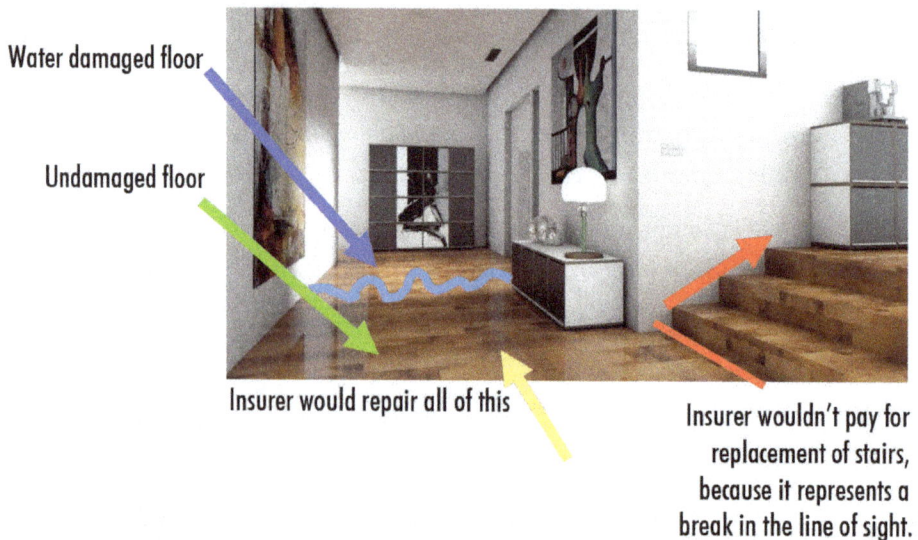

Water damaged floor

Undamaged floor

Insurer would repair all of this

Insurer wouldn't pay for replacement of stairs, because it represents a break in the line of sight.

Another item to consider is "cosmetic damage" of property. Cosmetic damage is a scratch, a small dent, or superficial damage that affects the look/appearance/function of the property in an inconsequential manner. If there is cosmetic damage to an item, the adjuster can offer a nominal amount to the owner, knowing the property will likely not be repaired. (Again, is the property owner profiting from insurance?) Some policies have exclusions for reimbursement for cosmetic damages.

Finally, there is a school of thought regarding minor damage to roofs, matching, and the concept of "harvesting" roof tiles. Florida's building code has a regulation, colloquially called the "25% Rule." It states that if more

---

23 ITEL, Itelinc.com, is one such company. This is not an endorsement of ITEL; I am simply giving an example of this kind of vendor.

than 25 percent of a roof or a section of a roof is covered for repair/replacement, the entire roof or roof section must be brought up to current code.

SECTION 708

REROOFING

708.1 General.

Materials and methods of application used for recovering or replacing an existing roof covering shall comply with the requirements of Chapter 15 of the Florida Building Code, Building or Chapter 9 of the Florida Building Code, Residential. Roof repairs to existing roofs and roof coverings shall comply with the provisions of this code.

Exception: Reroofing shall not be required to meet the minimum design slope requirement of 1/4:12 in Section 1507 of the Florida Building Code, Building for roofs that provide positive roof drainage (high-velocity hurricane zones shall comply with Sections 1515.2.2.1 and 1516.2.4 of the Florida Building Code, Building).

708.1.1

Not more than 25 percent of the total roof area or roof section of any existing building or structure shall be repaired, replaced or recovered in any 12-month period unless the entire roofing system or roof section conforms to requirements of this code.

Carefully reading the legalese, an adjuster will discover that the Florida regulation does not say if 25 percent of the roof or section is *damaged*, the roof or section must be brought up to code. It says if 25 percent has to be **replaced**, which is how the regulation will trigger the matching principle.

While a roof or section may need to be brought up to code, the carrier may be able to harvest roofing materials (such as clay tiles) from one structure to complete and match another structure, especially if, for example, the roofs are similar, such as you might find at an apartment complex. This may be a cost benefit for the carrier, rather than replacing the tiles for all buildings.

Rolling Totals

Earlier I mentioned "rolling totals." This is a concept encountered in automobile claims. A total loss refers to an item whose damage is more than its value, or it costs more to repair or replace the damage that the item is worth. A rolling total is a car that is a total loss and should be taken off the road.

Although the concept of a rolling total is used specifically for automobiles, it can be applied to any kind of property, which is why I mention it here. I should also mention that, unlike automobile losses, buildings and their contents do not have an unwritten rule that if the damage is more than 70% (or 80% or some other percent) of the value, the structure or personal property is a total loss.

Salvage is another practice usually reserved for auto claims, but it can also be utilized in certain property claims. As I mentioned previously, there is some value in practically anything, even if it is severely damaged.

That value—what someone would pay for a severely damaged product—is the "salvage value." Insurers use the salvage value to offset loss adjustment expenses, which is one of the reasons salvage is extremely important to carriers.

Insurance in Action (Total Losses)

Using our earlier example of a TV, the television is a "rolling total" because it's past its useful life expectancy, but it still worked perfectly before it was struck by lightning. Before the lightning incident, there was no reason to replace it. However, the TV was struck by lightning, the insured replaced it, and the cycle begins again. This is fairly straightforward.

Claims become more difficult, however, when the insured has been paid for a total loss but does not repair or replace the item. Let's look at another example.

Say a hailstorm severely damages a roof (shingles). The adjuster takes the damages and useful life expectancy into consideration and declares the roof a total loss. The carrier pays to have the entire roof replaced, but because there are no leaks (no functional damage), the insured pockets the money. Six months later, there is another hailstorm and the insured has interior water damage because the roof failed. What is covered?

The carrier would not pay to replace the roof (shingles) again because there was not a new roof to begin with. The roof had been declared a total loss after the first occurrence. So, in between the first and second hailstorms, the roof was a "rolling total." The roof (shingles) continued to serve its purpose, so it still had some monetary value. The monetary value is debatable though, because in the real world, no one would pay for damaged shingles. However, the adjuster must adjust the loss; so she assigns a monetary salvage value of $500 to the shingles/roof. This is the amount the carrier would pay, because now the rolling total value is truly $0.

The interior water damage claim is also tricky. It would not have occurred if the insured had protected his property and repaired the roof as he was paid to do, but interior water damage as a result from a covered peril is a covered loss under a standardized HO 03 05 10/12. Is the interior water damage a result of neglect, which is excluded under the policy? Is it covered? It is best to send a reservation of rights letter and discuss the matter with a supervisor and perhaps coverage counsel.

Value Policies

It seems to me that this may be a rule that is known, and because there are laws surrounding it, obviously it has been written down. Adjusters may not know about it, though.

The law I'm referring to is the Value Policy Law. As always, depending on the jurisdiction, if the insured suffers a total loss of his structure, he is entitled to the entire policy limit he purchased.

The thinking is that the insurer figured the premium based on the possibility of a total loss of the building. The insured paid that premium; therefore, the insured gets the entire policy limit.

The law mandates payment of the policy limit; so, there's no consideration of the coinsurance adjustment.

Settling Without a Proof of Loss

Most policies state the insured will submit a proof of loss to the carrier. A proof of loss is usually used in property insurance and is a formal document the insured signs and has notarized regarding a claim. The insurer uses the proof of loss to determine what is owed under the policy. State departments of insurance require that if the carrier insists on a signed and sworn proof of loss in order to make a payment, the insurer provides the document to the insured.

Insureds are often hesitant to sign proofs of loss because they are legal documents, and these individuals believe they will not be able to supplement their claims once they are signed. It is understandable that the insured might confuse a proof of loss with a release of all claims, which is generally reserved for third-party claimants, although there is a policyholder's release. This is similar to the release of all claims, except it is for a first-party claimant.

The purpose of a proof of loss is to provide the insurer with specific information pertaining to the claim. The policy determines what is in a proof of loss, but it often includes:

- Amount of loss claimed
- Documents supporting the amount of loss claimed
- Parties claiming the loss under the policy
- Date and cause of the loss
- All people/parties with an interest in the claim.

The majority of this information is already in the possession of the carrier.

- Amount of loss claimed
  - Damage estimate(s)
- Documents supporting the amount of loss claimed
  - Damage estimate(s)
  - Deed or title to the property, if needed
  - Photographs of the damaged property
- Parties claiming the loss under the policy
  - The insured
  - Mortgage holders or lienholders
  - This information is on the Declarations Page
- Date and cause of the loss
  - This information is in the claim file
- All people/parties with an interest in the claim.
  - Mortgage holders or lienholders
  - This information is on the Declarations Page

State departments of insurance also mandate that a carrier may not hold up settlement in one area of coverage to influence another, and it must timely pay a claim.

To put it simply:

> # Pay what you know you owe when you know you owe it.

Therefore, if an adjuster has an estimate with photographs, the adjuster should send the proof of loss, which she has filled out for the insured (so that the insured only has to sign and have the document notarized). She should not expect the insured to have the know-how to fill out a proof of loss himself.

Some carriers send the proof of loss to be signed and notarized with the check; others require the proof of loss to be returned before sending payment.

If the latter is the case, again, the adjuster should fill in the blanks for the insured and mail the proof to him with a request that he sign and notarize it in exchange for a check. Many policyholders will be hesitant to do this because they fear it will close their claim, especially if they do not agree with the damage assessment.

It is a violation of the unfair claims handling practice guidelines to hold up settlement of a claim for a piece of paper. The insurer should settle the claim for the undisputed amount and continue to resolve the disputed amount.

An insurer's delay in payment of a loss is a common basis for bad faith claims. The key, again, is determining what is meant by the term "reasonable delays." Most jurisdictions state an insurer may have opened itself up to bad faith claims handling for delay in payment of policy benefits, and/or that the insurer acted unreasonably or without proper cause.

Generally speaking, jurisdictions don't require the insured to dot all the I's and cross all the T's. Courts look for substantial, rather than strict, compliance with the provisions of a proof of loss; therefore, it is always better to err on the side of caution and make an advance payment when the adjuster is able to.

The carrier can always obtain a "full" proof of loss at the end of the claim when all damages are agreed.

This means *you can settle a claim without a proof of loss*. And you should do so if the claim has become stagnant. If necessary, speak to your supervisor to get the claim off center.

What if the insured doesn't cash the check?

This is fine.

It is invariably better to enlarge a copy of the check you sent to the insured which he did not cash because he disagreed with the assessment for a jury than to enlarge letter after letter after letter stating you will not give him money, even though that might be your right under the policy (never mind that it was his duty to submit the proof of loss). Juries are just not going to side with the carrier on this one.

If the insured doesn't cash the check, and it goes stale, reissue it. Or, hopefully by this time you will have reached an agreement on total damages so you can void the first check and write a new check for the whole amount.

A word on proofs of loss. They are not "final." The insured can supplement them.

Insurers point to the fact the document states "The Whole Loss and Damage was $xxx.xx." There is nothing on the proof of loss form which states it is a "full and final settlement."

Contents

Contents damage may be adjusters' least favorite coverage of property because it can be extremely tedious. All too often, adjusters toss a contents worksheet (see Appendix) at an insured and expect them to know how to fill it out.

Thinking of yourself as a layperson and not an adjuster, do you know the manufacturer, model, serial number, date purchased, and purchase price of the pillows and blankets on the couch in your living room? As an adjuster, do you know this? No one knows this. It's impossible to think a layperson with no insurance experience would know this.

To ask him to fill out this kind of form at a time of loss is necessary, but there is a better way. Leaving out a catastrophic situation, assign an appraiser to go and help the insured fill out this form. Or employ a restoration vendor who is called to help immediately clean up the damage and is skilled at this type of claim.

This leaves the adjuster to spot check the work. eBay and other bidding sites are good choices for determining the current actual cash value of a product. For example, the ubiquitous television may be for sale on eBay for $140. The insured has replacement cost, and the policy states ACV is paid until the item is repaired or replaced. So, the adjuster could offer the $140, and more importantly, she could back up the reasoning for her offer.

Vizio 55 inch tv (39 Tesla) #2 Read!
Pre-Owned
$135.00   Apr-26 13:57
Buy It Now
Pickup only: Free
View similar active items
Sell one like this

philips 55 4k tv - Android Television
Pre-Owned
$140.00   Mar-31 01:47
Buy It Now
Pickup only: Free
View similar active items
Sell one like this

TCL 55" US5800 4K UHD LED ROKU SMART TV Local Pickup Only
Pre-Owned
$140.00   Jun-13 02:29
59 bids
Pickup only: Free
View similar active items

Wrap Up

There is a lot of information in this chapter, and it barely scratches the surface of property damage insurance. If you take anything away from this chapter, let it be that adjusters adjust claims. While it may be corporate procedure not to offer GCOP on roof claims (regardless of how many roofs are involved), there should be some consideration for the claims an insured puts forth.

Summarily dismissing a claim out of hand "because that's not what we pay for" will result in a bad faith claim. As mentioned in Chapter 9, the adjuster's notes must be able to support her thought process. And if you went to your supervisor to ask for consideration, your notes should reflect that in the notes as well.

It is possible for insureds to "profit" from insurance, but they don't get to "double dip." If they pocket the funds, you will deduct that payment from the next claim.

Keep up to date with the states' regulations and rules regarding settling of claims. Remember that adjusters need to know the laws as much as lawyers do.

11

General Liability Coverage Unwritten Claims Rules Written Down

Personally, I enjoy general liability insurance. I disagree with the current trend of separating adjusters into monoline handling of claims. Adjusters can become more valuable by learning various lines of coverage. But no one asked me, and there is a certain logic to having specialty adjusters, if that is the point of a monoline adjuster.

Most of the adjusters I know are intimidated by general liability claims, thinking they are more complex than property damage claims. In truth, I find the only difficult part is dealing with Medicare and determining the logic of a governmental agency, which was discussed in Chapter 4. I hope to dispel some of those fears in this chapter.

Coverage vs. Liability

Laypeople often confuse coverage with liability; younger adjusters do, as well. You need to know and understand the difference.

Coverage has been discussed in other chapters and applies to the policy. What constitutes a duty owed to the claimant (e.g., business invitee, trespasser, etc.) is better covered in other books. However, this concept of coverage versus liability is one of the fundamentals that is often overlooked or thought to be so self-evident that it is not specifically addressed.

Coverage is based on the insurance policy language, which is the contract between the insurance company and the insured.

Liability is imposed by law. Liability can be imposed by contract, negligence, vicarious liability, and any number of other legal principles. Negligence is failing to act as a reasonable person would.

There are 4 steps in determining liability:

A. Is there **A** duty owed?

B. Was that duty **B**reached?

C. Is there a **C**ausal relationship between the breach of duty and damages?

D. Did the breach of duty create **D**amages?

If any of these elements do not exist in the claim, then there is no negligence, and therefore, no liability. The claim can be denied.

50 Shades of Grey

There is no such thing as a perfect claim file. This makes many adjusters uncomfortable.

The claimant has an obligation to prove his damages, but it is often in the adjuster's best interest to obtain the medical invoices and records herself. Medical authorizations signed by the claimant allow the adjuster to obtain injury invoices and records.

Settlement, however, should not be held up because the adjuster cannot obtain every scrap of documentation. There are times when the adjuster needs to make a decision based on the available information. This is the time to get comfortable with the grey areas of the file.

CPT/ICD-10 Codes

Current Procedural Terminology, or CPT, is an expansive, important code set published and maintained by the American Medical Association (AMA). It is, along with the International Classification of Disease (ICD), one of the most important code sets for the adjuster to become familiar with.

CPT codes are used to describe tests, surgeries, evaluations, and any other medical procedure performed by a healthcare provider on the claimant. As you might imagine, this code set is extremely large and includes codes for thousands upon thousands of medical procedures.

Each CPT code is five characters long and may be numeric or alpha-numeric, depending on which category it falls into. CPT codes also have a number of modifiers. These modifiers are two-digit additions to the CPT code that describe certain important facets of the procedure, like whether the procedure was bilateral or was one of multiple procedures performed at the same time. CPT modifiers are relatively straightforward, but are very important for coding accuracy.

Office Visit CPT Coding Guidelines for New Patients

Office Visit Code	History	Exam Type	Decision-Making
99201	Focused	Focused	Straightforward
99202	Expanded Focus	Expanded Focus	Straightforward
99203	Detailed	Detailed	Low Complexity
99204	Comprehensive	Comprehensive	Moderate Complexity
99205	Comprehensive	Comprehensive	High Complexity

One reason it is important for adjusters to know these codes, at least informally, is that a bodily injury adjuster may routinely see a CPT code of 99205 at an initial visit to a chiropractor's office for a whiplash injury.

Looking at the chart below, in order for a medical practitioner to bill for the 99205 code three things must occur (1) a comprehensive exam of and history from the patient; (2) highly complex medical decisions must be made; and (3) the severity of the patient's problem should also be complex ("moderate to high" is used in the chart). All of these things should take approximately 60 minutes.

New Patient Visit with CPT Codes (Detail)

CPT Code	99201	99202	99203	99204	99205
History & Exam					
• Focused	X				
• Expanded Focus		X			
• Detailed			X		
• Comprehensive				X	X
Decision-Making					
• Straightforward	X	X			
• Low			X		
• Moderate				X	
• High					X
Presenting Problem (severity)					
• Minor	X				
• Low to Moderate		X			
• Moderate			X		
• Moderate to High				X	X
Time (Face to Face in minutes)	10	20	30	45	60

Let's go over a brief example. For legality purposes, I am not a doctor. I am literally making up this scenario as I write it.

> Our claimant, Simon, is involved in a motor vehicle accident and suffers whiplash, which is a sprain/strain of his spine (usually thoracic and cervical). He goes to the emergency room via ambulance.

When Simon sees the emergency room doctor, she will obtain a medical history.

- Has Simon ever injured his neck or spine before?
- Did Simon lose consciousness?
- Which medications is Simon taking?
- Does Simon have any allergies?

This is a 10,000-foot medical history. The doctor doesn't need to obtain information about every papercut Simon has ever had for this kind of injury. She will order an X-Ray to see if anything is broken; she may test some reflexes to make sure Simon's neuropathways are still functioning; she will likely poke and prod his neck and upper back to see if that area is tender. Again, not a real in-depth exam.

The doctor has a problem (motor vehicle accident) with a focused history and exam (limited in scope). This exam will probably take 10 to 20 minutes (although if you've ever been in a car accident, you know Simon will spend hours in the ER).

The doctor's decision-making is fairly straightforward, meaning she can advise Simon to apply RICE (Rest, Ice, Compression, and Elevation) to his back and neck. She may give him a prescription for pain relief and muscle spasms. Easy peasy.

Therefore, the CPT code for Simon's medical visit should be 99201 or 99202.

Here's another example:

> Brandon comes into the ER as a gun-shot victim. He arrives via ambulance. He has surgery to remove the bullet and check for any internal bleeding. When he is able, the doctor will obtain a thorough medical history from him, beginning with any surgeries Brandon had as a child; what medicines he takes; allergies; pre-existing illnesses; etc. If Brandon can't provide this information (because he's in surgery or incapable), the hospital staff will obtain this history from a family member. This is a detailed and comprehensive history and exam.

The medical decision-making is complex, and the problem is severe; therefore, the CPT code for Brandon should be 99204 or 99205.

Jumping back to Simon, who later seeks treatment from a chiropractor. The chiropractor performs the same medical history and initial exam as Simon's ER doctor but bills the at-fault carrier the CPT code 99205. That would be fraud. The chiropractor did not spend 60 minutes with Simon, learning about every pimple he ever had. Neither did Simon present with a complex medical problem (albeit, if you have suffered from whiplash, you might say it's complex).

In addition to the CPT codes, you should be familiar with ICD-10 codes which consist of two parts.

- CD-10-CM diagnosis coding, which is used in all U.S. health-care settings

- ICD-10-PCS inpatient procedure coding, which is used in U.S. hospital settings

ICD-10 affects diagnosis and inpatient procedure coding for everyone covered by the Health Insurance Portability Accountability Act (HIPAA), not just those who submit Medicare or Medicaid claims:

- Claims for services provided on or after the compliance date should be submitted with ICD-10 diagnosis codes.

- Claims for services provided prior to the compliance date should be submitted with ICD-9 diagnosis codes.

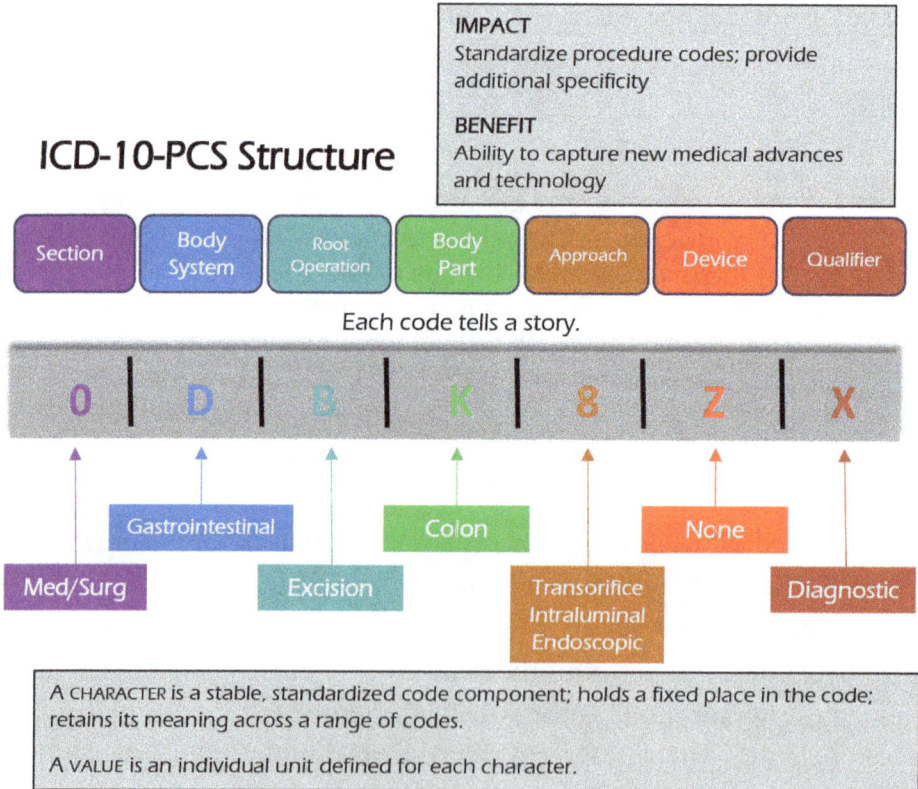

ICD-10-PCS Structure

IMPACT
Standardize procedure codes; provide additional specificity

BENEFIT
Ability to capture new medical advances and technology

| Section | Body System | Root Operation | Body Part | Approach | Device | Qualifier |

Each code tells a story.

| 0 | D | B | K | 8 | Z | X |

Gastrointestinal — Colon — None

Med/Surg — Excision — Transorifice Intraluminal Endoscopic — Diagnostic

A CHARACTER is a stable, standardized code component; holds a fixed place in the code; retains its meaning across a range of codes.

A VALUE is an individual unit defined for each character.

Both appear in the HCFA form discussed in Chapter 5.

If You Ain't First, You're Last

Negotiating liability settlements are particularly nerve wrecking to young adjusters.

Let's get this out of the way:

You are going to get yelled at.

The claimant will yell at you because he's not happy with the settlement; the attorney will yell at you as an intimidation method; the insured will yell at you because you accepted liability, and he thinks he is not at fault; your boss will yell at you because you're not sending out your 30-day letters on time (or for some other reason). Welcome to claims adjusting.

Knowing this will help the adjuster get her job done, because the yelling is just part of the job. It's no reflection of the adjuster, personally.

Claimants and attorneys believe there is one price for settlement, and that the insurer's "settlement range" is an incentive for adjusters to lowball the claim settlement value. This is not accurate for a number of reasons.

1. Adjusters are paid well, but very few adjusters receive incentives or bonuses.

2. It would be an ethics violation for adjusters to receive incentives for settling cases below value.

3. It would be bad faith for adjusters to receive incentives for settling cases below value.

4. The settlement range means that the claim is worth the same between these two numbers.

That last one confuses people, but think of it this way: the speed limit on the highway is 65 mph. You can drive 55 mph, and you are legal. You will get yelled at, though (back to the YELLING!). If you drive 35 mph, you will likely get a ticket for driving too slowly because you've now placed others in danger (bad faith, unethical behavior, low-balling a settlement to tie it back to a claim). If you drive 85, you will likely get a ticket for driving too fast (and get yelled at by the manager). There's a range in driving, and there's a range for settlement.

Negotiating settlement of a claim is not a win-lose situation. The adjuster will not be the "loser" if she settles at the high end of the range. That's the "legal speed limit" so to speak.

One of the reasons young adjusters are nervous about negotiating settlements is they simply don't know how. First the adjuster must know the strengths and weaknesses of the case. This means being able to intelligently discuss the facts of the case with the claimant and/or the attorney. These strengths and weaknesses are the beginning of the backbone of the case valuation.

How do you arrive at the settlement value of a case? There are several methods.

1. Individual Case Method
   a. Claim is settled strictly on the facts involved in the case.
   b. Because of this, settlement ranges can vary widely from adjuster to adjuster.
   c. This method is best used on serious injuries in order to consider all the issues relevant to the claim.
2. Roundtable Techniques
   a. This involves the claim file being evaluated by two or more claims professionals.
   b. This method tends to work best when it is used by a senior adjuster or overseen by a supervisor with experience.
   c. This is time consuming, but a good way to learn.
3. Formula Methods
   a. A mathematical formula determines the settlement.
   b. This usually is seen as "3 times meds," meaning the settlement value is worth three times the medical invoices.
      i. This is a popular valuation method with laypeople and claimant attorneys. They think it means the valuation of the claim is fair—and they believe *every* claim is settled at three times the medical invoices. However, this is not the case. Imagine a motor vehicle accident in which a person was immediately killed. There would be no medical invoices, except perhaps the ambulance. So, is a settlement of approximately $4,500 fair for the loss of a person's life? (Ambulance invoice $1,500 x 3=$4,500 settlement.)

4. BATNAs
    a. Best Alternative to Negotiated Agreement (or Defense Cost Settlement)
    b. A settlement should not exceed the combined value of the cost of litigating the case, plus the highest probable jury award.
    c. This accurately reflects four critical factors:
        i. The risk to the claimant of a defense verdict
        ii. The proportionate share of liability for the claimant
        iii. The numerous variables that affect a jury's likely award
        iv. A reasonable estimate of damages the claimant is likely to prove
    d. You must also take into consideration the cost of the in-house attorney.
5. Expert Systems (computer evaluation)
    a. This is a computer program designed to simulate the thought processes of experienced, knowledgeable adjusters.
    b. The "data" is arrived at by interviewing claims professionals and entering their responses into the system.
    c. Colossus is a well-known valuation system.

The majority of liability adjusters seem to wait on the demand letter from the claimant or the attorney; there is no reason for this. The adjuster's job is to bring the claim to conclusion, and the conclusion must be fair to the insured, the insurer, and the claimant.

Adjusters will always be accused of "lowballing" the offer. You will not come in "last" if you are the first to make an offer. The adjuster knows the file better than anyone.

Insurance in Action (Negotiating Settlement)

Despite all the above, which can be found in other insurance books, I found it helpful to roleplay to reenforce what I was learning. I'm not with you, so we'll keep it simple and go through a slip-and-fall claim here.

The insured is Industrial Music, a store which sells vinyl records. Steve is a regular client and goes every Third Thursday, when Industrial Music receives new releases. One particularly cold, snowy, icy Thursday, Steve made his routine jaunt to Industrial Music upon finishing a few after-work beers with some coworkers.

It had been snowing all day, and Industrial Music shoveled the sidewalk leading up to the door around lunchtime. Unfortunately, it did not put down ice melt because the local hardware store was sold out. The sidewalk was icy. A layer of snow also covered the ice where Industrial Music previously had shoveled because the snowfall had not stopped.

Since it was winter, it was dark, but Steve was familiar with the parking lot, which was adequately lit. Below are the adjuster's notes about the strengths and weaknesses of Steve's claim, which can be found in her file notes.

Strengths/Weakness Chart for Steve's Bodily Injury Claim to Discuss with Attorney	
STRENGTHS	**WEAKNESSES**
Steve was familiar with the property	Industrial Music employee saw the trip-and-fall
Steve appeared intoxicated	Industrial Music employee has no evidence of intoxication
Steve had soft-tissue injury	Steve sought treatment immediately after the fall
Steve treated with a chiropractor	Accident occurred in New York, a very pro-plaintiff state
Steve overtreated (Level 3 exams; back-to-back X-rays)	Steve has an attorney who seems ready to file suit
Steve apparently had an intervening incident (broken ankle)	
No time off work	
Hospital bill appears to be unrelated	
Questionable liability; no duty breached	Lot was adequately lit, but it was nighttime and that could be a detriment
Suspicious medical records; missing medical bills	

So, when the adjuster calls Steve's attorney to settle the case, the conversation might look something like the following:

Adjuster: Hello, Mr. Steve's Attorney, this is Adjuster for Industrial Music calling about Steve LastNameUnknown. Do you have a minute to talk? I'd like to discuss settling his claim.

Attorney: Steve's not finished treating. He has a broken ankle he's treating for.

Adjuster: Yes, I saw that, but that injury is not a result of this slip-and-fall accident. The date of that accident is three weeks later. Steve originally saw a chiropractor immediately after this slip-and-fall who stated Steve sustained a sprain/strain of the cervical and thoracic neck/back areas. It would seem the ankle is not related, so I will not consider those medical invoices.

Attorney: We'll see about that. I'll sue you over that denial of claim.

Adjuster: OK. That's fine. It is your prerogative to sue. However, in reviewing the invoices and medical records for the slip-and-fall, Steve suffered soft tissue injury. He did not have any time off work, which would further support our case, as he was not injured enough to miss work. He overtreated by having two X-Rays back-to-back...

Attorney: You'll have to take up any alleged overtreatment with the doctor. Your insured owes us everything Steve incurred.

Adjuster: First, chiropractors are not recognized doctors by the American Medical Association. Second, we owe reasonable and customary medical charges. Third, Steve is familiar with the insured's property, as he goes there every month. Fourth, the property is adequately lit. Fifth, the insured did not breach its duty to a business invitee. They shoveled the sidewalk leading up to the door. Finally, Steve admitted to drinking prior to the loss.

Attorney: It is not illegal for someone to have a drink before going to look at new records.

Adjuster: No, it is not. For these reasons, I am able to offer Steve $5,000 to settle his claim. This encompasses his $3,872.62 medical invoice for the chiropractor. As I stated before, I am excluding the treatment concerning the broken ankle.

Attorney: That's ridiculous. We won't settle for that. This case is worth at least $20,000. You can let your insured know to expect papers declaring the suit.

Adjuster: Again, that's your prerogative. I would ask you to send me a courtesy copy of the suit papers so I can get them to our defense attorney. I will also send you a letter and a release with my offer so you can discuss it with your client.

And that's the conversation. The adjuster went over all the strengths of the case, and she did not allow the attorney to fluster or bully her.

It's always a good idea to write the attorney a letter immediately after making an offer. The attorney is ethically bound to discuss all offers with his client. A letter is a good method to ensure this is done.

It's also an excellent idea to immediately send the insured a letter informing them you made an offer to settle, but the attorney has threatened to file suit. Instruct the insured to contact the carrier immediately upon service of the suit. The adjuster's failure to do this leaves the insurer open to bad faith claims handling; failure for the insured to contact the carrier leaves him open to receipt of a default judgment and a carrier who will not defend him.

Disagreeing with the Settlement Offer

The insurance company *offers* settlement; the insured and the claimant *demand* settlement. Thus, there is an "offer" and a "demand."

As mentioned several times previously, the adjuster's job is to adjust the claim and to settle the claim—fairly to all parties involved. So, it is silly to waste time waiting for a demand if the adjuster has all the information available to arrive at a settlement figure.

It is more likely that there will be disagreements over the value of the claim when it comes to liability losses than with property claims. Both are resolved the same way. The adjuster asks for additional information from the claimant or attorney to support why they believe the value of the claim is different than the amount the adjuster calculated. Similar to property claims, the answer cannot simply be, "Because I said so," or "Because I want more money."

Likewise, the adjuster must review the documents submitted by the claimant or the attorney and not dismiss them outright. If the adjuster disagrees with the documents, this should be noted in the file followed by a letter to all relevant parties explaining the reason for declining the new amount. Of course, if the new documents make a good case and the adjuster accepts the revised total, she will write a new release, send it out, alert the insured as to the settlement offer, and in all cases pick up the phone and speak with the claimant/attorney to let them know.

Partial Bodily Injury Settlements

It is a sad fact of life that some people in the United States do not have health insurance. To overgeneralize, if a person does not have health insurance, they usually do not have the means to seek treatment for injuries and pay for that medical treatment out of their pocket in the hopes of being reimbursed later. Yet, this is what liability carriers ask third-party claimants to do.

Unlike first-party claimants, where the insurer has a fiduciary duty, a contract, and the threat of bad faith for delaying the settlement of a claim, these obligations do not apply in a third-party context. The insurer must pay for claims the insured becomes "legally liable" for—meaning if the carrier doesn't want to get into trouble with the insured for ignoring a third-party claim, the insurer should pay equal attention to the third-party claimant as it would a first-party claimant. But the insurer, in its duty to protect the insured from the third-party claimant, will insist on a release of all claims before settlement can be procured.

A release of all claims cannot be sent until the claimant (assume for a liability claim, this will always be a third party; for property insurance, the claimant will always be the first party) has completed treatment. Therein lies the dilemma for the claimant who cannot afford treatment.

Adjusters will have been told they cannot offer an advance pay for medical invoices for claimants. ***This is not true.*** They can and should pay in advance if it is advantageous for controlling the claim. Having said this, offering a partial settlement to a claimant almost never happens.

There are forms for the partial settlement or receipt for advance payment on a bodily injury claim. If the insurer does not have them, defense counsel will. See the Appendix for examples. It is important to note the receipt for the advance payment is not a release, and it is equally important to state verbally and in writing that the advance payment will be deducted from the final settlement.

As mentioned previously, this is a good way to retain control over a file. The claimant may think the only way to get treatment is to go through an attorney, but if the adjuster is able, the insurer can pre-pay for certain treatments.

What is difficult, however, is that a liability carrier is not a health carrier. An adjuster will be called by providers wanting to send their invoices on a routine basis. Yes, the adjuster needs these invoices, because they will have to be considered for settlement of the claim. No, the liability carrier does not pay these invoices as they come in—like a health carrier—because, again, a release of all claims must be obtained to complete the claim.

Insurance in Action (Partial Settlements)

An example may be helpful to understand the partial-settlement theory.

On May 1, 2020, Mark was involved in a terrible auto accident which resulted in his being airlifted from the scene. Mark sustained multiple fractures, including his pelvis, neck, back, and left femur. He had to be cut out of the car, and while waiting for this to happen, he suffered severe burns to the front of his body. Needless to say, Mark has extraordinary medical invoices, not only from the hospital immediately after the loss, but for follow-up visits and surgeries.

Mark's auto insurer paid the medical payments coverage on May 5, 2020. But it has not paid the under-insured motorist coverage because the at-fault party, our insured, has a $2 million limit for liability.

Mark's doctors want him to have another skin graft surgery, which would cost approximately $30,000. Mark has been off work since the accident and will continue to be off work for two weeks after the skin graft surgery. Mark has depleted his savings and does not have the money for the surgery. The hospital requires a deposit of $15,000. On August 15, 2020, Mark approached the adjuster about reimbursement of his current medical invoices (totaling $75,000), lost wages, and the deposit.

Liability is clear, and the medical invoices and lost wages are reasonable, given the types of injuries Mark sustained. However, it is not common for a liability carrier to pay all of these expenses upfront. Conventional insurance wisdom is that Mark will be motivated to conclude his treatment in order to be paid and settle the claim.

Normally, the adjuster will accept the invoices and lost wage information from Mark but will not move to pay or take action on any of these bills until the end of treatment, the statute of limitations is due to expire, or by court order to oversimplify things and keep the story moving along. Fortunately, Mark's wife, Rhonda, is working and they are able to pay for their groceries, utilities, etc. Unfortunately, since they are down one salary, they are falling behind in other bills, such as Mark's medical invoices.

Let's take a quick side step and discuss health insurance. Mark has health coverage through his employer. Why isn't the health carrier paying these invoices? The hospital and doctors submitted their invoices to the health carrier. The health insurer's adjuster saw the cause of the injuries was an automobile accident. That's not among the health carrier's covered cause of loss, so the carrier denies payment for all bills related to this accident. Health carriers have different rules than the property and casualty insurers. They can deny claims and force their insureds to file their claims with someone else.[24]

Stepping back into our liability claim, it's now August 15, 2020—about two-and-a-half months post-loss, and Mark has a hospital and helicopter invoice of $55,000 hanging over his head. Remember he's not working and doesn't have the money to pay for these bills. To ensure they are paid, the hospital and the airlifting service file a lien on Mark's mobile home. This means he can't sell his house until his bills are paid off. Or rather, if he does sell his home, the hospital and helicopter will get the first $55,000 as payment of their services.

According to the normal handling of liability claims, since Mark doesn't have any money for the skin graft surgeries, physical therapy, prescription medicine, or other doctor invoices and his health carrier is not paying for any of this, Mark simply doesn't receive these treatments. This may affect him adversely not only physically because he can't heal properly, but also mentally and emotionally because he's dealing with pain.

Looking at This Another Way

On August 15, 2020, our adjuster receives Mark's demand of $75,000. She discusses it with her supervisor. The supervisor authorizes an offer of the $15,000 deposit and two weeks' lost wages, for a total of $18,500. This is not everything Mark needs, but it's a little something to help him get treatment. His deposit is paid; he can get the surgery. Because he and Rhonda are using her salary to stay afloat elsewhere, he can take the advancement of his two-week salary, $3,500, and pay a little to the hospital and a little to the

---

24 Remember: as a property and casualty adjuster, you can't force someone to file a claim with another insurer. The unfair claims handling guidelines, which are usually laws and regulations, say so.

airlifting service. Yes, it's only keeping the wolves at bay, but it prevents a lien on his house.

Mark agrees to the advance, partial payment of $18,500. The adjuster sends a receipt of advance payment. Mark signs, notarizes, and sends the receipt back to the adjuster. When the adjuster has the signed and notarized receipt of advance payment, she can make payment to Mark.

Upon settlement of the claim, the adjuster will deduct the advance payment. In reality, a claim with an injury this serious would result in liens, due to the length of time between the accident and payment. I've shown this settlement on the following page with fictional numbers as an example.

Initial Hospital Charges	$35,000
Airlifting Invoices	$20,000
2 Skin Graft Surgeries	$60,000
Physical Therapy	$13,000
Lost Wages	$120,000
Specific Damages	$248,000
General Damages	$848,000
Total Settlement Offer	**$1,096,000**
Less Advance Pay	$18,500
Subtotal	$1,077,500
Less Hospital Liens (E/R and Surgeries)	$95,000
Net Settlement Offer (the check Mark receives)	**$982,500.00**

Chiropractors

Here's a quick side note about treatment in bodily injury claims. The majority of soft tissue claims appear to be treated by chiropractors.

As mentioned in the earlier Insurance in Action section, the American Medical Association (AMA) does not recognize chiropractors as "medical doctors." This may be a matter of the association splitting hairs, because chiropractors do receive chiropractic degrees and are awarded the title "doctor."

Chiropractors typically complete 8 years of education before they are licensed. This consists of the 4 years at a university and 4 years in a chiropractic graduate program. They study general anatomy, clinical orthopedics, imaging interpretation, ethics, and complete a clinical internship with rotations. The American Chiropractic Association (ACA) states that its program requires as many classroom hours as medical school.

The chiropractic student will then take the state licensing board test, and once he has obtained his license and certification, he will be a "Doctor of Chiropractic."

Health insurers and Medicare/Medicaid all recognize chiropractors as "physicians." The ACA further states that federal statutes consider chiropractors physicians.

Chiropractors have often been derided by liability adjusters as offering a massage for a sprain. However, it's wise to withhold judgment and attempt to understand who is treating the claimant and the methods they've used when evaluating a claim.

Time Demands

Often the claimant, with the help of an attorney, will demand settlement from the adjuster with a time limit for acceptance. Failure of the adjuster to acknowledge the demand within the time limit can have dire consequences. If the insurer rejects, overlooks, or misses a policy limits time demand, an excess settlement of the policy limits could be the result.

Claimant attorneys have many reasons to submit time demands. The time demands may relate to issues other than policy limits, but this is where adjusters most frequently see them.

Remember the carrier has a duty to the insured to settle the case. This duty means the insurer should accept a reasonable settlement offer which is within the limits of the policy. When liability is clear, serious consideration must be given to the demand. That is not to say that questionable liability automatically means the claimant's demand is unreasonable. Again, the insurer owes a duty to the insured to investigate a claim and to determine if there is liability on the part of the policyholder.

Sometimes attorneys do not play fairly. Adjusters may see this when dealing with a time demand. A claimant attorney may attempt to set up the adjuster to fail by deliberately sending a time demand for policy limits to the carrier's home office, rather than the adjuster's mailing address. This can delay the demand from reaching the adjuster, which could leave the adjuster only a few days to address the loss. Another set up is a demand that occurs immediately after the loss and which does not give the carrier time to adequately investigate the claim. A third set up is a demand requiring unreasonable conditions of settlement, such as a printed, public apology from the policyholder for the accident.

Even if the time demand is faulty, it is imperative the adjuster immediately acknowledge the demand and request additional information if a liability decision cannot be immediately reached. The adjuster should also send a letter to the policyholder informing him of the demand.

Naturally, the adjuster should notate the file of all correspondence and the steps she is taking regarding her continued investigation into the loss.

One of the best-known time demands is called a *Stowers* demand in Texas. A number of requirements must be met for the time demand to be effective, such as offering a full and final release of all claims. As with any claim, adjusters must know their states' rules and regulations regarding the acceptance and rejections of time demands. Failure can open the carrier up to bad faith claims handling allegations.

Wrap Up

Adjusters should know by this stage in their career the difference between coverage and liability. They should be comfortable knowing they will not have a perfect file because there is no such thing as a perfect file; therefore, occasionally they will need to make decisions based on incomplete information. Tools to help the adjuster better handle her claims include recognizing that settlement negotiations are not a win-lose proposition and the ability to offer an advance payment in order to keep control of the file.

12

The Art of Adjusting

Parents like to offer nuggets of wisdom when their children go out into the adult world.

Don't talk to strangers.

Spend less than you earn.

Neither a borrower nor a lender be.

This final chapter is a hodge-podge of advice and things an adjuster should know at the interim stage of her career. These are mostly soft skills, which are very often overlooked, and rarely taught, but I am hoping this advice will help make your work a little easier.

You Are a Professional

The U.S. Bureau of Labor Statistics and I have very different views of being an insurance adjuster. The bureau believes the outlook for 2019 through 2029 will see a 6 percent decline in insurance claim jobs. It believes you need only a high school diploma to obtain work as an entry-level adjuster or appraiser. The former may be true, but I have never seen high school grads with zero higher ed hired as adjusters.

Adjusters must know how to analyze complex legal ideas, think on their feet, communicate with different people and different personality types, be detail oriented, and have a certain level of math skills. This complete skill set is not something that usually comes out of high school.

The mental calisthenics alone necessitate a bachelor's degree, which does not need to be in insurance or risk management, contrary to popular belief. In fact, I think people with other majors and adults looking for a change from other careers make better adjusters. They have transferable skill sets. Take a journalist, for example, who is trained to investigate a story. What do claims adjusters do? They investigate claims. The ability to investigate is transferable skill set.

For the most part, an adjuster is a licensed professional. She must obtain an adjuster license to handle claims. While it is true that in some states (e.g. Illinois, Kansas, and Missouri) an adjuster does not need a license, adjusters in these states likely operate under the company license. Despite not having an individual license, the adjuster may need annual continuing education, such as classes regarding the Californian Fair Claims Settlement Practices Law.

Like doctors and attorneys, adjusters must take ethics courses. These requirements for the license show you are in a profession, not a job. You have a career.

Insurance is a well-regulated field, and like doctors and attorneys, adjusters are professionals.

Adjusters are white collar. They work behind a desk for the most part. Appraisers are usually in the field, but they, too, are considered white collar. Adjusters are paid annually, not hourly. Their median salary in May 2020, per the US Bureau of Labor Statistics, was $68,130. That's a professional's salary.

I am harping on this fact because adjusters need to act like professionals since they are professionals. They should have self-respect and hold their heads high. Adjusters help people in their time of need, like doctors and attorneys. Be proud of this fact.

Under-Promise and Over-Deliver

You're probably familiar with Murphy's Law, which states "If something can go wrong, it will." It's because of this law the adjuster will want to under-promise and over-deliver. This means when a claimant (either first- or third-party) asks how long something will take to get done (and adjusters hear this question quite often), add a few days to what you believe to be the correct answer. Something always comes up to delay things unexpectedly.

For example, if the adjuster is reviewing an appraiser report, and it takes her two hours to do so and submit a proof of loss to the insured, I would tell the insured to expect something by the close of business *tomorrow*. The insured will be pleasantly surprised when he receives the proof of loss in a few hours, since he expected it the next day.

This is not manipulation. Far from it. This is managing expectations.

As a side note, this tends to work well for both your boss and in your personal life.

Over-Communicate

Everyone hates the adjuster who hides behind voicemail.

Everyone.

Sometimes an actual phone call is the only thing that will do. First, it quickly resolves the issue at hand; second, it reduces the chance of being misinterpreted, and third, it's polite. If the adjuster will deny an insured's or claimant's claim, the adjuster must respect the insured/claimant enough to pick up the phone and speak to the individual.

Because the insured and the claimant are individuals. They are humans. They are not claim numbers. They have feelings. They have been through a traumatic event (the accident). The adjuster must show them some respect.

When the phone rings, pick it up. I, personally, am more stressed seeing the blinking red voicemail light because I wonder what horrors (or yelling) await me. Picking up the phone immediately often has a soothing effect.

Despite the above advice, there are some cheats the adjuster can employ when necessary.

I find sending letters and emails advising the insured and claimant of the claim status drastically reduces phone calls. I would send emails stating, "I followed up with the appraiser for the status of the estimate. I have not heard back. I will diary this for another week and keep you informed."

Again, this managed expectations, because in reality, I would put a note in my calendar to follow up with the appraiser in three days if I hadn't heard anything (under-promise and over-deliver).

I am aware that Millennials and Gen Z prefer texting for communicating with others. I'm not a fan of this method of staying in touch unless the claims system can record the text. If the adjuster is using a personal number to text the insured or claimant, they must then forward that message into the claim system for record keeping. Remember, departments of insurance mandate that files be documented, and texting someone about the claim must become part of the claim file.

Of course, there's always that one person we don't want to talk to.

NOTE: Use the following advice judiciously and rarely!

Know the time to call so a voicemail can be left, then send an email for the person to respond to. For example, if you are dealing with a particularly unpleasant attorney, call him before 9 a.m. or during lunch. Then send an email. It's easier to respond to an email than to call back.

Conference Calls Are Your Friend

Overgeneralizing, oversimplifying, and insulting probably everyone, most agents are familiar with insureds who want the most coverage at the cheapest price—two things which are polar opposites. The agent can be the adjuster's best ally (and vice versa).

Before calling the insured to inform him of a forthcoming reservation of rights or letter of denial, it is in the adjuster's best interest to call the agent and alert him. For one thing, the agent may have a key piece of information which will help the adjuster find coverage for the claim. Second, you will alert the agent that any minute, he's likely to receive an angry phone call from the insured demanding to know why such-and-such isn't covered. Third, it will help the agent sell a better policy (if he knows what he's doing).

There are times when the adjuster is caught between the agent and the insured. Perhaps the insured simply doesn't understand all aspects of his policy and/or believes the adjuster is "being mean." I have found it helpful in these circumstances to have the insured's agent on the phone while I spoke with the insured. The agent is usually someone the insured trusts because both live in the same town. They may have even met when the policy was originally placed. So, it can be advantageous to use this relationship to help the insured.

Why Am I Paying Premiums??

Immediately upon learning there is a coverage question or that his claim is being denied, the insured will inquire, "Why am I paying my premiums?"

This is often preceded or followed by a statement like, "I've been paying premiums for XXX (number of) years."

Which is generally followed by, "Well, you want to take my money, but you sure don't want to pay anything!"

And the conversation almost always ends with, "I'm going to take my business to another company!"

When this occurs, it's a good idea to briefly review the coverages the insured has, again, although you will have done this at the *beginning* of the claim, pursuant to the good faith claims handling guidelines from the state department of insurance.

Finally, advise the insured to contact his agent (have the agent's information on hand so you can provide excellent customer service and be helpful). Of course, the agent will already be aware a call may be coming because, smart little adjuster that you are, you've already alerted him, as discussed above.

Always Prepare the File for Litigation

This is somewhat self-explanatory. If the file is handled with the thought that everything (and I mean **EVERYTHING**) will be second guessed, twisted, tortured, and then blown up in 3-foot-tall court exhibits for the jury to use its 20/20 hind-vision on, you will be much less likely to experience allegations of bad faith claims handling, and you will be just fine when you're named in the lawsuit. Yep.

You Will Be Sued

That's right. Just like getting yelled at, the plaintiff attorney will name the adjuster in most lawsuits. If the adjuster follows good faith claims guidelines for the state, there should not be an issue. (Ahem, that means protect yourself by documenting everything, handling your job like the professional you are, and committing this entire book to memory.) Defense counsel should be able to remove any adjuster who takes these steps from the lawsuit.

Naming the adjuster in the lawsuit is usually a bullying tactic by plaintiff counsel. Don't let it affect or influence you. It likely means you're doing your job correctly.

You Will Have a Formal Complaint Lodged Against You

This is the third truism of being an adjuster. It's not a matter of *if* you will have someone complain about you; the only questions are *when* and *to whom* they will complain. If it's the insured lodging the complaint, they will go to the state department of insurance who will investigate the issue.

When you receive the complaint, ***do not dally in your response.*** In fact, most states have a deadline (10 to 15 days) by which the insurer must respond. Failure to respond will result in monetary fines against the carrier.

The insured will write a paragraph or paragraphs explaining which actions he perceives as having been mishandled. The best way to respond to a department of insurance complaint is allegation by allegation.

For example, the insured might write:

> I reported this claim on July 1, 2019, but I was not contacted until August 31, 2019. The claim has been one delay after another. The adjuster did not come out to my house to inspect my home until September 5, 2019, at which time I had been out of my home for 2 months. I repeatedly followed up for the status, but the adjuster hides behind her voicemail and does not return calls. On September 10, I received a copy of the estimate and a check for $753.86 which my insurance company states are for the repairs. My contractor's estimate is $10,591.17. I am not being fairly paid for this loss.

A response to this could be:

> The insured reported the claim on July 1, 2019, and Nicole Brown, the adjuster, attempted contact with the insured on the same date. She spoke with Mrs. Perkins on July 2, 2019, who stated she was the named insured's wife. The adjuster explained coverage and stated she would assign an appraiser to inspect the home. Mrs. Perkins acknowledged.
>
> Ms. Brown assigned State Appraisal Service to inspect Mr. Perkins' home on July 2, 2019. State Appraisal Service attempted three times to reach Mr. and Mrs. Perkins, according to its report dated July 15, 2019. Ms. Brown sent a letter to

Mr. and Mrs. Perkins and attempted to call them on three separate occasions: July 17, 2019; July 24, 2019; and August 1, 2019. There was no response to messages left on the voicemail for (501) 555-1212.

Ms. Brown issued another letter and attempted contact on August 31, 2019 and reached Mr. Perkins. He apologized for the delay and stated he has been busy with work. Ms. Brown assigned State Appraisal Service again, who was unable to inspect Mr. Perkins' home until August 31, 2019, due to delays on Mr. Perkins' part. Please see State Appraisal Service's September 1, 2019, report.

A check was sent to the Perkins on September 8, 2019, for $753.86, which represents the covered loss. The Perkins have an actual cash value policy, which does not cover depreciation. Further there was uncovered water damage, represented in Mr. Perkins' contractor's estimate. Attached is the declination of coverage with the explanation of settlement sent to Mr. Perkins with the indemnity check.

The explanation is a great deal longer than the complaint, which is generally the case. The insurer must back up why the complaint is incorrect (if the complaint is, indeed, incorrect). Of course, if the complaint is correct, the insurer needs to take steps to correct the issue. The point is: be specific in the response to the department of insurance.

Just Like Grandma

I mentioned this earlier: claimants (first- and third-party) are humans. They have the same hopes and dreams we all do. They love someone. They hate someone (it might just be you, for the moment). They have favorite foods. They have favorite pets.

So, treat them the way you would like your grandma to be treated.

As an adjuster, you will be overworked (we've discussed this previously, as well). Adjusting is not a Monday-Friday, 9-5 job. I have never known it to be and doubt this will change, going forward. So slow down and take the time to explain the steps of the claim to the claimant. Doing so may seem like a bother now, but it will save you a headache (and potential lawsuit) in the long run. Enlist a trusted adviser to increase your credibility. This, too, will save you time in the long run.

Use your empathy. If empathy isn't your strong suit, fake it until you make it. Or watch YouTube videos to learn how.

Take care of your claimants. As an adjuster, you are the promise keepers of the policy, and you are a professional at your craft.

Knowledge Is Power

Many young adjusters lack confidence. They don't realize they are professionals; they don't respect themselves; and they don't recognize they know more about the file than anyone else. They have reviewed the policy; they have reviewed the estimate, the photos, the medical records, etc.; they are familiar with the rules, regulations, and laws of the state.

Don't let anyone bully you.

When speaking with a claimant or attorney, be able to answer their questions. Alternatively, if you don't know the answer, say so. It's a worse crime to lie and lose credibility than confess to not knowing everything. State in a calm, assertive manner that you don't know, but you will research the issue and call them back by XXX time/date. (Then put this on your calendar so you don't forget and lose face by failing to keep that promise.)

Attorneys, public adjusters, and contractors will often use the excuse that something cannot be done because of XYZ statute or regulation. Ask for the exact code, statute, ruling, or regulation and then look it up. Put the results of your research in the file. This will offer support if the insurer has to increase the indemnity payment. Or, you may have just called the other party's bluff attempt to hoodwink the insurer for a larger payment (which would be fraud).

As a side note, if you discover there is a local rule about something, be sure to share it with your team and supervisor. This is a good political move and shows you are a "team player." Your employer will like that.

Could You Lower Your Voice, Please?

In case you missed it: people yell at adjusters. This is because they have experienced a loss and are angry and confused. The reality of how claims adjusting works is not portrayed well in 30-second TV commercials. Adjusters rarely come out and write a check on the spot for the full damages.

Claimants often don't understand why something is not covered if they have "all-risk" coverage (which, again, ***does not exist – REVIEW CHAPTER 02***). They don't understand why insurers cannot pay medical invoices as they treat (because the ***carriers are not health insurers***). They do not understand why they must prove their damages (because ***not everything is covered or reasonable***).

Claimants are frustrated, and many express that frustration through profanity and yelling (guilty!). The key to helping the claimant is to do your part to keep from escalating the situation. No one teaches that in college or risk management classes. So here it goes:

When someone yells at you, lower your voice and speak softly.

You will get a call where someone yells at you.

Stop what you are doing.

Do not respond. Do not interrupt. Do not say anything.

It will be hard to remember this in the heat of battle.

The person will eventually stop to come up for air. They may even ask you if you are still on the line because you've been quiet and not engaging. When they do, ***whisper***, "Yes, I am here. I am listening to you. Please go on."

Here's what you've done by speaking softly:

- You've made them, essentially, lean into you in order to hear you (even though this is taking place over the phone).

- You haven't contradicted them (yet).

- You've invited them to continue to unload their frustrations (which is needed).

- You have, in essence, validated their concerns (extremely important!).

Sometimes the claimant simply wants to get his frustrations off his chest.

When the claimant says he has nothing more to say, the adjuster should recap the claimant's statements in a low voice—not necessarily a whisper this time. Ask if you've properly understood what the claimant said.

Again, this validates the claimant's perception and makes him feel heard.

Then you can go over, bit by bit, what is troubling the claimant. If the situation becomes tense again, use the same steps. If the conversation doesn't seem to move forward, inform the claimant in an empathetic manner that seem to be having a circular argument and you will send a letter outlining the issues. You can then terminate the call.

Here is an example of how this type of call may unfold:

> Mike, the first-party claimant, calls his adjuster, Ruth, concerning the settlement for his claim, which involved roof and interior water damage. Mike is livid, and as soon as Ruth answers the call, he spews a series of obscenities and insults Ruth in a loud manner.
>
> Ruth does not engage and listens to Mike's complaints. Mike speaks for approximately three minutes, listing the ways Ruth has not adjusted the claim correctly and what his contractor has told him about similar claims. He threatens to file a complaint with the department of insurance and to file suit for bad faith.
>
> Mike stops, mid-torrent, to ask if Ruth is still there, because he has not heard her say anything. He is afraid she hung up, which makes him even angrier. Ruth says in a soft voice, "I'm here Mr. Black. I'm taking notes so I can discuss this with you. Do you have anything else to add?"
>
> Mike is taken aback, first, that Ruth has not hung up on him, and second, that she is taking notes and listening to what he is saying. He tells her has nothing further to add.
>
> Ruth continues in a calm, soft voice, similar to the tone a therapist might use, "Mr. Black, you said your contractor told you he could not repair your damage for our estimated cost and the amount you received in the check. Is that correct?"
>
> Mike acknowledges she is correct so far.
>
> "OK. I can have an appraiser go out to look at the damage again. When the appraiser calls to set up an appointment, make sure your contractor is there. I want them to go over the damages together so we can agree on a price for repairs.
>
> "In the meantime, you can cash that first check. It won't prohibit you from filing what's called a supplemental claim.
>
> "Next, I want to address some concerns about the estimate and your contractor. You have a replacement cost policy. This means we will pay the actual cash value, and once you complete

repairs, we will pay the remainder, holding back depreciation. It's kinda like we're giving you seed money to start repairs. We don't pay the entire thing up front. I'll send you a letter with the policy language in it explaining why we do this.

"Also, you may recall I sent a letter about the previous interior water damage which is not covered because it's not a result of this loss. We can open another claim for you, but there would be another deductible."

Mike objects to this, stating he had not experienced a prior loss. Ruth counters, stating the photographs from the first inspection show multiple water damaged areas on the ceiling in locations where the roof was not leaking on the outside.

Mike states his contractor told him water "migrated" to those areas. Ruth again counters, in a soft voice, that it is unlikely the water migrated from the northwest corner of the house to the southeast corner where the current loss occurred. This would mean that water would have had to run through the entire home, and there is no evidence of that having occurred; therefore, the northeast corner water damage must be from a previous loss.

Mike begins to raise his voice again. This time Ruth interrupts, stating they are having a circular argument, and she will send a letter to him outlining the carrier's position. Ruth reiterates she will assign an appraiser and wants the contractor there to perform a joint inspection. She thanks Mike and terminates the call.[25]

Ruth immediately informs her supervisor she terminated an insured's call, in case Mike contacts her supervisor to file a complaint about her. Ruth also calls the agent to let him know about her call with Mike and see if she can help explain the issues to the insured. She then updates her file notes and assigns the appraiser.

---

25 A circular argument is one that goes in circles. No matter what is said, the argument always comes back to one point. In this instance, Mike has water damage; therefore, all the water damage in his house must be from the current claim. In all likelihood, he had prior water damage but did not see it until the recent water damage occurred. Since he didn't previously observe it, in his mind, the damage did not exist previously.

Also, it is good manners when terminating the call to let the other person know the call is being terminated. In this instance, Ruth would say, "Mr. Black, we're having a circular argument. I am going to send you a letter outlining our position. Since we can't agree right now, I'm going to hang up." It feels abrupt, but there's really no reason to keep going around in circles.

Ruth was not able to address the threats to file a complaint or suit with Mike, but she can address those in the letter. See the next section for discussion on this topic.

There may come a time when this method will not work and the claimant does not want to be placated. Depending on your carrier's policies, this might be the time to terminate the call.

You may be thinking, *I'm supposed to treat the claimant like I want my grandma treated. I don't want the adjuster to hang up on my grandma.*

Yes, well...

The adjuster also has other grandmothers to take care of and can't sit on the phone all day talking in circles. Also, Ruth attempted three times to explain the carrier's denial of pre-existing damages to the northeast corner of the insured's home. Mike either was hard-of-listening or honestly didn't understand. Regardless, it didn't behoove Ruth to stay on the phone indefinitely.

The point of this example is to demonstrate that Ruth didn't immediately begin to yell back or talk over Mike. Neither did she ignore his complaints. She didn't immediately hang up on him when he challenged her. She attempted, in good faith, to explain the logic of the carrier's denial of the northeast water damage. She's a professional and acted like one.

A final note about terminating a call with someone. Again, depending on the carrier's internal rules and regs, the adjuster may well have the right to hang up the phone on the caller. Adjusters do not have to open themselves up to being berated and insulted. People don't, for the most part, speak that way to other professionals, like doctors and attorneys; therefore, it's beyond me why they feel they can do it to an insurance professional.

The same rule would apply if the caller were using profanity and calling the adjuster insulting names, making racist or sexist remarks, etc. Except this time, the adjuster could immediately nip it in the bud.

I won't give an example because I don't want to type out the kind of vitriolic diatribe that spews from some people's mouths. Once that kind of language starts, again, in a calm, soft voice while the verbal attack is ongoing, the adjuster should state, "Mr. PersonWhoIsCallingMeNames, I must ask you to speak to me in a more respectful manner, or I will be forced to terminate the call."

If the caller does not stop, state in the same tone of voice a second time, "Again, Mr. PersonWhoIsCallingMeNames, I will not speak with you if you continue to speak to me in this un-business-like manner. I will terminate the call if you do not stop."

If the caller continues, the adjuster can state in a soft, low voice, "Because you are using profanity and insults, I am terminating this call. I will not speak to you until you can address me in a more respectful way. I am hanging up now."

Again, the adjuster should immediately:

- Inform her supervisor she hung up on a caller and the reasons why.

- If the caller was the insured, she should contact the agent to let him know the insured may be upset by the adjuster's actions.

- A note should go into file that the call was terminated and why (insults/profanity/racist/sexist remarks).

- A letter should be sent to the claimant, stating the adjuster must insist on written correspondence with the caller until a more professional tone can be maintained.

Do I Need an Attorney?

Adjusters are asked this question quite often. The answer is:

I cannot advise you as to you whether you need an attorney; however, if you retain one, please have him/her send me a letter of representation.

And that's it.

As mentioned previously, adjusters are sued. They are also threatened with complaints and being sued.

If there is a threat of a lawsuit, answer in the manner the fictitious adjuster did in Chapter 11: ask for a copy of the pleadings. Make a note in the claim file that "***This file is being prepared in anticipation of litigation***," as discussed in Chapter 6.

Regarding Mike and Ruth's conversation, the rest of the story is as follows:

Ruth terminated the call before she could verbally address Mike's threats of a complaint to the department of insurance and of a lawsuit for bad faith claims handling. In her letter outlining the carrier's denial of the northeast corner water damage, Ruth states:

"In our conversation of May 15, 2020, you stated you would file a complaint with the department of insurance. You also stated you would contact an attorney and file suit for bad faith claims handling. Please have your attorney send a letter of representation and a copy of the pleadings to my attention. However, I would like you to know I am unable to accept service for the carrier. I will respond to the insurance department's query into your complaint when it is received.

"In the meantime, please have your contractor perform a joint inspection with the appraiser in order to arrive at an agreed price of repairs."

Again, Ruth would mark the file "This file is being handled in anticipation of litigation" because there was a threat of a lawsuit.

Promise Keepers

I've said throughout this book adjusters are the promise keepers of the insurance industry, and the policy is the promise. I've urged adjusters to treat claimants like they would want other adjusters to treat their grandma.

But how, exactly, is this done nowadays, when everyone is kept in their little pigeon holes? You're not likely to be happy with the answer to that question.

1. Take a vacation or personal-time-off (PTO) day.
2. Spend that day in the field with an appraiser.
3. Inspect houses; inspect cars; attend in-person recorded statements; go back to the appraiser's office and help write an estimate or a report for the desk adjuster.

If you can convince your boss that it's part of your continuing education, you can probably take the day off without burning a vacation day.

At some point, the adjuster will need to sit with an attorney in court and do boring stuff like legal research.

In essence, the adjuster needs to get out from behind her desk and meet the insured and claimant. She needs to look them in the eye so she understands what they are going through. She can then take this experience and extrapolate it to other claims, making her a better and stronger adjuster.

Wrap Up

This chapter is the heart of the book, even though it is at the end. But all of the things here build on what has already been discussed and what the adjuster has learned in the first part of her career as a professional. Honor your role as a promise keeper. Then remember your clients (insureds and claimants) are people and you pursued this profession for a reason.

Good luck!

Appendix

T his Appendix is a helpful little tool with a lot of information at your disposal. It comes out of a previous job I had where we saved every scrap of information to put on our intranet. That way, adjusters didn't have to reinvent the wheel.

You can visit my website, **TheArtOfAdjusting.com/Resources** to access this info at work, in your car, at the beach, in the grocery store, etc. You don't have to lug this book around everywhere you go. But if you do take the book every-where you go, people will know you are seriously intelligent, not to mention exceptionally cool.

These charts are current as of our publication date, but adjusters should be familiar with their own states' rules. As you know, things change, so I cannot guarantee the accuracy of the lists. Because laws and regulations can change without notice, you should contact an attorney if you have any ques-tions regarding these charts. These materials are provided for informational and educational purposes only and do not constitute legal advice or legal opinions because I am not an attorney.

Property Deadlines Per State

This is a list of first-party property statutes of limitations. Adjusters should be aware of their states' particular statutes of limitations and whether the insurer should notify an insured of the upcoming deadline to file suit. While it may seem counterintuitive, it is a good practice to let the insured know of the upcoming deadline, regardless of whether there is a regulation or statute dictating the same. The reason is transparency. You want the insured to trust you. It's true that many companies, would prefer not to inform the insured about the statute of limitations deadline if the state(s) where they do business remains silent on the issue. They worry about an increased slew of litigation. However, if the companies settle fairly, timely, and equitably, there should be nothing to worry about.

This chart is current as of our publication date, but adjusters should be familiar with their own states' rules. I cannot guarantee the accuracy of this list. Because laws and regulations can change without notice, you should contact an attorney if you have any questions regarding this chart. These materials are provided for informational and educational purposes only and do not constitute legal advice or legal opinions because I am not an attorney.

Property Deadlines Per State

State	Time	Statute
Alabama	2 years	AL Code § 6-2-38
Alaska	2 years	AK Stat. § 9.10.070
Arizona	2 years	AZ Rev. Stat. § 12-542
Arkansas	3 years	AR Stat. § 16-114-203
California	2 years	CA Code of Civ. Proc. § 335.1
Colorado	2 years	CO Rev. Stat. § 13-80-102
Connecticut	2 years	CT Gen. State. § 52-584
Delaware	2 years	DE Code Title 10, § 8119
District of Columbia	3 years	D.C. Code § 12-301
Florida	4 years	FL Stat. § 95.11
Georgia	2 years	GA Code § 9-3-33
Hawaii	2 years	HI Rev. Stat. § 657.7
Idaho	2 years	ID Code § 5-219
Illinois	2 years	IL State. Ch. 735, Art. 5, § 13-202
Indiana	2 years	IN Code § 34-11-2-4
Iowa	2 years	IA Code §. 614.1
Kansas	2 years	KS Stat. § 60-513

State	Time	Statute
Kentucky	1 year	KY Rev. Stat. § 413.140
Louisiana	1 year	LA Civ. Code Art. 3492
Maine	6 years	ME Rev. Stat. Title 14, Ch. 205, §752
Maryland	3 years	MD Code § 5-101
Massachusetts	3 years	MA Gen. Laws, Art. 260, § 2A, 4
Michigan	3 years	MI Comp Laws Sec. 600.5805(9)
Minnesota	2 years	MN Stat. § 541.05, 541.07
Mississippi	3 years	MS Code § 15-1-49
Missouri	5 years	MO Stat. Title 35, § 516.120
Montana	3 years	MT Code § 27-2-204, 27-2-207
Nebraska	4 years	NB Rev. Stat. § 25-207
Nevada	2 years	NV Rev. Stat. § 11.190
New Hampshire	3 years	NH Rev. State. § 508.4
New Jersey	2 years	NJ Stat. § 2A:14-2
New Mexico	3 years	NM Stat. § 37-1-8
New York	3 years	NY Civ. Prac. R. § 214
North Carolina	3 years	NC Gen. Stat. § 1-52
North Dakota	6 years	ND Cent. Code § 28-01-16, 28-01-18
Ohio	2 years	OH Rev. Code § 2305.10
Oklahoma	2 years	OK Stat. Title 12, § 95
Oregon	2 years	OR Rev. Stat. § 12.110
Pennsylvania	2 years	42 PA Con. Stat. § 5524
Rhode Island	3 years	RI Gen. Laws § 9-1-14
South Carolina	3 years	SC Code § 15-3-530
South Dakota	3 years	SD Comp. Laws § 15-2-14
Tennessee	1 year	TN Code § 28-3-104
Texas	2 years	TX Civ. Prac. & Rem. Code § 16.003
Utah	4 years	UT Code § 78-12-25
Vermont	3 years	VT Stat. Ann. Title 12, § 512
Virginia	2 years	VA Code § 8.01-243
Washington	3 years	WA Rev. Code § 4.16.080
West Virginia	2 years	WV Code § 55-2-12
Wisconsin	3 years	WI Stat. § 893.54
Wyoming	4 years	WY Stat. § 1-3-105

Liability Deadlines Per State

This is a list of third-party property statute of limitations. Adjusters should be aware of their states' particular statutes of limitations and whether the insurer should notify a claimant of the upcoming deadline to file suit.

This chart is current as of our publication date, but adjusters should be familiar with their own states' rules. I cannot guarantee the accuracy of this list. Because laws and regulations can change without notice, you should contact an attorney if you have any questions regarding this chart. These materials are provided for informational and educational purposes only and do not constitute legal advice or legal opinions because I am not an attorney.

Liability Deadlines Per State

State	Time	Statute
Alabama	2 years	AL Code § 6-2-38
Alaska	2 years	AK Stat. § 9.10.070
Arizona	2 years	AZ Rev. Stat. § 12-542
Arkansas	3 years	AR Stat. § 16-114-203
California	2 years	CA Code of Civ. Proc. § 335.1
Colorado	2 years	CO Rev. Stat. § 13-80-102
Connecticut	2 years	CT Gen. State. § 52-584
Delaware	2 years	DE Code Title 10, § 8119
District of Columbia	3 years	D.C. Code § 12-301
Florida	4 years	FL Stat. § 95.11
Georgia	2 years	GA Code § 9-3-33
Hawaii	2 years	HI Rev. Stat. § 657.7
Idaho	2 years	ID Code § 5-219
Illinois	2 years	IL State. Ch. 735, Art. 5, § 13-202
Indiana	2 years	IN Code § 34-11-2-4
Iowa	2 years	IA Code §. 614.1
Kansas	2 years	KS Stat. § 60-513
Kentucky	1 year	KY Rev. Stat. § 413.140
Louisiana	1 year	LA Civ. Code Art. 3492
Maine	6 years	ME Rev. Stat. Title 14, Ch. 205, §752
Maryland	3 years	MD Code § 5-101
Massachusetts	3 years	MA Gen. Laws, Art. 260, § 2A, 4

Liability Deadlines Per State

State	Time	Statute
Michigan	3 years	MI Comp Laws Sec. 600.5805(9)
Minnesota	2 years	MN Stat. § 541.05, 541.07
Mississippi	3 years	MS Code § 15-1-49
Missouri	5 years	MO Stat. Title 35, § 516.120
Montana	3 years	MT Code § 27-2-204, 27-2-207
Nebraska	4 years	NB Rev. Stat. § 25-207
Nevada	2 years	NV Rev. Stat. § 11.190
New Hampshire	3 years	NH Rev. State. § 508.4
New Jersey	2 years	NJ Stat. § 2A:14-2
New Mexico	3 years	NM Stat. § 37-1-8
New York	3 years	NY Civ. Prac. R. § 214
North Carolina	3 years	NC Gen. Stat. § 1-52
North Dakota	6 years	ND Cent. Code § 28-01-16, 28-01-18
Ohio	2 years	OH Rev. Code § 2305.10
Oklahoma	2 years	OK Stat. Title 12, § 95
Oregon	2 years	OR Rev. Stat. § 12.110
Pennsylvania	2 years	42 PA Con. Stat. § 5524
Rhode Island	3 years	RI Gen. Laws § 9-1-14
South Carolina	3 years	SC Code § 15-3-530
South Dakota	3 years	SD Comp. Laws § 15-2-14
Tennessee	1 year	TN Code § 28-3-104
Texas	2 years	TX Civ. Prac. & Rem. Code § 16.003
Utah	4 years	UT Code § 78-12-25
Vermont	3 years	VT Stat. Ann. Title 12, § 512
Virginia	2 years	VA Code § 8.01-243
Washington	3 years	WA Rev. Code § 4.16.080
West Virginia	2 years	WV Code § 55-2-12
Wisconsin	3 years	WI Stat. § 893.54
Wyoming	4 years	WY Stat. § 1-3-105

Made Whole States

The subrogation doctrine of making the insured whole prior to taking any reimbursement for the carrier is common throughout the states, although the definition may change depending on the state in which the loss occurred.

This chart is current as of our publication date, but adjusters should be familiar with their own states' rules. I cannot guarantee the accuracy of this list. Because laws and regulations can change without notice, you should contact an attorney if you have any questions regarding this chart. These materials are provided for informational and educational purposes only and do not constitute legal advice or legal opinions because I am not an attorney.

Made Whole States

State	Adheres to the Made Whole Doctrine	Does Not Adhere to the Made Whole Doctrine	Consult with Subrogation Attorney
Alabama	X		
Alaska		X	X
Arizona		X	
Arkansas	X		
California	X		
Colorado	X		X
Connecticut		X	X
Delaware		X	X
District of Columbia	X		
Florida	X		
Georgia	X		X
Hawaii		X	X
Idaho		X	
Illinois		X	X
Indiana	X		X
Iowa	X		X
Kansas		X	X
Kentucky			X
Louisiana	X		

State	Adheres to the Made Whole Doctrine	Does Not Adhere to the Made Whole Doctrine	Consult with Subrogation Attorney
Maine			X
Maryland		X	
Massachusetts		X	X
Michigan	X		X
Minnesota	X		
Mississippi	X		
Missouri		X	X
Montana		X	
Nebraska	X		X
Nevada			X
New Hampshire			X
New Jersey	X		X
New Mexico		X	X
New York	X		
North Carolina		X	X
North Dakota		X	X
Ohio	X		
Oklahoma	X		
Oregon			X
Pennsylvania	X		
Rhode Island	X		
South Carolina		X	X
South Dakota	X		
Tennessee	X		
Texas	X		X
Utah	X		
Vermont		X	X
Virginia			X
Washington	X		
West Virginia	X		
Wisconsin	X		X
Wyoming		X	X

Made Whole Specifics by State

Alabama

Adheres to the Made Whole Doctrine. The insurer may pursue subrogation after the insured is made whole. The insured has been made whole when the at-fault party has completely compensated for all the insured's losses; all sources of reimbursement must be considered in order to determine if the insured has been made whole. This applies to liability and property damage claims. The insurance policy can specifically state that the Made Whole Doctrine does not apply. The insurer must determine if the insured has been made whole.

Alaska

It does not appear Alaska adheres to the Made Whole Doctrine, but adjusters are encouraged to seek information from subrogation counsel.

Arizona

It does not appear Arizona adheres to the Made Whole Doctrine, but adjusters are encouraged to seek information from subrogation counsel. The 9th Circuit Court made the doctrine into a federal common law concerning health care insurance. There is no mention of liability or property insurance.

Arkansas

Adheres to the Made Whole Doctrine. The insurer may pursue subrogation after the insured is made whole. Unlike Alabama, the insurer cannot circumvent the doctrine with policy language. Note: The insurer should determine if the insured has been made whole prior to sending a subrogation demand to the at-fault party. Arkansas believes even a subrogation demand by the carrier is attempting to obtain reimbursement before the insured is made whole.

California

Adheres to the Made Whole Doctrine. The insurer may pursue subrogation after the insured is made whole. The insurance policy can specifically state that the Made Whole Doctrine does not apply. Note: The doctrine applies even for non-covered claims. Therefore, the insured must be wholly reimbursed by the at-fault party for losses he sustained that the insurer did not cover before the insurer can obtain reimbursement for its payments.

Colorado

Adheres to the Made Whole Doctrine. The insurer may pursue subrogation after the insured is made whole. C.R.S. § 10-1-135 codified the common laws surrounding subrogation claims, but there are few court rulings interpreting the statute. Therefore, it would be wise for the adjuster to consult with a subrogation attorney.

Connecticut

It does not appear Connecticut adheres to the Made Whole Doctrine, but adjusters are encouraged to seek information from subrogation counsel. The doctrine has been mentioned in bankruptcy cases. The Connecticut Court of Appeals opined, in one case, the insured must be fully reimbursed for his loss before the insurer can pursue subrogation.

Delaware

It does not appear Delaware adheres to the Made Whole Doctrine, but adjusters are encouraged to seek information from subrogation counsel.

District of Columbia

Adheres to the Made Whole Doctrine. The insurer may pursue subrogation after the insured is made whole. The insurance policy can specifically state that the Made Whole Doctrine does not apply.

Florida

Adheres to the Made Whole Doctrine. The insurer may pursue subrogation after the insured is made whole.

Georgia

Adheres to the Made Whole Doctrine which it calls the "Full Compensation Rule." The insurer may pursue subrogation after the insured is made whole. It was codified in 1998 § 33-24-56.1. The insurance policy can specifically state that the Made Whole Doctrine does not apply; however, the Georgia Supreme Court stated this was against public policy. Adjusters should discuss the case with subrogation counsel. Note: Subrogation for medical expenses and disability payments is not allowed.

Hawaii

It does not appear Hawaii adheres to the Made Whole Doctrine, but adjusters are encouraged to seek information from subrogation counsel. Courts state insureds should be made whole before an uninsured auto insurer may seek reimbursement from the at-fault party.

Conversely, Hawaii has not applied the doctrine in a routine subrogation case.

Idaho

It does not appear Idaho adheres to the Made Whole Doctrine, but adjusters are encouraged to seek information from subrogation counsel. The 9th Circuit Court made the doctrine into a federal common law concerning health care insurance. There is no mention of liability or property insurance.

Illinois

It does not appear Illinois adheres to the Made Whole Doctrine, but adjusters are encouraged to seek information from subrogation counsel. However, Illinois does recognize subrogation clauses in insurance policies. Note: The legislature passed § 23/50. 2012 IL Legis. Serv. P.A. 97-1042 (H.B. 5823) which allows for the reduction of payments by the insured's comparative fault.

Indiana

Adheres to the Made Whole Doctrine. The insurer may pursue subrogation after the insured is made whole. The insurance policy can specifically state that the Made Whole Doctrine does not apply, but standard wording of a policy may be insufficient to overcome Indiana statute § 34-51-2-19. Adjusters should seek advice of subrogation counsel.

Iowa

Adheres to the Made Whole Doctrine, which it calls the "Full Recovery Rule." The insurer may pursue subrogation after the insured is made whole. Note: Pain and Suffering does not need to be taken into account to determine if the insured has been made whole. There appears to be some confusion as to the policy's ability to supersede the Made Whole Doctrine. Adjusters should seek advice of subrogation counsel.

Kansas

Kansas has an anti-subrogation statute KS Admin. Regs. § 40-1-20 (1987); therefore, it does not appear Kansas adheres to the Made Whole Doctrine. However, if a policy was issued out of state, a question may arise if the statute applies to the contract. Adjusters should consult with subrogation counsel.

Kentucky

Kentucky believes the insured must be fully reimbursed for injuries or damages prior to the insurer seeking subrogation. However, the policy can overwrite the doctrine. Unfortunately, a court must undergo the analysis to determine if the Made Whole Doctrine is applicable. Adjusters should consult with subrogation counsel.

Louisiana

Adheres to the Made Whole Doctrine. The insurer may pursue subrogation after the insured is made whole. The insured has been made whole when the at-fault party has completely compensated for all the insured's losses. Note: It is the insured who must prove he has not been made whole by his settlement.

Maine

Maine appears to be conflicted about the Made Whole Doctrine. There is no case law discussing the doctrine, but the state prefers the insured to be fully compensated by an uninsured motorist before the insurer can pursue subrogation. Adjusters should consult with subrogation counsel.

Maryland

Maryland straight-up says it does not adhere to the Made Whole Doctrine.

Massachusetts

It does not appear Massachusetts adheres to the Made Whole Doctrine, but adjusters are encouraged to seek information from subrogation counsel.

Michigan

Adheres to the Made Whole Doctrine. The insurer may pursue subrogation after the insured is made whole. Michigan remains silent regarding if the insurer can circumvent the doctrine with policy language. Adjusters should consult with subrogation counsel. Note: The Michigan Supreme Court opined an insurer is not entitled to reimbursement unless the insured is fully compensated including attorney fees and costs.

Minnesota

Adheres to the Made Whole Doctrine, which it calls the "Full Recovery Rule." The insurer may pursue subrogation after the insured is made whole. The insurance policy can specifically state that the Made Whole Doctrine does not apply.

Mississippi

Adheres to the Made Whole Doctrine. The insurer may pursue subrogation after the insured is made whole. The insured has been made whole when the at-fault party has completely compensated for all the insured's losses.

Missouri

It does not appear Missouri adheres to the Made Whole Doctrine, but adjusters are encouraged to seek information from subrogation counsel.

Montana

Montana states it is public policy for the insured to be completely reimbursed for all costs, including attorney fees. The carrier may not pursue subrogation until it determines if the insured has been made whole. Medical Payments (Med-Pay) may not be subrogated in an auto policy.

Nebraska

Adheres to the Made Whole Doctrine. The insurer may pursue subrogation after the insured is made whole. The state appears conflicted if a policy can overwrite the doctrine with policy language. Adjusters are encouraged to seek information from subrogation counsel.

Nevada

Nevada appears conflicted about the Made Whole Doctrine. The Supreme Court of Nevada declared the insured must be made whole prior to the carrier seeking reimbursement, but a policy can specifically state that the Made Whole Doctrine does not apply. Adjusters should contact subrogation counsel.

New Hampshire

Adheres to the Made Whole Doctrine as it applies to health carriers. Adjusters are encouraged to seek information

from subrogation counsel. There is no mention of liability or property insurance.

New Jersey

Adheres to the Made Whole Doctrine. The insurer may pursue subrogation after the insured is made whole. The insurance policy can specifically state that the Made Whole Doctrine does not apply, but standard wording of a policy may be insufficient to overcome the doctrine. Therefore, adjusters should seek advice from subrogation counsel.

New Mexico

While New Mexico does not have the Made Whole Doctrine, it does allow for the insurer and insured to split the settlement on a pro-rata basis. Adjusters are encouraged to speak with subrogation counsel.

New York

Adheres to the Made Whole Doctrine. The insurer may pursue subrogation after the insured is made whole. The insured has been made whole when the at-fault party has completely compensated for all the insured's losses.

North Carolina

It does not appear North Carolina adheres to the Made Whole Doctrine, but adjusters are encouraged to seek information from subrogation counsel.

North Dakota

It does not appear North Dakota adheres to the Made Whole Doctrine in regard to health insurers. There is no mention of liability or property insurers, but adjusters are encouraged to seek information from subrogation counsel.

Ohio

Adheres to the Made Whole Doctrine. The insurer may pursue subrogation after the insured is made whole. The insured has been made whole when the at-fault party has completely compensated for all the insured's losses. The insurance policy can specifically state that the Made Whole Doctrine does not apply.

Oklahoma

Adheres to the Made Whole Doctrine. The insurer may pursue subrogation after the insured is made whole. The insured has been made whole when the at-fault party has completely compensated for all the insured's losses. The insurance policy can specifically state that the Made Whole Doctrine does not apply.

Oregon

Oregon appears conflicted about the Made Whole Doctrine. The Court of Appeals declared the insured must be made whole prior to the carrier seeking reimbursement, but the doctrine is not the law of the land. Adjusters should contact subrogation counsel.

Pennsylvania

Adheres to the Made Whole Doctrine. The insurer may pursue subrogation after the insured is made whole which includes attorney fees.

Rhode Island

Adheres to the Made Whole Doctrine. The insurer may pursue subrogation after the insured is made whole. The in-

sured has been made whole when the at-fault party has completely compensated for all the insured's losses. It does not appear the insurance policy can specifically state that the Made Whole Doctrine does not apply.

South Carolina

While South Carolina does not have the Made Whole Doctrine, it does allow for the insurer and insured to split the settlement on a pro-rata basis. However, there is a caveat, in that if the insured believes the carrier is being unfair in taking its portion, subrogation would not be allowed. Adjusters are encouraged to speak with subrogation counsel.

South Dakota

Adheres to the Made Whole Doctrine. The insurer may pursue subrogation after the insured is made whole. The insured has been made whole when the at-fault party has completely compensated for all the insured's losses. The insurance policy can specifically state that the Made Whole Doctrine does not apply.

Tennessee

Adheres to the Made Whole Doctrine. The insurer may pursue subrogation after the insured is made whole. The insured has been made whole when the at-fault party has completely compensated for all the insured's losses. Note: It is the insured who must prove he has not been made whole by his settlement. The insured may spoil the carrier's right of subrogation if he settles with the at-fault party, knowing the carrier will pursue subrogation, and the settlement does not make the insured whole. In other words, if the insured knows the at-fault party's settlement will not fully reimburse him, but he settles anyway, the carrier loses its ability to pursue subrogation from the at-fault party because the insured has admitted he is not being made whole and will never be made whole.

Texas

Texas adheres to the Made Whole Doctrine, but it is one of the most misunderstood provisions. The insurance policy can specifically state that the Made Whole Doctrine does not apply. Note: Texas courts state the party who is filing suit for reimbursement must be the one to demonstrate the insured has been made whole in order to obtain reimbursement. Because this rule is often misunderstood, adjusters are encouraged to speak with subrogation counsel.

Utah

Adheres to the Made Whole Doctrine. The insurer may pursue subrogation after the insured is made whole. The insured has been made whole when the at-fault party has completely compensated for all the insured's losses. The insurance policy can specifically state that the Made Whole Doctrine does not apply.

Vermont

Vermont is odd in that it interprets the sole reason for subrogation to make the insurer, rather than the insured, whole. Adjusters are encouraged to speak with subrogation counsel.

Virginia

Adjusters are encouraged to speak with subrogation counsel.

Washington

Adheres to the Made Whole Doctrine. The insurer may pursue subrogation after the insured is made whole. The insured has been made whole when the at-fault party has completely compensated for all of the insured's losses. Note: The insured is allowed to obtain his general damages (pain and suffering) before the insurer is reimbursed, but the insured must be careful not to do anything that will prejudice the carrier's rights.

West Virginia

Adheres to the Made Whole Doctrine. The insurer may pursue subrogation after the insured is made whole. The insured has been made whole when the at-fault party has completely compensated for all the insured's losses. The insurance policy can specifically state that the Made Whole Doctrine does not apply.

Wisconsin

Adheres to the Made Whole Doctrine. The insurer may pursue subrogation after the insured is made whole. The insured has been made whole when the at-fault party has completely compensated for all the insured's losses. Note: There is a legislatively sanctioned subrogation right which overrides routine subrogation claims. This usually involves uninsured and underinsured motorist coverage as well as Medical Payments (MedPay) coverage, which was not discussed in this book. Adjusters are encouraged to speak with subrogation counsel.

Wyoming

It does not appear Wyoming adheres to the Made Whole Doctrine, but adjusters are encouraged to seek information from subrogation counsel.

Direct-Action States

In most insurance liability claims, in order to reach into the insurer's pocketbook, the third-party claimant must sue the insured who, then, turns to his carrier for a defense. The carrier will evaluate the cost of the lawsuit (often called the "cost of defense") in addition to reviewing the merits of the claim and either settle or fight the suit. However, in Direct-Action States, the legislatures created statutes which avoid this circuitous route and allows the third-party claimant to directly sue the insurer.

This chart is current as of our publication date, but adjusters should be familiar with their own states' rules. I cannot guarantee the accuracy of this list. Because laws and regulations can change without notice, you should contact an attorney if you have any questions regarding this chart. These materials are provided for informational and educational purposes only and do not constitute legal advice or legal opinions because I am not an attorney.

Direct Action States

State	Direct Action	State	Direct Action
Alabama	No	Illinois	No
Alaska	No	Indiana	No
Arizona	No	Iowa	Yes
Arkansas	No	Kansas	Yes
California	No	Kentucky	No
Colorado	No	Louisiana	Yes
Connecticut	Yes	Maine	No
Delaware	No	Maryland	No
District of Columbia	No	Massachusetts	No
Florida	No	Michigan	No
Georgia	Yes	Minnesota	No
Hawaii	No	Mississippi	No
Idaho	No	Missouri	No

State	Direct Action	State	Direct Action
Montana	No	Rhode Island	Yes
Nebraska	Yes	South Carolina	No
Nevada	No	South Dakota	No
New Hampshire	No	Tennessee	No
New Jersey	Yes	Texas	No
New Mexico	No	Utah	No
New York	No	Vermont	No
North Carolina	No	Virginia	No
North Dakota	No	Washington	No
Ohio	No	West Virginia	No
Oklahoma	No	Wisconsin	Yes
Oregon	No	Wyoming	No
Pennsylvania	No		

Direct Action Specifics by State

Alabama
There are no direct-action statutes.

Alaska
There are no direct-action statutes.

Arizona
There are no direct-action statutes.

Arkansas
There are no direct-action statutes.

California
There are no direct-action statutes.

Colorado
There are no direct-action statutes.

Connecticut
Connecticut believes the insurer is legally responsible. Connecticut statute (D.G.S.A. § 38a–321) allows direct action only after the third-party claimant obtains a final judgment against the insured and only if the judgment has not been satisfied within 30 days of proclamation. Note: The third-party claimant, when he seeks payment from the carrier, steps into the shoes of the insured. Therefore, he has the same rights and duties as the insured under the policy and may be subject to any of the policy defenses the carrier had against the insured.

Delaware
There are no direct-action statutes.

District of Columbia
There are no direct-action statutes.

Florida
There are no direct-action statutes.

Georgia
Georgia's direct-action statute (Ga Code Ann § 46–7–12) limits direct-action to motor vehicle claims. Note: There is not a direct-action cause if the accident occurs outside of Georgia.

Hawaii

There are no direct-action statutes.

Idaho

There are no direct-action statutes.

Illinois

There are no direct-action statutes.

Indiana

There are no direct-action statutes.

Iowa

Iowa's direct-action statute (Iowa Code § 516.1) applies to all liability policies issued in Iowa. Note: Before the third-party claimant can bring his direct-action lawsuit, he must show he has a judgment, and it remains unsatisfied.

Kansas

Like Georgia, Kansas limits direct-action to automobile accidents (KS Code § 66–1, 128). Note: The insurer can be the sole party in the suit; in other words, the insured does not need to be a party to the direct-action lawsuit in Kansas.

Kentucky

There are no direct-action statutes.

Louisiana

Louisiana is probably the first state adjusters think about when they hear "direct-action lawsuit." Its broad direct-action statute (La. Rev. Stat. 22:1269) has been attacked throughout the years.

Extremely recently, Act 37 has come into effect—as of January 1, 2021. Under this act, jurors will not be told there is insurance coverage for several reasons, which is beyond the scope of this text. In a twist of logic, the act requires the court to read instructions to the jurors which would inform them there is insurance coverage in place. But the act specifically states the jurors will not be told the identity of the insurer. Adjusters should consult with counsel in this matter.

Maine

There are no direct-action statutes.

Maryland

There are no direct-action statutes.

Massachusetts

There are no direct-action statutes.

Michigan

There are no direct-action statutes.

Minnesota

There are no direct-action statutes.

Mississippi

There are no direct-action statutes.

Missouri

There are no direct-action statutes.

Montana

There are no direct-action statutes.

Nebraska

Again, Nebraska's direct-action statute (Neb Rev Stat § 44–508) is limited to auto accidents. It is further limited to cases involving the insured's bankruptcy or inability to satisfy a judgment.

Nevada

There are no direct-action statutes.

New Hampshire

There are no direct-action statutes.

New Jersey

New Jersey, like other states, has a limited direct-action statute (NJ Rev. Stat.

§ 17:28–2) for automobile accidents. However, the damage must be caused by animals.[26] Note: Third-party claimants do not have the right to sue for bad faith in their direct-action lawsuits.

New Mexico
There are no direct-action statutes.

New York
There are no direct-action statutes.

North Carolina
There are no direct-action statutes.

North Dakota
There are no direct-action statutes.

Ohio
There are no direct-action statutes.

Oklahoma
There are no direct-action statutes.

Oregon
There are no direct-action statutes.

Pennsylvania
There are no direct-action statutes.

Rhode Island
The third-party claimant can only pursue a direct-action against the insurer when he has obtained a judgment solely against the insured (RI Gen Laws § 27–7–2). Note: The claimant can begin a direct-action lawsuit against the carrier if he can convince a jury that he made a good faith effort to serve the insured.

South Carolina
There are no direct-action statutes.

South Dakota
There are no direct-action statutes.

Tennessee
There are no direct-action statutes.

Texas
There are no direct-action statutes.

Utah
There are no direct-action statutes.

Vermont
There are no direct-action statutes.

Virginia
There are no direct-action statutes.

Washington
There are no direct-action statutes.

West Virginia
There are no direct-action statutes.

Wisconsin
Like Iowa, Wisconsin direct-action statute (§ 632.24) applies to all types of liability policies. It expands the statute to include bonds and does not require the third-party claimant to obtain a judgment against the insured prior to commencing suit.

Wyoming
There are no direct-action statutes.

---

26 I think this is meant to allow third-party claimants to sue a carrier directly for "free-range" animals. Clearly deer, armadillos, and mosquitos don't have policies with Animal, Nature, Insect Mutual Assurance, LLC (ANIMAL). Adjusters should seek advice of counsel.

Independent Counsel States

In Chapter 6, I discussed the requirement to retain a second (or third, depending on how you look at it) attorney if a Reservation of Rights letter is sent to the insured. The reasoning for this is the belief that coverage issues create a conflict of interest between the insurer and the insured.

As a side note, the duty to provide independent counsel arises when there is a material conflict of interest between the insurer and the insured. This means the insurer reserves its right to deny coverage based on the result of a disputed issue.

This chart is current as of our publication date, but adjusters should be familiar with their own states' rules. I cannot guarantee the accuracy of this list. Because laws and regulations can change without notice, you should contact an attorney if you have any questions regarding this chart. These materials are provided for informational and educational purposes only and do not constitute legal advice or legal opinions because I am not an attorney.

Independent Counsel States

State	Independent Counsel Needed	State	Independent Counsel Needed
Alabama	No	Illinois	Maybe
Alaska	Yes	Indiana	No
Arizona	No	Iowa	Maybe
Arkansas	Maybe	Kansas	Yes
California	Yes—commonly called *Cumis* Counsel	Kentucky	No
Colorado	No	Louisiana	Maybe
Connecticut	No	Maine	No
Delaware	Maybe	Maryland	Yes
District of Columbia	Maybe	Massachusetts	Yes
Florida	Yes	Michigan	Maybe
Georgia	Maybe	Minnesota	Maybe
Hawaii	No	Mississippi	Yes—commonly called *Moeller* Counsel
Idaho	No	Missouri	Yes

State	Independent Counsel Needed	State	Independent Counsel Needed
Montana	Yes	Rhode Island	Yes
Nebraska	No	South Carolina	No
Nevada	Yes	South Dakota	Yes
New Hampshire	Yes	Tennessee	No
New Jersey	Yes	Texas	Yes
New Mexico	Yes	Utah	Maybe
New York	Maybe	Vermont	No
North Carolina	No	Virginia	No
North Dakota	No	Washington	No
Ohio	Maybe	West Virginia	No
Oklahoma	Maybe	Wisconsin	Yes
Oregon	No	Wyoming	Maybe
Pennsylvania	Yes		

Independent Counsel Specifics by State

Alabama

There is no requirement for independent counsel.

Alaska

If there is a conflict between the insurer and the insured, independent counsel is needed. Alaska has determined that the following do not constitute a conflict of interest: (1) a claim for punitive damages; (2) a claim of damages in excess of the policy limits; (3) claims in a lawsuit where the carrier denies coverage, unless the insurer reserves its right on the issue for which coverage is denied. See Alaska Stat. §21.89.100(b) and (c).

Arizona

There is no requirement for independent counsel.

Arkansas

There is no requirement for independent counsel according to the State of Arkansas. However, Federal District courts in Arkansas believe that the insured has a right to select independent counsel.

California

The California legislature adopted Cal. Civ. Code Ann. §2860 to address an insured's right to independent counsel. This codified the court decision in *San Diego Navy Fed. Credit Union v. Cumis Ins. Soc'y*, 208 Cal. Rptr. 494 (Cal. Ct.

App. 1984) which prompted adjusters everywhere to ubiquitously refer to independent counsel as "*Cumis* counsel."

There are times when a conflict does not exist per California, such as when punitive damages or demands in excess of policy limits are claimed. Not every Reservation of Rights letter creates a conflict of interest; the conflict is created when coverage is dependent on the facts in the lawsuit.

Finally, there are several caveats regarding independent counsel, such as Cumis counsel must have at lease "five years of civil litigation practice which includes substantial defense experience in the subject at issue in the litigation," and the insured may waive his right to independent counsel.

Colorado

There is no requirement for independent counsel.

Connecticut

There is no requirement for independent counsel.

Delaware

There is no requirement for independent counsel, but a trial court opined that if there is a conflict of interest, the insurer should provide independent counsel. Confusingly, the court referred to the attorney assigned by the insurer as "independent counsel."

District of Columbia

If an insured can prove a conflict of interest exists, he is entitled to independent counsel.

Florida

While Florida recognizes the right to independent counsel, it believes the ethical rules governing attorneys are sufficient to protect the insured. Therefore, both the insured and the insurer must be "mutually" agreed to the choice of the attorney. In the instance of a reservation of rights for late notice, the insured may have the ability to choose his counsel without agreement of the insurer. See Fla. Stat. § 627.426(2) regarding the insurer's ability to deny the claim.

Georgia

There is no requirement for independent counsel per the State of Georgia, but like Arkansas, the 11th Circuit Court of Appeals opined there is a need for independent counsel. The court stated it relied on George law but didn't quote which law it was referring to.

Hawaii

There is no requirement for independent counsel.

Idaho

There is no requirement for independent counsel.

Illinois

Illinois appears to be conflicted in this matter, and it is best to consult coverage counsel. While the Appellate Court of Illinois refused to opine that a reservation of rights automatically creates a conflict of interest, it also stated that the insurer's right in negating coverage does not create an adequate conflict to prevent it from defending the insured.

Indiana

There is no requirement for independent counsel.

Iowa

There is no requirement for independent counsel. However, there is a court case which stated that if the insured is prejudiced by the insurer's defense, a conflict could exist and independent counsel could be needed. See *First Newton Nat'l. Bank v. General Cas. Co.*, 426 N.W.2d 618, 630 (Iowa 1988) (citing *Howard v. Russell Stover Candies, Inc.* 649 F.2d 620, 625 (8th Cir. 1981).

Kansas

The Supreme Court of Kansas held that if there is a conflict of interest between the insured and the insurer as discussed in the Reservation of Rights letter, the correct way to resolve the issue is for the insurer to hire independent counsel to defend the insured.

Kentucky

There is no requirement for independent counsel.

Louisiana

If an insured can prove a conflict of interest exists, then he is entitled to independent counsel. The main issue, as with all the states which permit independent counsel, revolves around determining if a conflict of interest is created when comparing the allegations in the suit to the policy and if the insurer provides a "less than vigorous defense" to the insured.

Maine

There is no requirement for independent counsel.

Maryland

A reservation of rights does not automatically create a conflict, but independent counsel must be appointed in the event of an actual conflict. Similar to Alaska, demands for amounts in excess of policy limits do not automatically create a conflict.

Massachusetts

Massachusetts' Supreme Judicial Court held that a reservation of rights creates a conflict, and the insurer will pay for the insured's independent counsel.

Michigan

If an insured can prove a conflict of interest exists, he is entitled to independent counsel.

Minnesota

An actual conflict of interest, rather than the appearance of a conflict, is the trigger for independent counsel. The Minnesota courts advise insurers to file a Declaratory Judgment Action on the coverage issue prior to trial in order to avoid the issue of a conflict of interest.

Mississippi

Mississippi's Supreme Court, like Massachusetts, believes that a reservation of rights letter creates a per se conflict of interest, but the conflict is only for the claim parts which the insurer has reserved rights on. See *Moeller v. Am. Guarantee & Liab. Ins. Co.*, 707 So. 2d 1062, 1071 (Miss. 1996).

Missouri

Insurers must provide independent counsel to the insured. The insured may reject the insurer's defense under a reservation of rights; if he does, the insurer has three options: (1) defend without a reservation of rights; (2) withdraw from defending the insured; or (3) file a Declaratory Judgment Action to determine coverage.

Montana

Insurers must provide independent counsel to the insured based on the Montana Supreme Court. See *Safeco Ins. Co. v. Liss*, 2005 Mont. Dist. LEXIS 1073, at *40–*41 (Mont. Dist. Ct. Mar. 11, 2005 and *State Farm Fire and Cas. Co. v. Schwan*, 308 P.3d 48 (Mont. 2013).

Nebraska

There is no requirement for independent counsel.

Nevada

In 2015 Nevada's Supreme Court, inspired by California's Cumis rule, stated the insurer is obligated to provide independent counsel when there is a conflict.

New Hampshire

If there is a conflict of interest, the insurer must provide independent counsel to the insured.

New Jersey

If there is a conflict of interest, the insurer must provide independent counsel to the insured. When a reservation of rights is issued, the insurer can only control the defense with the insured's consent; therefore, it is possible that independent counsel does not have to be used.

New Mexico

New Mexico seems to agree with other states in that if there is a conflict, and the insured objects to the reservation of rights, the insurer can pay for independent counsel or insist the insured himself pay for the independent counsel. *See Rhode Island.*

New York

If the insurer defends under a reservation of rights, the insured is permitted to have independent counsel. Earlier court decisions opined that independent counsel was not needed in unless the defense counsel was placed in a conflict of serving two masters with opposing interests. It would be beneficial to discuss with coverage counsel.

North Carolina

There is no requirement for independent counsel.

North Dakota

There is no requirement for independent counsel.

Ohio

If there is a conflict of interest, the insurer must provide independent counsel to the insured. However, the Ohio Appeals Court did not say that a reservation of rights automatically grants independent counsel.

Oklahoma

Oklahoma is very nearly word for word like New York. It is best to speak with coverage counsel.

Oregon

There is no requirement for independent counsel.

Pennsylvania

If there is a conflict of interest, the insurer must provide independent counsel to the insured. Punitive damages are uninsurable in Pennsylvania, and a denial does not represent a conflict of interest requiring that the insurer provide independent counsel to the insured.

Rhode Island

New Mexico seems to agree with other states in that if there is a conflict, and the insured objects to the reservation of rights, the insurer can pay for independent counsel or insist the insured himself pay for the independent counsel. *See New Mexico.*

South Carolina

There is no requirement for independent counsel. Like Florida, South Carolina believes the South Carolina Rules of Professional Conduct for attorneys bars her from representing parties with conflicting interests; so, it is the attorney's ethical duty to determine if a conflict exists.

South Dakota

If there is a conflict of interest, the insurer must provide independent counsel to the insured.

Tennessee

There is no requirement for independent counsel. Again, Tennessee believes an attorney's Rules of Professional Conduct bars him from representing parties with conflicting interests. Interestingly, if the insured hires independent counsel himself, he is not entitled to reimbursement for that attorney's costs.

Texas

If there is a conflict of interest, the insurer must provide independent counsel to the insured. Not only must the insurer pay for the independent counsel but also a non-waiver does not allow the insurer to shirk its payment responsibility. There are some carve-outs to this rule, such as when the insurer defends unconditionally.

Utah

Utah has a conflicted view of independent counsel, and it is best to discuss with coverage counsel. The Eighth Circuit Court of Appeals believes it is impossible for an attorney to "adequately and fairly represent two parties in litigation," but does not believe a reservation of rights creates a conflict.

Vermont

There is no requirement for independent counsel.

Virginia

There is no requirement for independent counsel.

Washington

There is no requirement for independent counsel.

West Virginia

There is no requirement for independent counsel.

Wisconsin

If there is a conflict of interest, the insurer must provide independent counsel to the insured. An actual conflict of interest based on opposing defenses of insured and the coverage analysis of the insurer must exist.

Wyoming

It is best to discuss with coverage counsel. There are no cases on this issue, but a 1995 court case opined that when an insurer reserves rights it loses the right to control the defense.

Depreciation of Labor States

Chapter 10 discusses depreciation and three methods for determining Actual Cash Value (ACV). Depreciation is a hotly debated topic in the insurance world. Everyone knows materials like two-by-fours and roofs are depreciable. The question that comes into play is whether intangible things, such as labor, can be depreciated.

Courts vary on their interpretation of ACV, but almost all have supported the depreciation of intangibles like labor and even taxes if the policy specifically allows for it. Therefore, while a state may say "no" in this chart, if the policy allows for it, you might be able to depreciate across the board. I, again, urge you to speak with an attorney about this if there is a question.

This chart is current as of our publication date, but adjusters should be familiar with their own states' rules. I cannot guarantee the accuracy of this list. Because laws and regulations can change without notice, you should contact an attorney if you have any questions regarding this chart. These materials are provided for informational and educational purposes only and do not constitute legal advice or legal opinions because I am not an attorney.

Depreciation of Labor States

State	Depreciation of Labor	State	Depreciation of Labor
Alabama	Maybe	Iowa	Unknown
Alaska	Unknown	Kansas	Yes
Arizona	Unknown	Kentucky	Maybe
Arkansas	Yes	Louisiana	Unknown
California	No	Maine	Unknown
Colorado	Maybe	Maryland	Unknown
Connecticut	Unknown	Massachusetts	Unknown
Delaware	Unknown	Michigan	Unknown
District of Columbia	Unknown	Minnesota	Maybe
Florida	Yes	Mississippi	Yes, with limitations
Georgia	Unknown	Missouri	Yes
Hawaii	Unknown	Montana	No
Idaho	Unknown	Nebraska	Yes
Illinois	Maybe	Nevada	Unknown
Indiana	Yes	New Hampshire	Unknown

State	Depreciation of Labor	State	Depreciation of Labor
New Jersey	Unknown	South Dakota	Unknown
New Mexico	Unknown	Tennessee	No
New York	Unknown	Texas	Maybe
North Carolina	Yes	Utah	Unknown
North Dakota	Unknown	Vermont	No
Ohio	Maybe	Virginia	Unknown
Oklahoma	Yes	Washington	No
Oregon	Unknown	West Virginia	Unknown
Pennsylvania	Yes, with exceptions	Wisconsin	Unknown
Rhode Island	Unknown	Wyoming	Unknown
South Carolina	Yes		

Depreciation of Labor Specifics by State

Alabama

Maybe. Depending on the policy's definition of ACV, depreciation of labor may be allowed. ACV must be defined as physical deterioration, depreciation, and/or obsolescence. If the policy remains mute on the subject, then the insurer may not depreciate labor.

Alaska

There is no court case or regulation specifically discussing this point.

Arizona

There is no court case or regulation specifically discussing this point.

Arkansas

Ark. Code Ann. § 23-88-106 allows the depreciation of labor starting August 1, 2017. The policy, however, must have specific, preapproved language for this to be effective.

California

State regulation 10 C.C.R. § 2695.9(f)(1) does not allow the depreciation of labor.

Colorado

Yes, labor may be depreciated by an insurer when determining ACV. See *Basham v. United Servs. Auto. Ass'n*, No. 16-cv-03057, 2017 U.S. Dist. LEXIS 118729 (D. Colo. July 28, 2017).

The Colorado Division of Insurance states in Bulletin No. B-5.1, which is dated May 8, 2007, "Insurers shall be prohibited from deducting contractors' overhead and profit in addition to depreciation when policyholders do not repair or replace the structure."

Connecticut

There is no court case or regulation specifically discussing this point.

Delaware

There is no court case or regulation specifically discussing this point.

District of Columbia

Unknown.

Florida

An insurer may depreciate labor costs.

Georgia

There is no court case or regulation specifically discussing this point.

Hawaii

There is no court case or regulation specifically discussing this point.

Idaho

There is no court case or regulation specifically discussing this point.

Illinois

Maybe. Illinois state law does not automatically allow insurers to depreciate labor. It's best to seek advice of counsel.

Indiana

An insurer may depreciate labor.

Iowa

There is no court case or regulation specifically discussing this point.

Kansas

An insurer may depreciate labor.

Kentucky

Kentucky state courts have refused to answer the question regarding labor depreciation. Federal court stated labor should not be depreciated when ACV is not defined in the policy. It's best to seek advice of counsel.

Louisiana

There is no court case or regulation specifically discussing this point.

Maine

There is no court case or regulation specifically discussing this point.

Maryland

There is no court case or regulation specifically discussing this point.

Massachusetts

There is no court case or regulation specifically discussing this point.

Michigan

There is no court case or regulation specifically discussing this point.

Minnesota

Minnesota appears to take depreciation of labor on a case-by-case basis. It's best to seek advice of counsel.

Mississippi

Yes, with limitations. The Mississippi Insurance Department stated in Bulletin 2017-8 that no law in Mississippi prohibits depreciation of labor, but if an insurer is going to do it, it should clearly state so in the policy. In a 2020 case, the Fifth Circuit Court of Appeals, reading Mississippi law, denied an insurer's motion to dismiss because "actual cash value" was not defined in the policy. Both the insurer and the insured had reasonable interpretations of the term; therefore, the court sided with the insured.

Missouri

An insurer may depreciate labor unless the policy strictly prohibits it.

Montana

Montana Code Ann. § 33-24-10 does not allow for depreciation of labor. The Montana Insurance Commissioner issued an Advisory Memorandum reinforcing the idea that labor may not be depreciated in property claims.

Nebraska
An insurer may depreciate labor because a Nebraska court found that ACV is depreciation of the entire item, and the insured would not be "underindemnified by receiving the depreciated amount of both materials and labor." See Henn v. American Family Mut. Ins. Co., 894 N.W.2d 179 (Neb. 2017)

Nevada
There is no court case or regulation specifically discussing this point.

New Hampshire
There is no court case or regulation specifically discussing this point.

New Jersey
There is no court case or regulation specifically discussing this point.

New Mexico
There is no court case or regulation specifically discussing this point.

New York
There is no court case or regulation specifically discussing this point.

North Carolina
In a 2020 decision, a North Carolina court stated labor costs may be depreciated in determining ACV.

North Dakota
There is no court case or regulation specifically discussing this point.

Ohio
Maybe. In 2020, the 6th Circuit Court of Appeals, in looking at Ohio law, found that an insurer cannot depreciate labor if the policy does not define depreciation. This is a more modern interpretation than the Ohio Department of Insurance which conducted a market survey in 2011 and found the depreciation of labor to be an "exception."

Oklahoma
Yes, insurers may depreciate labor in the determination of ACV.

Oregon
There is no court case or regulation specifically discussing this point.

Pennsylvania
Yes, with exceptions. If there is a partial loss, absent language in the policy, the insurer may not depreciate labor. Contrarily, if the policy defines ACV as "the cost to repair or replace the damaged property less deduction for physical deterioration (depreciation) and obsolescence..." (London v. Insurance Placement Facility, 703 A.2d 45, 49-50 (Pa. Super. Ct. 1997)) and a RCV policy as one that provides actual cash value payment until repairs are completed, then depreciation of labor is permissible. One court found it acceptable to depreciate labor and tax if there is a "holdback" of the depreciation until repairs are complete See Papurello v. State Farm Fire & Cas. Co., No. 15-1005, 2015 U.S. Dist. LEXIS 154536 (W.D. Pa. Nov. 16, 2015). It's best to seek advice of counsel.

Rhode Island
There is no court case or regulation specifically discussing this point.

South Carolina
As of May 12, 2021, the court found a carrier can depreciate the cost of labor when the estimated cost to repair or re-

place the property includes both materials and embedded labor components.

South Dakota
There is no court case or regulation specifically discussing this point.

Tennessee
The Tennessee Supreme Court stated insurers may not depreciate labor.

Texas
Maybe. A Texas court suggested that labor costs may be depreciated. In Tolar v. Allstate Texas Lloyd's Co., 772 F. Supp. 2d 825, 831 (N.D. Tex. 2011), the court determined that "(b)ecause GCOP (General Contractor Overhead & Profit), sales tax, repair costs, and property value together represent the total replacement cost value, it follows naturally that GCOP, sales tax, repair costs, and property value ought to be depreciated together to reach the ACV payment." There are other cases which state repair costs may not be depreciated for partial losses.

These cases are newer than the Texas Department of Insurance bulletin which states "The deduction of prospective contractors' overhead and profit and sales tax in determining the actual cash value under a replacement cost policy is improper, is not a reasonable interpretation of the policy language, and is unfair to insureds." (B-0045098) The insurance commission further stated in 2008's bulletin B-0068-08 that the deduction of GCOP and sales tax is akin to an unfair settlement practice and in violation of Insurance Code §541.060 and §542.003 and Texas Administrative Code Title 28, §21.203. It's best to seek advice of counsel.

Utah
There is no court case or regulation specifically discussing this point.

Vermont
The department of insurance states that labor does not break down or lose value over time. Therefore, depreciation of labor is prohibited by "8 V.S.A. § 4724(9)(F) and is an unfair claim settlement practice in violation of 8 V.S.A. § 4723 (the Vermont Insurance Trade Practices Act)." See Insurance Bulletin Number 184.

Virginia
There is no court case or regulation specifically discussing this point.

Washington
No. In a 2016 court opinion the court opined that policy language was ambiguous when the insured depreciated labor costs. The court said the policy defined ACV as "the amount it costs to repair or replace property with like kind and quality less depreciation for physical deterioration and obsolescence." See Lains v. American Family Mut. Ins. Co., No. C14-1982-JCC, 2016 WL 4533075, at *2 (W.D. Wash. Feb. 2, 2016).

West Virginia
There is no court case or regulation specifically discussing this point.

Wisconsin
There is no court case or regulation specifically discussing this point.

Wyoming
There is no court case or regulation specifically discussing this point.

Sample Letters

This section of the Appendix offers sample letters. They are honed from my 22 years as an adjuster. I realize nearly every insurer has its own form letters which may be better than my sample letters. However, the insurer may be trying too hard to check too many boxes, and the letters might not quite fit. Or, adjusters don't have the training to know when or why they are updating the letters. Hopefully these explanations and examples help.

Reservation of Rights Letters

Some insurers insist that coverage counsel pen reservation of rights letters. In some instances, this is a good idea, but for the most part, attorney ROR letters are convoluted and difficult to understand. Plus, departments of insurance don't necessarily like them, and there may be the fact that privilege between the attorney and the insurer has been pierced. The key thing to note in an ROR is to say "coverage may not apply." It may not apply because you, as the adjuster, have not finished your investigation yet.

I want to point out that I created several coverage issues for the sample letter. The reason is that it is good form to separate the coverage issues and policy language to make the letter easier for the insured to read and understand.

Declination Letters

The letter of declination is almost the same as an ROR, except it will say that "coverage does not apply." Unlike the ROR, you wouldn't necessarily rub salt into the wound and announce in great big letters "YOUR CLAIM IS DENIED." First, that's rude; second, it's best to have some compassion for your insured.

Another way to think about this is to think that the Reservation of Rights letter closes a door to coverage, but opens a window, so if there has been a mistake in the investigation, the adjuster can correct it. A declination letter will close the window.

Also, a quick word of warning: When you tell the insured that such-and-such is not covered by the policy, that is a verbal denial. Failing to follow up with a written letter outlining the policy language is a breach of good-faith claims handling practices. An unfortunate number of adjusters do not send that letter out.

Subrogation Letters

There is usually nothing wrong with the insurer's subrogation letter. In fact, they usually have entire departments devoted to nothing but subrogation, and those adjusters can be very precise because it is what they do, day in and day out.

In this example, I've alerted our fictitious at-fault carrier to the fact the insured has some uncovered expenses that will need to be reimbursed. Insurers can do this since, for the most part, the insured must be completely reimbursed before they receive subrogation funds. However, if the at-fault carrier does not want to pay the first-party carrier, that is their right, and if the first-party carrier must seek arbitration to enforce the subrogation, it would only be able to do so for the funds it paid. Therefore, the adjuster would be wise to pen a letter confirming this with the insured to avoid later misunderstandings.

The sample estimate has a sublimit for slab leaks. This means the most the insurer can pay is the damage up to the sublimit policy limit of $2,500. If the total damages were $953.84, that would be the most the insurer would pay for this type of loss; in our instance, our damages go over this amount. I ignored the sublimit for the settlement letters in order to show a "clean" settlement letter. Just pretend, for this letter, the insured has recoverable depreciation, he's completed repairs, and there is no sublimit.

30-Day Letters

Nearly every department of insurance has a deadline for settling a first-party claim. Some deadlines are 15 days; some are 45 days. At my previous adjusting companies, we simply called this message a "30-day letter," since it was a letter which would go out every 30 days to let the insured know why we couldn't settle the claim. The good-faith claims handling guidelines from state departments also explain that if the insurer cannot settle a claim within that time, it needs to inform the insured.

How the carrier informs the insured is up to the carrier if it is not spelled out in the guidelines (for example, written correspondence). I strongly recommend a letter. The letter can be emailed, but I recommend some version of a letter.

The reason is simple: a letter is a formal document. An email is not. If the adjuster updates the insured about his claim via email by simply saying, "I am still waiting for your contractor to send me his prices on the supplemental damages he discovered," this does not convey the weight of a letter attached as an email. Further an insured could miss the fact that this is an actual update to his claim.

Settlement Letters

Depending on the carrier, the settlement letter can simply be something as simple as "Here's your check." This does not meet with the majority of departments of insurance definitions explaining how the payment applies to each coverage. Other carriers have the insured sign a proof of loss prior to sending a check. Both letters are shown. These letters don't necessarily follow the estimate at the back of the book because I'm attempting to show how a letter might look. However, there are so many iterations of claims, settlements, and policies that writing sample letters for each scenario could likely be a book in itself.

Some states like Texas and California want the insured to be notified of any and all offers made to the claimant for liability policies. There are examples of those letters.

I also included sample denial liability letters.

Finally, there is an estimate which I used in the book and referenced in the letters.

Sample Reservation of Rights Letter

Date

Via Email and Certified Return Receipt Requested:
Insured@insured.com
(certified receipt number)

NOTICE OF RESERVATION OF RIGHTS

Insured Name
Insured Address
Insured City, State, Zip

Re: Insured:
     Policy Number:
     Date of Loss:
     Company File Number:

Dear Insured:

I received notice of an occurrence that took place at (insured property address) on (date of loss).[27] I am the adjuster investigating the loss you sustained as a result of (peril).

The insurance policy issued to (Named Insured) provides coverage subject to the terms and conditions listed in the policy. As a result of this occurrence and my investigation, a coverage question has arisen under (policy number). Please note that I am continuing to investigate your loss under a reservation of rights, and upon completion of my investigation, I will provide you with my coverage opinion.

The nature of the coverage question is as follows:

You stated your property at (insured property address) sustained (peril) on (date of loss).[28]

You stated your property at 123 Apple St., Idyllic Town, SC, 55555 sustained interior water damage from a burst pipe on 02/01/2020. You have an CP 00 10 10/12 base form and a CP 10 30 10/12 special causes of loss form. There may not be coverage for your interior water damage under Policy HO98876 which states interior water damage from a burst pipe may not be

---

27 I find most letters are written in first person, plural (we/us/our/ours). Why? I've been told it's because the adjuster is representing the insurer. Poppycock! The adjuster already represents the insurer. The adjuster is not the Queen of England. Own the file. Own the investigation. Use first person, singular (I/me/my/mine).

28 For the sake of the letter, I am filling in the blanks here so you are better able to see what the letter should look like.

covered unless you do your best to maintain heat in the building or turn off the water. I draw your attention to the following policy language located on pages 1, 3-4 of 20 of the CP 10 30 10/12 special cause of loss form:

A. Covered Causes of Loss

When Special is shown in the Declarations, Covered Causes of Loss means direct physical loss unless the loss is excluded or limited in this policy.

B. Exclusions

1. *We will not pay for loss or damage caused directly or indirectly by any of the following. Such loss or damage is excluded regardless of any other cause or event that contributes concurrently or in any sequence to the loss.*

   ...

2. *We will not pay for loss or damage caused by or resulting from any of the following:*

   ...

   g. *Water, other liquids, powder or molten material that leaks or flows from plumbing, heating, air conditioning or other equipment (except fire protective systems) caused by or resulting from freezing, unless:*

      (1) *You do your best to maintain heat in the building or structure; or*
      (2) *You drain the equipment and shut off the supply if the heat is not maintained.*

You told me in our conversation of February 16, 2020, you did not turn off or drain the water to the structure and the heat was maintained at 65 degrees. However, when the appraiser inspected the property, he found the thermostat set at 55 degrees. Therefore, the heat may not have been adequate for the building.

Further, the appraiser reports the building is vacant. There may not be coverage for water damage to your structure if the building is vacant based on pages 1 and 12 of 16 of the CP 00 10 10/12 base form, which defines a vacant building as one that has ongoing operations in at least 31% of the structure:

A. Coverage

We will pay for direct physical loss of or damage to Covered Property at the premises described in the Declarations caused by or resulting from any Covered Cause of Loss.

...

6. *Vacancy*

    a. *Description Of Terms*

        (1) *As used in this Vacancy Condition, the term building and the term vacant have the meanings set forth in (1)(a) and (1)(b) below:*

            (a) *When this policy is issued to a tenant, and with respect to that tenant's interest in Covered Property, building means the unit or suite rented or leased to the tenant. Such building is vacant when it does not contain enough business personal property to conduct customary operations.*

            (b) *When this policy is issued to the owner or general lessee of a building, building means the entire building. Such building is vacant unless at least 31% of its total square footage is:*

                (i) *Rented to a lessee or sublessee and used by the lessee or sublessee to conduct its customary operations; and/or*

                (ii) *Used by the building owner to conduct customary operations.*

        (2) *Buildings under construction or renovation are not considered vacant.*

The appraiser reports the entire structure did not have ongoing business operations in it. You informed the appraiser the structure had been vacant for three (3) years. Therefore, there may not be coverage for the interior water damage based on the following policy language in the special form cause CP 00 10 10/12 pages 1 and 12 of 16 which states:

A. *Coverage*

We will pay for direct physical loss of or damage to Covered Property at the premises described in the Declarations caused by or resulting from any Covered Cause of Loss.

...

    b. *Vacancy Provisions*

If the building where loss or damage occurs has been vacant for more than 60 consecutive days before that loss or damage occurs:

> *(1) We will not pay for any loss or damage caused by any of the following, even if they are Covered Causes of Loss:*
>
> *(a) Vandalism;*
>
> *(b) Sprinkler leakage, unless you have protected the system against freezing;*
>
> *(c) Building glass breakage;*
>
> *(d) Water damage;*
>
> *(e) Theft; or*
>
> *(f) Attempted theft.*

At this time, it has not been determined if your policy applies to this loss. I will continue to investigate your loss, but I wanted to bring the above policy provision to your attention. No act by me or a company representative while investigating, negotiating settlement of the claim or defending a lawsuit shall be construed as waving, invalidating, forfeiting or modifying any of the insurer's rights and defenses under the policy we have issued.

There may be other reasons why coverage may not apply. Please note that other provisions of your policy which may be relevant to your loss are also reserved herein and (the carrier) reserves the right to rely on all such provisions. It is (the carrier's) intent to incorporate by reference all the terms and conditions of the policy through this reservation of rights. Further (the carrier) reserves the right to deny coverage at a later date based on any and all conditions, exclusions, and other limiting provisions of the policy and circumstances of the loss.

If you have information or documentation which you feel is important to my adjustment of this claim, please forward it to me for review.

If you have any questions or concerns, please do not hesitate to contact me.

Sincerely,
Adjuster
Title
Phone number
Email address

Enc: Policy language

cc: Retail Agent
RetailAgent@retailagent.com

Sample Letter of Declination

Date

Via Email and Certified Return Receipt Requested:
Insured@insured.com
(certified receipt number)

Insured Name
Insured Address
Insured City, State, Zip

Re: Insured:
 Policy Number:
 Date of Loss:
 Company File Number:

Dear Insured:

I received notice of an occurrence that took place at (insured property address) on (date of loss). I am the adjuster investigating the loss you sustained as a result of (peril).

The insurance policy issued to (Named Insured) provides coverage, subject to the terms and conditions listed in the policy. I completed my investigation into your (type of loss) at (property) on (date of loss).

Recap of the first coverage issue. Mention the policy which applies to the loss. Tell how the policy does not apply to the loss.

Quote the Policy

Recap of the second coverage issue. Mention the policy which applies to the loss. Tell how the policy does not apply to the loss.

Quote the Policy

Based upon the results of my investigation and the policy language noted above, (First-Party Carrier) is unable to afford coverage for the damages to your property because the policy excludes coverage for (cause of loss). No payment will be issued for this loss at this time.

No act by me or a company representative while investigating, negotiating settlement of the claim, or defending a lawsuit shall be construed as waving, invalidating, forfeiting, or modifying any of the insurer's rights and defenses under the policy we have issued.

There may be other reasons why coverage may not apply. Please note that other provisions of your policy which may be relevant to your loss are also reserved herein and (First-Party Carrier) expressly reserves all of its rights under the policy, including any additional grounds for disclaimer of coverage, including but not limited to those set forth above, if subsequent information indicates that such action is warranted. It is (the carrier's) intent to incorporate by reference all the terms and conditions of the policy through this reservation of rights. Further (the carrier) reserves the right to deny coverage at a later date based on any and all conditions, exclusions, and other limiting provisions of the policy and circumstances of the loss.

Please be advised that my coverage position is based on the information currently available to me. If you have any information that would alter our coverage position concerning this matter, please forward it to us for further evaluation.

If you have any questions or concerns, please do not hesitate to contact me.

Sincerely,
Adjuster
Title
Phone number
Email address

Enc: Policy language

cc: Retail Agent
       RetailAgent@retailagent.com

Sample Subrogation Letter

Date

Via Email and Regular Mail:
AtFaultCarrierAdjuster@atfaultcarrier.com

At Fault Carrier Adjuster
At Fault Carrier
At Fault Carrier Address
Insured City, State, Zip

Re: My Insured:
    My Policy Number:
    Date of Loss:
    My Company File Number:
    Your Insured:
    Your Policy Number:
    Your Company File Number

Dear At Fault Adjuster:

I received notice of an occurrence that took place at (insured property address) on (date of loss). I am the adjuster investigating the loss (My Insured) sustained as a result of (peril).

My investigation reveals (Your Insured) is at fault for this loss. Therefore, I am seeking rights of subrogation for moneys we paid to (My Insured). The total amount of damages is $15,000. This figure was determined in the following manner:

Whole Loss and Damage to (Insured property)	$10,000
My Insured Deductible	$1,000
Net Payment by (1st Party Insurance Carrier)	$9,000
Uncovered Expenses Incurred by (My Insured)	$4,000
Total Owed to (1st Party Insurance Carrier)	$9,000
Total Owed to (My Insured)	$5,000

(My Insured) asked that I pursue subrogation on his behalf for the uncovered expenses. If you would like, you may make a check for $5,000 to (My Insured) and another check for ($9,000) to (First-Party Carrier) as subrogee for (My Insured). You may mail the check(s) to:

Insurance Company Information

If you have any questions or concerns, please do not hesitate to contact me.

Sincerely,
Adjuster   .
Title
Phone number
Email address

Enclosure: Police Report
              Estimate
              Receipts
              Copies of Checks

cc: My insured
       (Without his email or physical address)

Sample Settlement Letter Without Proof of Loss

Date

Via Email:
Insured@insured.com

Insured Name
Insured Address
Insured City, State, Zip

Re: Insured:
     Policy Number:
     Date of Loss:
     Company File Number:

Dear Insured:

I received notice of an occurrence that took place at (insured property address) on (date of loss). I am the adjuster investigating the loss you sustained as a result of (peril).

Enclosed is an estimate and a check made payable to (First-Party Insured) and (Anyone Else?) for $6,674.65. This figure was determined in the following manner:

Whole Loss and Damage (Building)	$9,382.54
Whole Loss and Damage (Contents)	$1,368.04
Less Deductible	$2,500.00
Less Recoverable Depreciation	$1,575.93
Net Settlement	**$6,674.65**

You bought replacement cost coverage on your policy; therefore, you have recoverable depreciation available up to the amount of $1,575.93. In order to avail yourself of this coverage, you must notify us and repair or replace the property within 6 months (180 days), per your policy. Please keep your receipts for the repair or purchase of new items for my review.

Please note, (First-Party Carrier) is unable to instruct your contractors to begin repairs. If additional damages are discovered, please contact me immediately.[29]

If you have any questions or concerns, please do not hesitate to contact me.

Sincerely,
Adjuster
Title
Phone number
Email address

Enc: Estimate
     Check

---

29 Insureds and claimants often ask the adjuster if they have the insurer's permission to begin repairs. This is a double-edge sword. On the one hand, insurer's do not own the property, so they cannot authorize repairs. On the other, the insurer must see the damage to write an estimate. On the third hand, insureds and claimants have heard horror stories about adjusters denying newly discovered or additional damages because repairs have begun; therefore, they want assurances it's OK to begin repairs. Remember, they are not familiar with the claims process. My best method is to tell the insured or claimant, I cannot authorize repairs because I don't own the property, and the insured or claimant should do what they would do if there was no insurance to handle the damage. However, if additional damage is found, to contact me and I'll send an appraiser out to reinspect with the chosen contractor.

Sample Settlement Letter with Proof of Loss

Date

Via Email:
Insured@insured.com

Insured Name
Insured Address
Insured City, State, Zip

Re: Insured:
    Policy Number:
    Date of Loss:
    Company File Number:

Dear Insured:

I received notice of an occurrence that took place at (insured property address) on (date of loss). I am the adjuster investigating the loss you sustained as a result of (peril).

Enclosed is an estimate and a copy of the Sworn Statement of Proof of Loss for $6,674.65. This figure was determined in the following manner:

Whole Loss and Damage (Building)	$9,382.54
Whole Loss and Damage (Contents)	$1,368.04
Less Deductible	$2,500.00
Less Recoverable Depreciation	$1,575.93
Net Settlement	**$6,674.65**

Pursuant to the terms and conditions of the policy, please have the Proof of Loss (the last page of this letter) signed and notarized and returned to my office. You may send the signed and notarized proof of loss to my office, to my attention by email or fax. My email address is adjuster@firstpartycarrier.com and the fax number is (555) 555-5555. If you choose to send the executed proof of loss by post, my mailing address is as follows:

Insurance Company Address

Once I receive the copy of the signed and notarized Sworn Statement of Proof of Loss, I will issue the check made payable to (My Insured) and (Anyone Else?).

You bought replacement cost coverage on your policy; therefore, you have recoverable depreciation available up to the amount of $1,575.93. In order to avail yourself of this coverage, you must notify us and repair or replace the property within 6 months (180 days), per your policy. Please keep your receipts for the repair or purchase of new items for my review.

Please note, (First-Party Carrier) is unable to instruct your contractors to begin repairs.

If you have any questions or concerns, please do not hesitate to contact me.

Sincerely,
Adjuster
Title
Phone number
Email address

Enc: Estimate
     Proof of Loss

Sworn Statement in Proof of Loss

$_____	_____
Amount of Policy at Time of Loss	Policy Number
___/___/_____ ___/___/_____	_____
Date Issued Date Expires	Agent

To the _____ of _____

At the time of loss, by the above indicated policy of insurance you insured _____ against loss by _____ to the property described under Schedule "A", according to the terms and conditions of the said policy and all forms, endorsements, transfers, and assignments attached thereto.

1. Time and Origin: A _____ loss occurred about the hour of _____ o'clock ___ M on the _____ day of _____, 20_____. The cause and origin of the said loss were: _____.

2. Occupancy: The building described, or containing the property described, was occupied at the time of the loss as follows, and for no other purpose whatsoever: _____.

3. Title and Interest: At the time of the loss the interest of your insured in the property described herein was _____. No other

person or persons had any interest therein or encumbrance thereon, except: _____.

4. Changes: Since the said policy was issued there has been no assignment thereof, or change of interest, use, occupancy, possession, location, or exposure of the property described, except: _____.

5. Total Insurance: The total amount of insurance upon the property described by this policy was, at the time of the loss, $_____, besides which there was no policy or other contract of insurance, written or oral, valid or invalid.

The Whole Loss and Damage of the Property was	$
Less Depreciation	$
Less Deductible	$
Net Settlement for the Claim is	$
Recoverable Depreciation	$

The said loss did not originate by any act, design, or procurement on the part of your insured, or this affiant; nothing has been done by or with the privity or consent of your insured or this affiant, to violate the conditions of the policy, or render it void; no articles are mentioned herein or in annexed schedules but such as were destroyed or damaged at the time of said loss; no property saved has in any manner been concealed, and no attempt to deceive the said company, as to the extent of said loss, has in any manner been made. Any other information that may be required will be furnished and considered a part of this proof.

The furnishing of this blank or the preparation of proofs by a representative of the above insurance company is not a waiver of any of its rights.

SIGNATURE: _____

SIGNATURE: _____

NOTARY: State of _____;

County of _____; SS

On this _____ day of _____, 20_____, before me appeared _____ who is known to be the person(s) named herein and who voluntarily executed this release.

_____ _____ _____
Notary Signature   Date   Commission Expires

Home Contents Inventory Worksheet

Your homeowners insurance provides coverage for the contents of your home, up to the limit you selected with your insurance agent. Because you have suffered from a loss to your personal property, your adjuster needs your help in providing a list of all your possessions (contents) that was damaged or stolen, along with its estimated value and age at the time of loss.

Here is some of the information your adjuster will need:

Getting Started:

- Start now, even if your information is incomplete. A good home inventory includes a detailed list of your possessions, including receipts, descriptions, and photos of your home contents.

  - Start with new purchases and add older items later.

  - Group your possessions into logical categories, e.g., by hobby, by room in your home, etc.

- Be specific. For example: Sony 42-inch flat panel LED television. Better yet, write down the serial number. This will ensure the item is valued correctly.

  - Include a detailed record of antiques, jewelry, major appliances and collector's items.

- Scan invoices for large items purchased in case proof of ownership is needed.

- Photograph or videotape each room in your home, including inside closets, storage buildings, the attic, and the garage. Open drawers and photograph the contents.

  - Be sure to include those items in the worksheet.

- Don't miss items you rarely use, such as holiday decorations, sports equipment and tools.

- Email or mail your photographs and supporting documents to your adjuster when you have it.

    - Be careful not to submit the same item twice, as this will slow down the adjustment of your claim.

    - Put your name, date of loss, policy number, and claim number on all the documents you send to your adjuster.

    - Keep a copy of all the documents for your records.

LIVING ROOM/DEN

Name		Policy #	
Date of Loss		Claim #	

Item	Manufacturer	Model, Serial Number	Date Purchased	Purchase Price
Sofa				
Loveseat				
Recliner				
Chairs				
Ottoman				
Coffee Table				
End tables				
Curtains, blinds, wall decor				
Television				
Entertainment center				
Stereo				
CDs, DVDs, tapes, records				
Video game console				
Video games				
Sound system				
Bookcases				
Books				
Pillows, Blankets				

HOME OFFICE/FAMILY ROOM

Name		Policy #		
Date of Loss		Claim #		

Item	Manufacturer	Model, Serial Number	Date Purchased	Purchase Price
Chairs				
Ottoman				
Desk				
Coffee/end table				
Bookcases/books				
Computer/Laptop				
Computer Monitor				
External hard drive				
Computer peripherals				
Fax Machine/phone				
Scanner/copier				
Area rugs				
Curtains, blinds, wall decor				
Storage/chests				
Lamps				
File Cabinets				
Office supplies (pens/paper)				

DINING ROOM

Name		Policy #	
Date of Loss		Claim #	

Item	Manufacturer	Model, Serial Number	Date Purchased	Purchase Price
Table				
Chairs				
Buffet				
China cabinet				
China				
Serving table, cart				
Serving dishes				
Crystal				
Silverware				
Tea, coffee sets				
Linens				
Liquor cabinet				
Curtains, blinds				
Art, wall décor				
Table				
Chairs				
Buffet				
Area rugs				
Lamps				
Mirrors				

KITCHEN

Name			Policy #	
Date of Loss			Claim #	

Item	Manufacturer	Model, Serial Number	Date Purchased	Purchase Price
Stove				
Refrigerator				
Refrigerator contents				
Cabinets				
Freezer				
Freezer contents				
Table				
Chairs, stools				
Microwave				
Electric grill				
Coffee maker				
Toaster				
Blender, processor				
Mixer				
Toaster oven				
Waffle iron				
Television				
Radio				
Dishes				
Glasses				
Pots and pans				
Bowls				
Silverware				
Cooking utensils				
Cookbooks				

Item	Manufacturer	Model, Serial Number	Date Purchased	Purchase Price
Pantry items, food				
Linens				
Spices				
Knickknacks				
Lamps				
Art, wall décor				
Telephone				

LAUNDRY/UTILITY/CRAFTS ROOM

Name		Policy #	
Date of Loss		Claim #	

Item	Manufacturer	Model, Serial Number	Date Purchased	Purchase Price
Clothes washer				
Clothes dryer				
Table				
Cabinets				
Vacuum cleaner				
Cleaning tools				
Cleaning supplies				
Clothes washer				
Clothes dryer				
Table				
Cabinets				
Vacuum cleaner				
Cleaning tools				
Cleaning supplies				
Shelving units				
Iron, ironing board				
Sewing machine				
Sewing supplies				
Craft supplies				
Storage containers				
Carpet shampooer				
Telephone				
Art, wall décor				
Knickknacks				
Area rugs				
Curtains, blinds				

BEDROOMS

Name		Policy #	
Date of Loss		Claim #	

MASTER BEDROOM

Item	Manufacturer	Model, Serial Number	Date Purchased	Purchase Price
Bed				
Mattress, box springs				
Night tables				
Sofa, loveseat				
Chairs				
Ottoman				
Dressers				
Storage/chest				
Armoire				
Dressing table				
Bed linens, pillows				
Computer				
Computer monitor				
Computer peripherals				
Entertainment center				
Television				
Stereo				
Stereo equipment				
DVD player/ DVDs				
CDs, tapes, records				
Sound system				
Telephone				
Alarm clock, radio				
Bookcases				

Item	Manufacturer	Model, Serial Number	Date Purchased	Purchase Price
Books				
Curtains, blinds				
Art, wall décor				
Knickknacks				
Blankets				
Lamps				

WOMEN'S CLOTHING

Item	Brand	Model, Serial Number	Date Purchased	Purchase Price
Dresses				
Shirts, blouses				
Skirts				
Sweaters				
Dress pants				
Suits				
Jeans, casual pants				
Coats				
Shoes, boots				
Jewelry				
Accessories				

MEN'S CLOTHING

Item	Brand	Model, Serial Number	Date Purchased	Purchase Price
Dress pants				
Suits				
Jeans, casual pants				
Sweaters				
Shirts				
Coats				
Sporting apparel				
Ties				
Shoes, boots				
Gloves, hats				
Belts, accessories				
Watches, jewelry				

CHILDREN'S CLOTHING

Item	Brand	Model, Serial Number	Date Purchased	Purchase Price
Pants				
Shirts				
Jumpers				
Skirts & dresses				
Baby items				
Sporting apparel				
Shoes, boots				
Coats				
Gloves, hats				
Belts, accessories				

BEDROOM 1 _____

(Please add description; i.e., boy's room, blue room, etc.)

Item	Manufacturer	Model, Serial Number	Date Purchased	Purchase Price
Bed				
Mattress, box springs				
Night tables				

BEDROOM 2 _____

(Please add description; i.e., girl's room, yellow room, etc.)

Item	Manufacturer	Model, Serial Number	Date Purchased	Purchase Price
Bed				
Mattress, box springs				
Night tables				

Repeat this until all bedrooms are inventoried. Follow the same pattern as the master bedroom.

BATHROOMS

Name		Policy #	
Date of Loss		Claim #	

BATHROOM 1 _____

(Please add description; i.e., downstairs ½ bath, blue bathroom, etc.)

Item	Manufacturer	Model, Serial Number	Date Purchased	Purchase Price
Dressing table				
Cabinets (unattached)				
Chair				
Clothes hamper				
Storage containers				
Shelves (unattached)				
Towels, linens				
Electric razor				
Curling/flat iron				
Hair dryer				
Toiletries				
Medicine				
Scale				
Shower curtain				
Curtains, blinds				

BATHROOM 2 _____
(Please add description; i.e., upstairs master bathroom, green bath, etc.)

Item	Manufacturer	Model, Serial Number	Date Purchased	Purchase Price
Dressing table				
Cabinets (unattached)				
Chair				

Again, repeat until all bathrooms are inventoried.

OUTDOOR/SEASONAL/GARAGE/SHED

Name	Policy #
Date of Loss	Claim #

Item	Manufacturer	Model, Serial Number	Date Purchased	Purchase Price
Patio/porch furniture				
Bicycles, sports equipment				
Holiday decorations				
Garden/yard tools, containers, supplies				
Planters, plants				
Lawn mower, weed trimmer, leaf blower				
Sprinklers, hoses				
Ladders				
Toolbox				
Tools				
Outdoor games, toys				
Freezer, refrigerator, contents				
Cooking equipment				
Pet supplies				
Hobby supplies				

ATTIC

Name		Policy #	
Date of Loss		Claim #	

Item	Manufacturer	Model, Serial Number	Date Purchased	Purchase Price
Holiday decorations				
Dehumidifier, heater				
Hobby supplies				
Storage, shelving units (unattached)				

BASEMENT

Name	Policy #
Date of Loss	Claim #

Item	Manufacturer	Model, Serial Number	Date Purchased	Purchase Price
Holiday decorations				
Toolbox				
Tools				
Outdoor games, toys				
Freezer, refrigerator, contents				
Pet supplies				
Dehumidifier, heater				
Hobby supplies				
Storage (removable)				

ADDITIONAL ITEMS

Name		Policy #	
Date of Loss		Claim #	

Item	Manufacturer	Model, Serial Number	Date Purchased	Purchase Price

Sample Liability Status Letter to Insured

Date

Via Email:
Insured@insured.com

Insured Name
Insured Address
Insured City, State, Zip

Re: Insured:
    Policy Number:
    Date of Loss:
    Company File Number:
    Claimant:

Dear Insured:

I received notice of an occurrence that took place at (loss location) on (date of loss). I am the adjuster investigating the loss.

(Claimant) has completed (his/her) treatment due to the (accident type) on (date of loss). (He/She) has demanded $10,000 to settle the claim. I offered $3,500, plus medical invoices for a total settlement in exchange for a Full and Final Release of All Claims in the amount of $7,548.62.

(Claimant) stated (he/she) would like to think about my offer.

Should you receive suit papers, please contact me immediately. Failure to do so may jeopardize your coverage.

If you have any questions, please contact me.

Sincerely,

Adjuster
Title
Phone number
Email address

Sample Liability Settlement Letter to Claimant

Date

Via Email:
Claimant@claimantemail.com

Claimant Name
Claimant Address
Claimant City, State, Zip

Re: Insured:
    Policy Number:
    Date of Loss:
    Company File Number:
    Claimant:

Dear Claimant:

I received notice of an occurrence that took place at (loss location) on (date of loss). I am the adjuster investigating the loss due to a (accident description).

I received and reviewed your demand of $10,000. You suffered from sprain/strain of your cervical and thoracic spine and sought chiropractic care. Your medical invoices total $4,048.62.

I offered $7,548.62 in exchange for a full and final release, and you accepted.

Attached you will find a Release of All Claims (Husband and Wife). You and your spouse must sign the release of all claims, and it must be notarized.

Please return it to my attention. You may send the signed and notarized release to my office, to my attention by email or fax. My email address is adjuster@firstpartycarrier.com and the fax number is (555) 555-5555. If you choose to send the executed proof of loss by post, my mailing address is as follows:

Insurance Company Address

Once I receive the copy of the signed and notarized release, I will issue the check made payable to you and (your spouse) (and/or anyone else).

If you have any questions, please contact me.

Sincerely,
Adjuster
Title
Phone number
Email address

Enc: Release of All Claims (Husband & Wife)

Sample Liability Denial Letter to Claimant

Date

Via Email:
Claimant@claimantemail.com

Claimant Name
Claimant Address
Claimant City, State, Zip

Re: Insured:
      Policy Number:
      Date of Loss:
      Company File Number:
      Claimant:

Dear Claimant:

I received notice of an occurrence that took place at (loss location) on (date of loss). I am the adjuster investigating the loss due to a (accident description).

I completed my investigation into your loss. I found (My Insured) neither acted nor failed to act negligently. Therefore, I must respectfully deny liability for this claim. There will be no payment at this time.

Pursuant to (state law/regulation) you have (statute of limitations) to complete your claim or file a lawsuit to protect your interests. Should you retain an attorney or file a suit, please have the attorney contact me and provide me with a copy of the lawsuit.

If you have any questions, please contact me.

Sincerely,

Adjuster
Title
Phone number
Email address

Sample Liability/Coverage Denial Letter to Claimant

Date

Via Email:
Claimant@claimantemail.com

Claimant Name
Claimant Address
Claimant City, State, Zip

Re: Insured:
     Policy Number:
     Date of Loss:
     Company File Number:
     Claimant:

Dear Claimant:

I received notice of an occurrence that took place at (loss location) on (date of loss). I am the adjuster investigating the loss due to a (accident description).

I completed my investigation into your loss. There is no coverage for this loss; (My Insured) has been issued a coverage declination letter. Because you are not a party to the policy, I am unable to forward you a copy of the declination or discuss it with you.

Therefore, I must respectfully deny liability for this claim. There will be no payment at this time.

Pursuant to (state law/regulation) you have (statute of limitations) to complete your claim or file a lawsuit to protect your interests. Should you retain an attorney or file a suit, please have the attorney contact me and provide me with a copy of the lawsuit.

If you have any questions, please contact me.

Sincerely,

Adjuster
Title
Phone number
Email address

GENERAL RELEASE - HUSBAND AND WIFE

KNOW ALL BY THESE PRESENT:

That we, _____ and _____
                (Husband)   (Wife)
husband and wife, residing at _____
and each being of lawful age, for the sole consideration of
_____ dollars ($) to be paid
to _____(husband)_____ and for the sole consideration of
_____ dollars ($) to be paid to
_____(wife)_____, have remised, released, and forever discharged and by
these present do, severally and jointly, for ourselves and for our heir(s), executors, administrators, and assigns, do hereby remise, release, and forever
discharge _____ and his,
her, their, and its successors and assigns, and each of their heirs, executors,
and administrators, and all other persons, firms, and corporations, of and
from any and all claims, demands, rights, and causes of action, of whatsoever kind or nature, arising from or by reason of any and all known and unknown, foreseen and unforeseen bodily and personal injuries, loss and damage to property, and the consequences thereof, resulting, and to result, from
a _____which happened on or about the _____
day of _____, 20___, at or near _____
_____.

It is further understood and agreed that this settlement is the compromise of
doubtful and disputed claims, and that the payments are not to be construed
as an admission of liability on the part of   by whom liability is expressly denied.

This release contains the ENTIRE AGREEMENT between the parties
hereto, and the terms of this release are contractual and not a mere recital.
We further state that we have carefully read the foregoing release and know
the contents thereof, and we sign the same as our own free acts.

WITNESS(ES):   SIGNATURE(S):

_____   _____
Witness   Signature (husband)

_____   _____
Witness   Signature (wife)

Claim Number _____   Date   /   /

SIGNATURE: _____

SIGNATURE: _____

NOTARY: State of _____

County of _____

On this _____ day of _____, 20_____, before me a
_____ who is known to be the person(s)
herein and who voluntarily executed this release.

_____   _____   _____
Notary Signature   Date   Commission Expires

RECEIPT FOR ADVANCE PAYMENT

(THIS IS NOT A RELEASE)

This is to acknowledge receipt of _____

_____dollars ($_____) paid on behalf of_____

_____ to be credited to the

total amount of any final settlement or judgment in my/our favor for alleged

damages resulting from an accident on _____, 20 _____

at _____.

I /We authorize that the above sum be distributed as follows:

_____

_____

_____

_____

_____

WITNESS(ES):   SIGNATURE(S):

_____   _____
Witness   Claimant

_____   _____
Witness   Claimant

Claim Number _____   Date   /   /

SIGNATURE: _____

SIGNATURE: _____

NOTARY: State of _____

County of _____

On this _____ day of _____, 20_____, before me a

_____ who is known to be the person(s)

herein and who voluntarily executed this release.

_____   _____   _____
Notary Signature   Date   Commission Expires

SAMPLE ESTIMATE

Insured:	John Doe		Home:	(555) 555-5555
Property:	5555 Main St.			
	Little Rock, AR 72211			

Claim Rep.:   Test Test

Estimator: Test Test

Claim Number: 1111111   **Policy Number:** 2222222/R02   **Type of Loss:** Water Damage

Date Contacted:	2/27/2021 12:00 AM			
Date of Loss:	2/18/2021 12:00 AM	Date Received:	2/27/2021 12:00 AM
Date Inspected:	3/6/2021 12:00 AM	Date Entered:	3/6/2021 12:12 PM

Price List: TXCS8X_MAR21
               Restoration/Service/Remodel
Estimate: 335595-1

335595-1

Kitchen

Main Level

Kitchen   Height: 8'

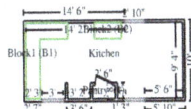

499.12 SF Walls	201.27 SF Ceiling
700.39 SF Walls & Ceiling	201.27 SF Floor
22.36 SY Flooring	39.24 LF Floor Perimeter
71.70 LF Ceil. Perimeter	

Missing Wall - Goes to Floor	3' X 6' 8"	Opens into Exterior
Missing Wall - Goes to Floor	2' 10" X 6' 8"	Opens into Exterior
Missing Wall - Goes to Floor	2' 10" X 6' 8"	Opens into Exterior

Subroom: Pantry (1)   Height: 8'

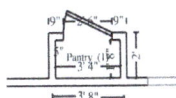

63.33 SF Walls	5.56 SF Ceiling
68.89 SF Walls & Ceiling	5.56 SF Floor
0.62 SY Flooring	7.50 LF Floor Perimeter
10.00 LF Ceil. Perimeter	

Door	2' 6" X 6' 8"	Opens into KITCHEN

QUANTITY	UNIT	TAX	O&P	RCV	AGE/LIFE	COND.	DEP %	DEPREC.	ACV
1. Contents - move out then reset - Small room									
1.00 EA	39.01	0.00	8.19	47.20	10/NA	Avg.	0%	(0.00)	47.20
2. Refrigerator - Remove & reset									
1.00 EA	37.97	0.00	7.98	45.95	10/NA	Avg.	0%	(0.00)	45.95
3. Range - gas - Remove & reset									
1.00 EA	136.96	0.00	28.77	165.73	10/NA	Avg.	0%	(0.00)	165.73
4. Dishwasher - Detach & reset									
1.00 EA	199.79	0.00	41.96	241.75	10/NA	Avg.	0%	(0.00)	241.75
5. Garbage disposer - Detach & reset									
1.00 EA	136.96	0.00	28.77	165.73	10/NA	Avg.	0%	(0.00)	165.73
6. Sink - double - Detach & reset									
1.00 EA	136.59	0.00	28.69	165.28	10/NA	Avg.	0%	(0.00)	165.28
7. R&R Snaplock Laminate - simulated wood floor - Standard grade									
206.77 SF	5.20	35.99	233.36	1,344.55	10/25 yrs	Avg.	40%	(362.60)	981.95
8. R&R Plumbing fixture supply line									
2.00 EA	21.82	0.99	9.38	54.01	10/20 yrs	Avg.	50%	(18.09)	35.92
9. R&R P-trap assembly - ABS (plastic)									
1.00 EA	59.68	0.57	12.66	72.91	10/25 yrs	Avg.	40%	(21.56)	51.35
10. Detach & Reset Countertop - Granite or Marble - Standard grade									
34.50 SF	26.51	0.00	192.07	1,106.67	0/150 yrs	Avg.	0%	(0.00)	1,106.67

335595-1   3/13/2021   Page: 2

CONTINUED - Kitchen

	QUANTITY	UNIT	TAX	O&P	RCV	AGE/LIFE	COND.	DEP %	DEPREC.	ACV
11. Detach & Reset Baseboard - 3 1/4"										
	46.74 LF	2.20	0.08	21.61	124.52	0/150 yrs	Avg.	0%	(0.00)	124.52
12. Paint baseboard - one coat										
	46.74 LF	0.85	0.31	8.40	48.44	10/15 yrs	Avg.	66.67%	(26.70)	21.74
13. Detach & Reset Cabinetry - lower (base) units										
	12.00 LF	53.28	0.00	134.27	773.63	0/50 yrs	Avg.	0%	(0.00)	773.63
14. Material Only Cabinetry - lower (base) units										
	3.00 LF	159.42	39.46	108.73	626.45	10/50 yrs	Avg.	20%	(103.54)	522.91
43. Apply anti-microbial agent to the floor										
	206.77 SF	0.24	5.52	10.53	65.67	0/NA	Avg.	0%	(0.00)	65.67
Totals: Kitchen			82.92	875.37	5,048.49				532.49	4,516.00
Total: Main Level			82.92	875.37	5,048.49				532.49	4,516.00
Total: Kitchen			82.92	875.37	5,048.49				532.49	4,516.00

Hallway
Main Level

Hallway/Entry Height: 8'

322.00 SF Walls	90.40 SF Ceiling
412.40 SF Walls & Ceiling	90.40 SF Floor
10.04 SY Flooring	37.33 LF Floor Perimeter
54.83 LF Ceil. Perimeter	

Missing Wall - Goes to Floor	2' 11" X 6' 8"	Opens into Exterior
Missing Wall - Goes to Floor	3' X 6' 8"	Opens into Exterior
Missing Wall - Goes to Floor	2' 7" X 6' 8"	Opens into Exterior
Door	2' 6" X 6' 8"	Opens into Exterior
Door	2' 6" X 6' 8"	Opens into Exterior

Subroom: Room2 (1) Height: 8'

88.00 SF Walls	10.33 SF Ceiling
98.33 SF Walls & Ceiling	10.33 SF Floor
1.15 SY Flooring	10.33 LF Floor Perimeter
14.33 LF Ceil. Perimeter	

| Door | 2' X 6' 8" | Opens into HALLWAY_ENTR |
| Door | 2' X 6' 8" | Opens into HALLWAY_ENTR |

QUANTITY	UNIT	TAX	O&P	RCV	AGE/LIFE	COND.	DEP %	DEPREC.	ACV
15. Contents - move out then reset - Small room									
1.00 EA	39.01	0.00	8.19	47.20	10/NA	Avg.	0%	(0.00)	47.20
16. R&R Snaplock Laminate - simulated wood floor - Standard grade									
100.74 SF	5.20	17.54	113.68	655.07	10/25 yrs	Avg.	40%	(176.67)	478.40
17. Detach & Reset Baseboard - 3 1/4"									
47.67 LF	2.20	0.08	22.05	127.00	0/150 yrs	Avg.	0%	(0.00)	127.00
18. Paint baseboard - one coat									
47.67 LF	0.85	0.31	8.57	49.40	10/15 yrs	Avg.	66.67%	(27.22)	22.18
44. Apply anti-microbial agent to the floor									
100.74 SF	0.24	2.69	5.14	32.01	0/NA	Avg.	0%	(0.00)	32.01
Totals: Hallway/Entry		**20.62**	**157.63**	**910.68**				**203.89**	**706.79**
Total: Main Level		**20.62**	**157.63**	**910.68**				**203.89**	**706.79**
Total: Hallway		**20.62**	**157.63**	**910.68**				**203.89**	**706.79**

Living Room

Main Level

Living Room Height: 8'

468.00 SF Walls	244.22 SF Ceiling
712.22 SF Walls & Ceiling	244.22 SF Floor
27.14 SY Flooring	57.50 LF Floor Perimeter
63.50 LF Ceil. Perimeter	

| Door | 2' 6" X 6' 8" | Opens into Exterior |
| Missing Wall - Goes to Floor | 3' 6" X 6' 8" | Opens into Exterior |

QUANTITY	UNIT	TAX	O&P	RCV	AGE/LIFE	COND.	DEP %	DEPREC.	ACV
19. Contents - move out then reset - Large room									
1.00 EA	77.94	0.00	16.36	94.30	10/NA	Avg.	0%	(0.00)	94.30

335595-1 3/13/2021 Page: 4

CONTINUED - Living Room

QUANTITY	UNIT	TAX	O&P	RCV	AGE/LIFE	COND.	DEP %	DEPREC.	ACV
20. R&R Snaplock Laminate - simulated wood floor - Standard grade									
244.22 SF	5.20	42.51	275.63	1,588.09	10/25 yrs	Avg.	40%	(428.27)	1,159.82
21. Detach & Reset Baseboard - 3 1/4"									
57.50 LF	2.20	0.09	26.59	153.18	0/150 yrs	Avg.	0%	(0.00)	153.18
22. Paint baseboard - one coat									
57.50 LF	0.85	0.38	10.35	59.61	10/15 yrs	Avg.	66.67%	(32.84)	26.77
42. Apply anti-microbial agent to the floor									
244.22 SF	0.24	6.50	12.44	77.55	0/NA	Avg.	0%	(0.00)	77.55
Totals: Living Room		**49.48**	**341.37**	**1,972.73**				**461.11**	**1,511.62**
Total: Main Level		**49.48**	**341.37**	**1,972.73**				**461.11**	**1,511.62**
Total: Living Room		**49.48**	**341.37**	**1,972.73**				**461.11**	**1,511.62**

Small Hallway

Main Level

Hallway   Height: 8'

68.11 SF Walls   16.25 SF Ceiling
84.36 SF Walls & Ceiling   16.25 SF Floor
1.81 SY Flooring   6.92 LF Floor Perimeter
16.50 LF Ceil. Perimeter

Door	2' 6" X 6' 8"	**Opens into Exterior**	
Missing Wall - Goes to Floor	2' 7" X 6' 8"	**Opens into Exterior**	
Door	2' 6" X 6' 8"	**Opens into Exterior**	
Door	2' X 6' 8"	**Opens into Exterior**	

QUANTITY	UNIT	TAX	O&P	RCV	AGE/LIFE	COND.	DEP %	DEPREC.	ACV
23. Detach & Reset Baseboard - 3 1/4"									
6.92 LF	2.20	0.01	3.19	18.42	0/150 yrs	Avg.	0%	(0.00)	18.42
24. Paint baseboard - one coat									
6.92 LF	0.85	0.05	1.26	7.19	10/15 yrs	Avg.	66.67%	(3.95)	3.24
25. Snaplock Laminate - simulated wood floor - Standard grade									
16.25 SF	4.21	2.83	14.96	86.20	10/25 yrs	Avg.	40%	(28.49)	57.71
41. Apply anti-microbial agent to the floor									
16.25 SF	0.24	0.44	0.82	5.16	0/NA	Avg.	0%	(0.00)	5.16

335595-1   3/13/2021   Page: 5

CONTINUED - Hallway

QUANTITY	UNIT	TAX	O&P	RCV	AGE/LIFE	COND.	DEP %	DEPREC.	ACV
Totals: Hallway		3.33	20.23	116.97				32.44	84.53
Total: Main Level		3.33	20.23	116.97				32.44	84.53
Total: Small Hallway		3.33	20.23	116.97				32.44	84.53

Kids Room
Main Level

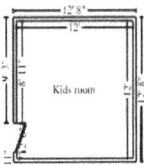

Kids room   **Height: 8'**

367.33 SF Walls	144.00 SF Ceiling
511.33 SF Walls & Ceiling	144.00 SF Floor
16.00 SY Flooring	45.50 LF Floor Perimeter
48.00 LF Ceil. Perimeter	

Door   2' 6" X 6' 8"   **Opens into Exterior**

QUANTITY	UNIT	TAX	O&P	RCV	AGE/LIFE	COND.	DEP %	DEPREC.	ACV
26. Contents - move out then reset									
1.00 EA	51.96	0.00	10.92	62.88	10/NA	Avg.	0%	(0.00)	62.88
27. R&R Snaplock Laminate - simulated wood floor - Standard grade									
144.00 SF	5.20	25.07	162.52	936.39	10/25 yrs	Avg.	40%	(252.53)	683.86
28. Detach & Reset Baseboard - 3 1/4"									
45.50 LF	2.20	0.08	21.04	121.22	0/150 yrs	Avg.	0%	(0.00)	121.22
29. Paint baseboard - one coat									
45.50 LF	0.85	0.30	8.19	47.17	10/15 yrs	Avg.	66.67%	(25.99)	21.18
39. Apply anti-microbial agent to the floor									
144.00 SF	0.24	3.84	7.34	45.74	0/NA	Avg.	0%	(0.00)	45.74
Totals: Kids room		29.29	210.01	1,213.40				278.52	934.88
Total: Main Level		29.29	210.01	1,213.40				278.52	934.88
Total: Kids Room		29.29	210.01	1,213.40				278.52	934.88

Fencing

QUANTITY	UNIT	TAX	O&P	RCV	AGE/LIFE	COND.	DEP %	DEPREC.	ACV
30. R&R Wood fence 5'- 6' high - cedar or equal									
16.00 LF	35.07	23.79	122.83	707.74	10/12 yrs	Avg.	83.33%	<416.90>	290.84
Totals: Fencing		**23.79**	**122.83**	**707.74**				**416.90**	**290.84**

Debris Removal

QUANTITY	UNIT	TAX	O&P	RCV	AGE/LIFE	COND.	DEP %	DEPREC.	ACV
31. Haul debris - per pickup truck load - including dump fees									
1.00 EA	114.25	0.00	24.00	138.25	10/NA	Avg.	NA	(0.00)	138.25
Totals: Debris Removal		**0.00**	**24.00**	**138.25**				**0.00**	**138.25**
Line Item Totals: 335595-1		**209.43**	**1,751.44**	**10,108.26**				**1,925.35**	**8,182.91**

[%] - Indicates that depreciate by percent was used for this item

[M] - Indicates that the depreciation percentage was limited by the maximum allowable depreciation for this item

Grand Total Areas:

1,875.90	SF Walls	712.04	SF Ceiling	2,587.94	SF Walls and Ceiling
711.98	SF Floor	79.11	SY Flooring	204.32	LF Floor Perimeter
0.00	SF Long Wall	0.00	SF Short Wall	278.86	LF Ceil. Perimeter
711.98	Floor Area	802.88	Total Area	1,910.80	Interior Wall Area
2,112.17	Exterior Wall Area	264.50	Exterior Perimeter of Walls		
0.00	Surface Area	0.00	Number of Squares	0.00	Total Perimeter Length
0.00	Total Ridge Length	0.00	Total Hip Length		

Coverage	Item Total	%	ACV Total	%
Above Slab leak	9,400.52	93.00%	7,892.07	96.45%
Below Slab leak	0.00	0.00%	0.00	0.00%
Other Structures	707.74	7.00%	290.84	3.55%
Total	10,108.26	100.00%	8,182.91	100.00%

Summary for Above Slab leak

Line Item Total	7,586.27
Material Sales Tax	166.65
Cleaning Mtl Tax	1.76
Subtotal	7,754.68
Overhead	775.52
Profit	853.09
Cleaning Sales Tax	17.23
Replacement Cost Value	**$9,400.52**
Less Depreciation	(1,508.45)
Actual Cash Value	**$7,892.07**
Less Deductible	(4,590.00)
Less Amount Over Limit(s)	(802.07)
Net Claim	**$2,500.00**
Total Depreciation	1,508.45
Less Residual Amount Over Limit(s)	(1,508.45)
Total Recoverable Depreciation	0.00
Net Claim if Depreciation is Recovered	**$2,500.00**

_____
Test Test

Summary for Other Structures

Line Item Total	561.12
Material Sales Tax	23.79
Subtotal	584.91
Overhead	58.49
Profit	64.34
Replacement Cost Value	**$707.74**
Less Non-recoverable Depreciation	<416.90>
Actual Cash Value	**$290.84**
Net Claim	**$290.84**

Test Test

335595-1   3/13/2021   Page: 9

Recap of Taxes, Overhead and Profit

	Overhead (10%)	Profit (10%)	Material Sales Tax (8.25%)	Cleaning Mtl Tax (8.25%)	Cleaning Sales Tax (8.25%)	Manuf. Home Tax (5%)	Storage Rental Tax (8.25%)	Total Tax (8.25%)
Line Items								
	834.01	917.43	190.44	1.76	17.23	0.00	0.00	0.00
Total								
	834.01	**917.43**	**190.44**	**1.76**	**17.23**	**0.00**	**0.00**	**0.00**

335595-1   3/13/2021   Page: 10

Recap by Room

Estimate: 335595-1

Area: Kitchen

Area: Main Level				
Kitchen			**4,090.20**	**50.20%**
Coverage: Above Slab leak	100.00% =		4,090.20	
Area Subtotal: Main Level			**4,090.20**	**50.20%**
Coverage: Above Slab leak	100.00% =		4,090.20	
Area Subtotal: Kitchen			**4,090.20**	**50.20%**
Coverage: Above Slab leak	100.00% =		4,090.20	

Area: Hallway

Area: Main Level				
Hallway/Entry			**732.43**	**8.99%**
Coverage: Above Slab leak	100.00% =		732.43	
Area Subtotal: Main Level			**732.43**	**8.99%**
Coverage: Above Slab leak	100.00% =		732.43	
Area Subtotal: Hallway			**732.43**	**8.99%**
Coverage: Above Slab leak	100.00% =		732.43	

Area: Living Room

Area: Main Level				
Living Room			**1,581.88**	**19.42%**
Coverage: Above Slab leak	100.00% =		1,581.88	
Area Subtotal: Main Level			**1,581.88**	**19.42%**
Coverage: Above Slab leak	100.00% =		1,581.88	
Area Subtotal: Living Room			**1,581.88**	**19.42%**
Coverage: Above Slab leak	100.00% =		1,581.88	

Area: Small Hallway

Area: Main Level				
Hallway			**93.41**	**1.15%**
Coverage: Above Slab leak	100.00% =		93.41	
Area Subtotal: Main Level			**93.41**	**1.15%**

Coverage: Above Slab leak	100.00% =	93.41

Area Subtotal: Small Hallway		**93.41**	**1.15%**
Coverage: Above Slab leak	100.00% =	93.41	

Area: Kids Room

Area: Main Level

Kids room		**974.10**	**11.96%**
Coverage: Above Slab leak	100.00% =	974.10	

Area Subtotal: Main Level		**974.10**	**11.96%**
Coverage: Above Slab leak	100.00% =	974.10	

Area Subtotal: Kids Room		**974.10**	**11.96%**
Coverage: Above Slab leak	100.00% =	974.10	
Fencing		**561.12**	**6.89%**
Coverage: Other Structures	100.00% =	561.12	
Debris Removal		**114.25**	**1.40%**
Coverage: Above Slab leak	100.00% =	114.25	

Subtotal of Areas		**8,147.39**	**100.00%**
Coverage: Above Slab leak	93.11% =	7,586.27	
Coverage: Other Structures	6.89% =	561.12	

Total		**8,147.39**	**100.00%**

Recap by Category with Depreciation

O&P Items			RCV	Deprec.	ACV
APPLIANCES			**511.68**		**511.68**
Coverage: Above Slab leak	@	100.00% =	511.68		
CABINETRY			**2,032.22**	**95.65**	**1,936.57**
Coverage: Above Slab leak	@	100.00% =	2,032.22		
CONTENT MANIPULATION			**207.92**		**207.92**
Coverage: Above Slab leak	@	100.00% =	207.92		
GENERAL DEMOLITION			**902.47**		**902.47**
Coverage: Above Slab leak	@	90.62% =	817.83		
Coverage: Other Structures	@	9.38% =	84.64		
FLOOR COVERING - WOOD			**2,997.44**	**1,198.98**	**1,798.46**
Coverage: Above Slab leak	@	100.00% =	2,997.44		
FENCING			**476.48**	**397.07**	**79.41**
Coverage: Other Structures	@	100.00% =	476.48		
FINISH CARPENTRY / TRIMWORK			**449.52**		**449.52**
Coverage: Above Slab leak	@	100.00% =	449.52		
PLUMBING			**225.10**	**38.92**	**186.18**
Coverage: Above Slab leak	@	100.00% =	225.10		
PAINTING			**173.69**	**115.80**	**57.89**
Coverage: Above Slab leak	@	100.00% =	173.69		
WATER EXTRACTION & REMEDIATION			**170.87**		**170.87**
Coverage: Above Slab leak	@	100.00% =	170.87		
O&P Items Subtotal			**8,147.39**	**1,846.42**	**6,300.97**
Material Sales Tax			**190.44**	**78.93**	**111.51**
Coverage: Above Slab leak	@	87.51% =	166.65		
Coverage: Other Structures	@	12.49% =	23.79		
Cleaning Mtl Tax			**1.76**		**1.76**
Coverage: Above Slab leak	@	100.00% =	1.76		
Overhead			**834.01**		**834.01**
Coverage: Above Slab leak	@	92.99% =	775.52		
Coverage: Other Structures	@	7.01% =	58.49		
Profit			**917.43**		**917.43**
Coverage: Above Slab leak	@	92.99% =	853.09		
Coverage: Other Structures	@	7.01% =	64.34		
Cleaning Sales Tax			**17.23**		**17.23**
Coverage: Above Slab leak	@	100.00% =	17.23		
Total			**10,108.26**	**1,925.35**	**8,182.91**

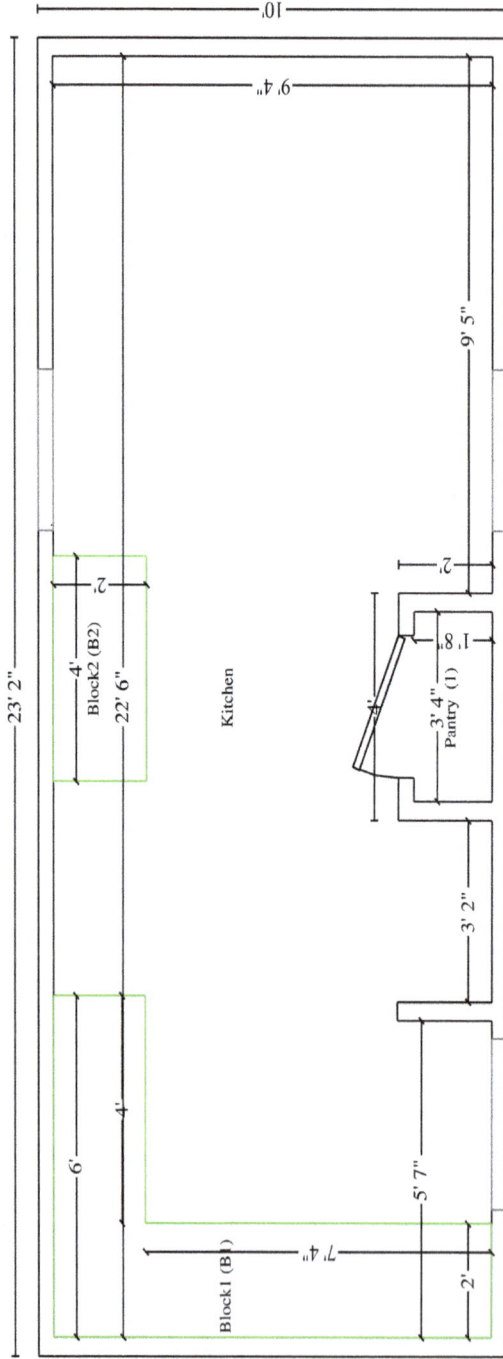

Kitchen - Main Level

Main Level

Page: 14

3/13/2021

335595-1

23' 2"

22' 6"

10'

9' 4"

9' 5"

Block2 (B2)

4'

2'

Kitchen

2'

3' 4"
Pantry (1)

1' 8"

3' 2"

6'

4'

Block1 (B1)

7' 4"

5' 7"

2'

Kitchen - Main Level

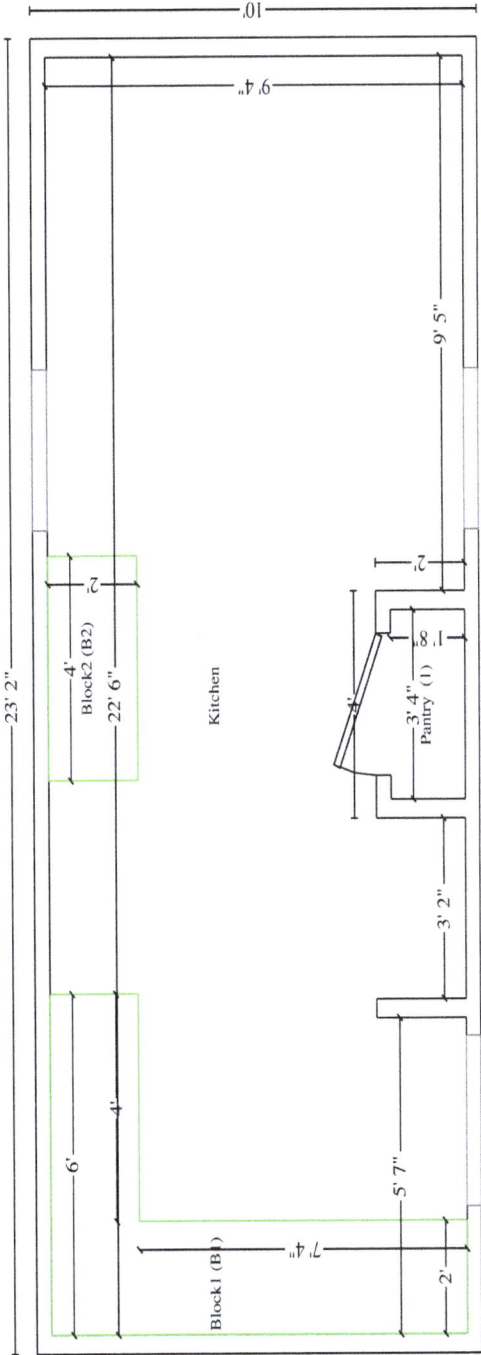

23' 2"

10'

9' 4"

9' 5"

22' 6"

Block2 (B2)

4'

2'

Kitchen

3' 4"

Pantry (1)

1' 8"

2'

3' 2"

6'

4'

5' 7"

7' 4"

Block1 (B1)

2'

3/13/2021

Main Level

N

Page: 15

Hallway - Main Level

335595-1

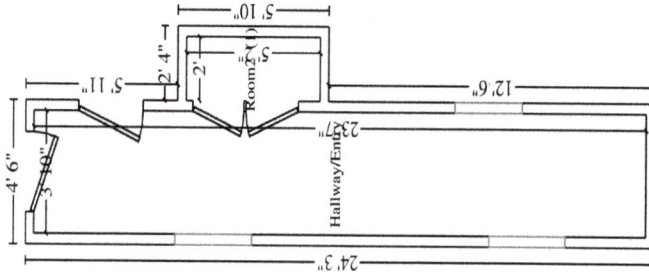

Hallway/Entry

24' 3"

23' 7"

12' 6"

4' 6"

3' 6"

5' 11"

2' 4"

2'

5' 3"

5' 3"

Room (O)

5' 10"

Living Room - Main Level

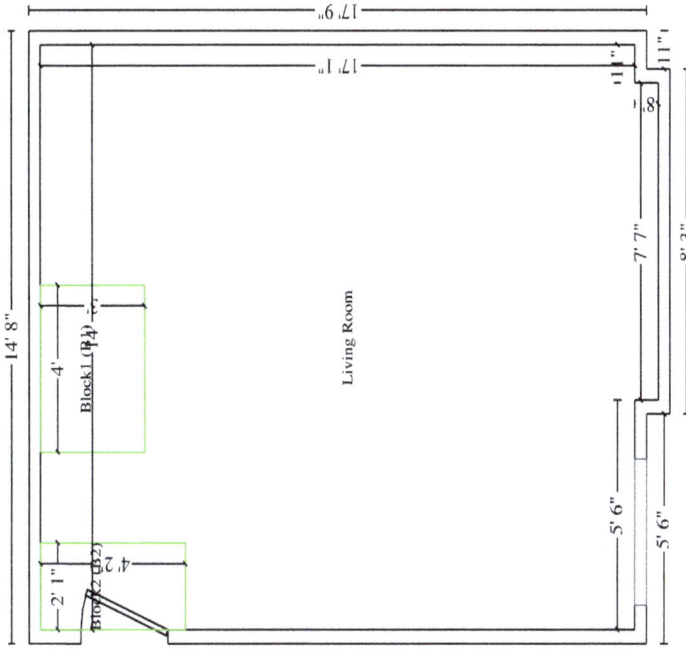

Living Room

14' 8"

17' 9"

17' 1"

11"

11"

8"

7' 7"

8' 3"

5' 6"

5' 6"

4'

Block1 (B4)

2' 1"

4' 2"

Block2 (B2)

335595-1

293

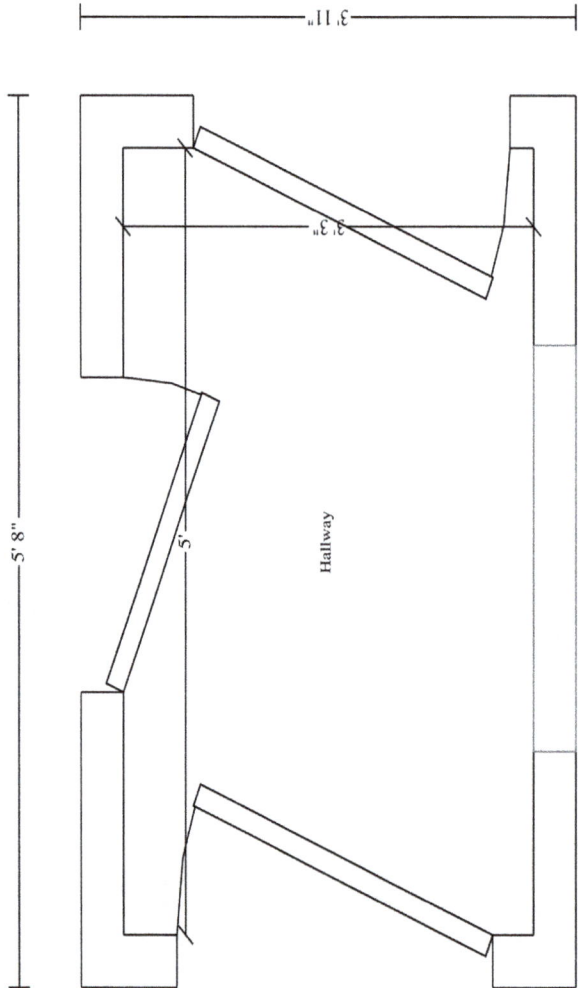

Small Hallway - Main Level

Hallway

5' 8"

3' 11"

3' 3"

5'

335595-1

Kids Room - Main Level

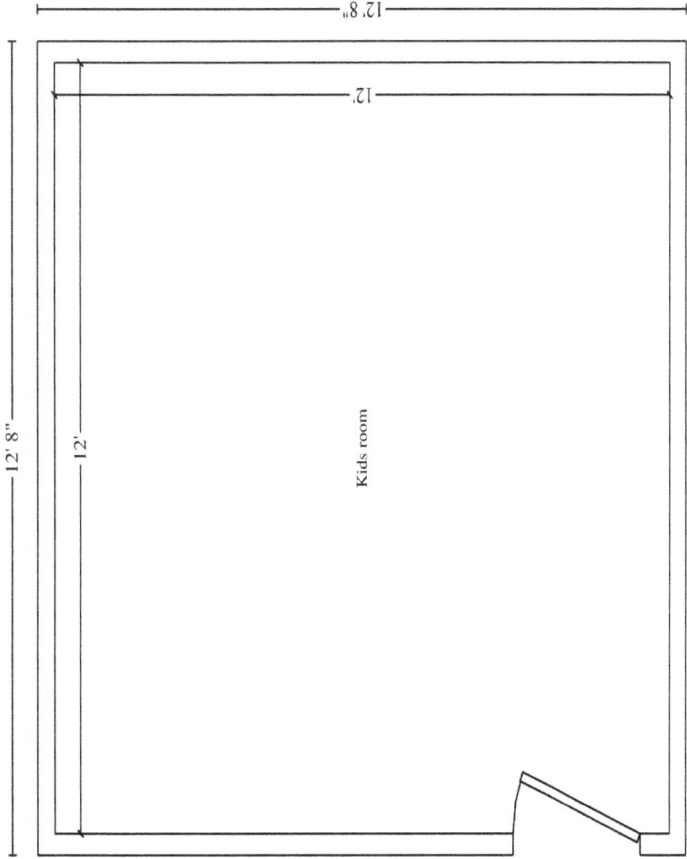

3/13/2021

Main Level

Page: 18

335595-1

12' 8"

12'

12' 8"

12'

Kids room

About the Author

Chantal M. Roberts, CPCU, AIC, RPA is passionate about teaching good-faith claims handling to adjusters.

She is a claims handling, practices, and procedures expert witness with 20-plus years' experience as a multi-lined claims adjuster. She is a self-described insurance nerd and actually enjoys talking about claims handling. She attempts to insert humor into a topic that is about as dry as burnt toast.

This is Chantal's first book. Chantal is available for hire to instruct adjusters on what she believes is the correct way to handle claims based on her experience both as an adjuster, a claims manager, and an expert witness. She is also a published author of several articles in professional journals with topics ranging from active shooters to COVID-19 claims handling to pitfalls in marijuana policies.

Chantal lives in Overland Park, Kansas, with her extremely tolerant husband, her loving dog, and a cat who ignores her.

CMR Consulting

CMRConsulting.net